W9-ACW-573

Praying for Slack

Praying for Slack

A Marine Corps Tank
Commander in Vietnam

Robert E. Peavey

To those who answered their country's call. Heroes, all.

First published in 2004 by Zenith Press, an imprint of MBI Publishing
Company, Galtier Plaza, Suite 200, 380 Jackson Street, St. Paul, MN 55101-
3885 USA

Zenith Press titles are also available at discounts in bulk quantity for industrial
or sales-promotional use. For details write to Special Sales Manager at
Motorbooks International Wholesalers & Distributors, Galtier Plaza, Suite
200, 380 Jackson Street, St. Paul, MN 55101-3885 USA.

ISBN 0-7603-2050-0

Edited by Eric Hammel
Cover design by Tom Heffron
Layout by Lynn Dragonette

Printed in the United States of America

Contents

Maps

Acknowledgments

While struggling to write this book, I used (and in some cases, abused) several friends and relatives. As the last person anyone ever expected to attempt such a project, I sought help and advice from anyone who would read the countless drafts, rewrites . . . and re-rewrites.

My best source of encouragement was my wife, Alica, who had faith when I doubted my abilities and kept me motivated to continue. My sons, Ian and Douglas, were both kind, but Doug pointed out the missing ingredient in an early manuscript by asking, "Dad, I read what you did. But I don't know how it felt."

Friends like Mark Anderson and Dean Kirby kept me on track and were of great help keeping me within grammatical bounds. My cousin, William Cocchi, also a good sounding board, helped me evaluate things from a nonmilitary perspective and keep terms understandable for all. Tom Flanagan will always be a friend for the fine maps he created for me.

And there's nothing like finding people who were there! The miracle of the Internet has put me in touch with countless veterans who I served with. Bob Embesi, Gary Gibson, and Tim Mayte in particular helped recall the details. After Bob read a short story of mine he suggested someone had to recount Operation Allen Brook, which had gone untold for thirty years.

Most important of all was the one person who kept giving me the positive feedback and support I needed through draft after draft: my mother. Without her and the letters of mine she had kept for thirty years, this book would have been impossible.

Thanks for the fireman boots, the bottles of Scotch, the dozens of care packages, and the endless letters that you sent during what was an equally horrible year for any mother.

You will never know what they meant to me.

Preface

Writing a book about one Marine's Vietnam experience was never my intent. What you are about to read was originally written in the form of several short stories. As I put the stories to paper, a hidden and suppressed anger surfaced within me. Writing, I found, was a catharsis for thirty years of pent-up frustration I had not previously been aware of.

After two years of work on these various stories, I saw that they could be strung together in roughly chronological order. I asked two close friends, both Vietnam-era Marine tank commanders, to take a look at what I had written and was surprised by their reaction. They encouraged me to turn the stories into the book that you now hold.

This, then, is a chronicle of experiences ranging from the humorous to the tragic. I wrestled with the dilemma of including derogatory slang words like "gooks" and "dinks", because the words we used aren't politically correct by today's standards. Nevertheless, those are the phrases and the language used by the men who fought that war. For me to change them to anything else would be unrealistic; doing so wouldn't honestly represent who we were or what we felt. It would not give you a true flavor of the men and our war. They are terms I left in Vietnam and don't represent who I am today.

The process of writing put my feelings in perspective. I was able to weigh and assess my anger, and deal with it constructively. More importantly, I realized just how very lucky I was to come out alive.

—Atlanta, 2004

"No event in American history is more misunderstood than the Vietnam War. It was misreported then, and it is misremembered now."

Richard M. Nixon, 1985

Chapter 1

How It All Began

It was a pitch-black night on the northernmost outpost in all of South Vietnam. The breeze off the ocean brought with it a chill that went right through me as I stood my watch. That's funny, I thought; this place can be so goddamned hot, and here I am shivering. The chill running through me was probably due more to the adrenaline pumping through my veins than the weather. I had no idea what to expect as I nervously scanned the sand dunes that lay before my tank. It was November 2, 1968, the first night after the bombing halt, LBJ's presidential order restricting offensive action against North Vietnam.

I was peering into the night for any signs or sounds of movement, scanning the dunes directly to the west and the China Sea two hundred meters directly behind me. As tank commander, I had the night's first watch—another ordinary watch, on an all but ordinary night, for Charlie now enjoyed unrestricted access into the DMZ (Demilitarized Zone), which lay just five hundred meters to the north of us.

It was close to midnight, near the end of my watch. Even today, I don't know what made me turn my head. Maybe it was a sixth sense, some kind of premonition.

Something tickled my consciousness and caused me to look to the northeast, almost over my right shoulder, toward the darkened North Vietnam coastline.

Out of the corner of my eye, something caught my attention. That's when I saw them. I picked up my binoculars and focused on them. "Motherfucker!" I said, half out loud, to no one in particular.

"You see something, TC?" asked Bob Steele, my loader, who always referred to me by the abbreviated title for tank commander. He had been trying to sleep on the back of the tank, above the engine.

"Yep. And you ain't gonna believe it!"

What I saw—so faint and so far off, several miles north of the DMZ—was so bizarre and so fantastic that I couldn't believe my eyes at first.

Coming toward me, straight down the coastline, was a long line of lights. Since the war had started, no one had witnessed anything like this. Moving lights were the last thing you expected to see across the DMZ. Then came a complete mental disconnect, for I began to realize just what they were—headlights. And if they were, then all of us were dead men—not tonight, maybe, but in a few days at the very least.

The rest of my tank crew had been trying to sleep, but had never really dozed off. None of us were ready to sleep on a night in which Charlie had a free timeout in the game. We were all just a little jumpy—this place would do that to you. Suddenly they all joined me, standing on the fenders next to the turret, wondering what it was that I had spotted.

Bob Truitt, my gunner, had already dropped down into the turret to swing the main gun in the direction of the faint lights. He located them in his sights then switched to the more powerful telescope. "Holy shit!" he muttered, his head up against the eyepiece.

It took each of my three crewmen a while to reach the same, hard-to-believe, conclusion. We were looking at an endless freeway of trucks driving due south, right down the beach.

Until now, Charlie wouldn't so much as smoke a cigarette at night. But after LBJ's order to restrict any offensive actions against North Vietnam, the NVA knew we couldn't shoot at them. So there they were, driving boldly down the coast and rubbing it ever so sweetly in our faces.

The sheer gall they were exhibiting really fried us. "Those little bastards!" I said through clenched teeth.

"The fuckin' nerve!" said Steele.

None of us could believe—or wanted to believe—they were so bold as to turn on the headlights of a goddamn convoy of trucks. It didn't take a brain surgeon to guess what those trucks were loaded with—ammunition, food, and supplies—courtesy of the President of the United States. It would be only days before the lethal contents of those trucks would be put to use on our side of the DMZ.

And so we sat, wide awake, mesmerized by the latest twist of a mismanaged war, wishing for permission to pump a couple of HE (high explosive) rounds into their smart asses. We were staring into our own death, almost powerless to prevent it. It seemed to be getting colder, but it wasn't. I began to feel sorry for my crew and myself; I could see how it was affecting them. How did I get into such a stupid situation? I began to wonder. It had been only nine months ago, on a similar dark, cold morning, that things went out of control—but all of that now seemed like years ago.

Nine months before, it had been an unusually chilly Southern California morning much like this on the DMZ. While chilly isn't strange for Southern California in February, that particular morning the air was damned near freezing. Odder still was that no one recognized the frigid cold snap for the harbinger it was. Recognition would come only days later. That morning's briskness was a silent starting gun for a series of events that would forever change me and most of the men around me.

To a casual passerby in that predawn darkness, as if any civilian would even be awake at 5 a.m., we must have appeared in the dark, cold air like a giant phantom locomotive, idling motionless at a station, steam venting from its vitals. But it wasn't steam. It was the combined breath of eighty men standing silently at attention waiting for the engineer's throttle. The engineer was a staff sergeant left over from the Korean War.

I'm freezing! I thought to myself. Come on, forget the headcount, and let's get going.

None of us had bothered to put on a field jacket, for once it warmed up, it would be something you would have to lug around the rest of the day. But that morning we had all been caught by surprise by just how cold it was. Five minutes of standing stationary had us all shivering, dying to get to the warm confines and hot coffee of the mess hall.

It was our next-to-last day before graduating the two-week NCO (non-commissioned officers') Training School at Los Pulgas, or simply Pulgas, as all Marines referred to it. It was one of several camps that made up the huge sprawling Camp Pendleton, a Marine Corps base on the California coast about forty miles north of San Diego.

Once fed and warmed with a couple cups of caffeine, we made our way back to our all-too-familiar classroom, glad to be out of the cold for a second time that morning. The classroom filled the entire interior of a Quonset hut whose concrete floor had long ago been bleached white from years of washing with lye soap. Quonset huts were the pre-fabs of their day. Their curved metal sides served as both wall and roof, making them look more like miniature airplane hangers than the barracks they really were—a throwback to what we young Leathernecks called the "Old Corps."

Crammed inside the hut were eighty wooden desk-chairs, each showing decades of abuse by a thousand NCO classes before ours. The building, in fact, looked every bit as weathered and worn as the sergeant major who ran the school.

Our class was made up of corporals from all over Pendleton. We had been sent by various unit commanders who thought we showed promise for future responsibility and higher rank. Many of us found ourselves outside our own units for the first time. People surrounded me from every MOS (military occupation specialty) imaginable. There were mechanics, truck drivers, artillerymen, amtrac crewmen, and cooks. I was one of three men with an MOS of 1811—tank crewman. Although there were a myriad jobs represented in the room, more than half the class was composed of 0300s, Marine riflemen—the backbone of the Marine Corps. Any other job existed merely to support them.

The NCO training program had been a little too much like boot camp—that beginning ten-week initiation that, once we completed it, earned us the title "Marine."

Most of us had put boot camp behind us at least a year and a half earlier. Yet here we were, facing it again. The previous thirteen days found us treated more like new recruits than the veteran Marines we thought we were. But it was part of a leadership program that was essential to advancing in rank: Before a man could start giving orders, he had to learn to take them.

My normal billet was at Las Flores, another of Pendleton's many camps. Flores was the home of the armored units of the 5th Marine Division, to which I had been assigned for the previous thirteen months after graduating from tank school. Living up to its Spanish name, Las Flores was indeed the flower of Camp Pendleton. The newest of all the bases, it looked less like a traditional Marine camp and more like a series of college dorms. The envy of Pendleton, it made my stay at Pulgas only that much harder to endure.

I'd been doing well in NCO School; I was in the upper twenty percent of a class due to graduate the next day. Things were finally winding down a little; it had been a tough two weeks. That day's schedule called for an all-morning lecture, which meant that we would be sitting inside, thank God. The topic was Marine Corps history, something the Corps holds in very high esteem. A history lesson would start with the Corp's founding in a Philadelphia tavern in 1775 and take us right up to present day. Most of us would never make it to World War II.

Two hours into the lesson found us finishing the Corps' exploits in the Caribbean between the two world wars. A loud crash sounded from the back of the room, startling everyone, including our instructor. It was the school's sergeant major, slamming open the door.

"Sergeant Lewis!" he growled, staring at our history teacher. "I will take over now." His startling entry got everyone's attention instantly. It was the very effect he desired, the way of a sergeant major. The door slammed for the second time as it shut behind him while he strutted up the aisle.

Staff Sergeant Lewis stepped aside without a word, and the sergeant major centered himself in the front of the room. We hadn't seen much of him since the first day we arrived, when he had "greeted" us. It was an address that only reinforced my limited experience with sergeant majors. Eighteen months in the Corps had taught me that changing one's direction was easier than crossing paths with a sergeant major. Simply fall within a sergeant major's field of view and you could easily find yourself assigned to any number of mindless jobs, like painting the rocks around a building or grooming the pebble walkways with a rake.

They were always tough old birds, and this one was no different. His chest was bedecked with half a dozen rows of ribbons that, to the trained eye, showed that he had served in China before World War II and fought in "The Big One" before serving in Korea, Lebanon, Vietnam, and a half dozen other garden spots around the globe. His weathered face revealed the hardship of thirty-plus years in "my Marine Corps"—a phrase he used often, as in, "You don't do that in my Marine Corp"—as if he owned it. But one ribbon on the top of endless rows—a Purple Heart with several stars across it—meant that he had been wounded in combat several times and probably did own a piece of the Corps. Next to it were a Silver Star and a Bronze Star, both medals for valor in combat.

Those of us sitting in the classroom could only look down at our solitary "fire watch" ribbon. We were "Snuffies," still wet behind the ears, with no combat experience. To say we were intimidated would be a gross understatement.

This sergeant major was born in the Old Corps, a reference to the endless Marine beach landings that were the legacy of World War II and Korea. Old Corps was a term of respect for those who served before us and who were now our mentors.

Thirty years of smoking and bellowing commands gave him a rough, raspy voice that only added to the impact of anything he had to say. And like all sergeant majors, he had a quality the Corps called "command presence," whose immediate impact almost paralyzed young Marines like us. His announcement to the class was direct and to the point—the only way a sergeant major knows how to speak. It would have an impact upon the rumors that would start right after his departure.

The sergeant major raised his clipboard and called out the names of three corporals. "Pack up your gear and report back to your unit immediately!"

Seventy-seven heads scanned the room as one, searching for the three men he had just named. On everyone's mind was the same question: What in hell had those guys done to get thrown out of NCO School one day short of graduation?

But nobody said a word. In the Marine Corps, you never asked why, you only reacted. We could only look with pity at the three bewildered faces as the three Marines packed their gear. NCO School wasn't something to be taken lightly. Each of our parent units expected us to graduate from the program. I couldn't imagine reporting back to my tank unit and having to tell SSgt. Robert Embesi, my platoon sergeant, that I had flunked out! I would find myself assigned, suddenly and forever, to wherever a body was needed for some shit detail. And every other corporal in that room, no matter what kind of unit he came from, had a Staff Sergeant Embesi to answer to.

The unlucky three weren't moving fast enough for the sergeant major's liking.

"Move it, Marines!" he boomed. "You've got five minutes to pack all your gear—and you won't be coming back! I will see you in my office in six minutes! Is that understood?"

"Yes, sir!" they replied in unison, not realizing the slip they had just uttered by addressing him as "sir." A sergeant major's presence was often so commanding that "sir" often seemed the natural reply, albeit the wrong one.

"Don't call me 'sir,' goddammit!" he shouted. "I work for a living! Now, you ladies only have five minutes. Move it!"

He stood, hands and clipboard on hips, glaring, until the trio hurriedly exited the room. From the looks on their faces, it was painfully obvious they had no idea what sin they had committed. The remainder of us could only guess what they had done. They were all from the same unit—after all, the sergeant major had said, "Return to your unit" not "units." We could only guess that, probably, they had celebrated their pending graduation from NCO School a little too early, gotten drunk, and caused a ruckus. Their rapid departure became a catalyst for the many rumors about to follow as our classmates exited the room.

"Sergeant Lewis, resume your class," the sergeant major commanded.

Staff Sergeant Lewis cleared his throat and resumed his role as instructor. It was obvious that even he didn't know what had just occurred. He was as wide-eyed as the rest of us. But only for a second. He tried to pick up where he had left off on Marine Corps history.

No one was listening. Seventy-seven minds were conjuring up what in hell had just happened.

The sergeant had just started in on World War II. Somewhere between the Marines' heroic defense on Wake Island and the first offensive of the war at Guadalcanal, a process, imperceptible at first, began to grow insidiously until it became an avalanche, impossible to stop—except with the truth: "Pssst! What unit were those guys from?"

"Motor-T," whispered back a corporal who sat next to me. By the time Staff Sergeant Lewis reached 1943, the entire class knew that our three departed classmates were from a motor transport outfit. In fact, they were truck drivers—an important clue that went unnoticed at first.

No sooner had we shared this vital information than the door banged open again. The sergeant major strutted up the aisle, ever-ready clipboard in one hand.

Once again he took over the class and called off eight more names from his board. "Pack up your gear," he ordered them, "and report back to your unit on the double!"

There it was again—not "units" plural, but that singular "unit"; and the second time that a specific group was told to report back to its regular unit. Something was unfolding: Why were the parent units calling their people back? We had no idea.

The sergeant major also had to tell this second group to move it. Not even Superman could move fast enough for a sergeant major. There were suddenly eight fewer NCOs than a moment before, eliminated.

On every military base, regardless of the branch of service, the rumor mill can take on enormous proportions. Life had just been breathed into the mill at Las Pulgas, and for all we knew, into all of Camp Pendleton as well.

"What the fuck is going on?" we whispered under our breath. Each of us in the room scanned the faces of the others, looking for the slightest indication that someone knew something—anything. All we saw were our own dumbfounded expressions mirrored back.

Staff Sergeant Lewis, equally perplexed by the morning's events, tried to drag us back to a history lesson about Tarawa—as if, all by himself, he could impede the grindings of the rumor mill.

"As I was saying, most of the Second Marine Division had to wade in water chest-high to reach a shore five hundred meters away. . . ."

For all we cared, he might as well have left the planet. No one was listening.

That same question—"Pssst! What unit were they from?"—raced around the room. Seconds later, back came the answer: "Thirteenth Marines."

That's really strange, I thought to myself. The 13th Marines was an artillery regiment made up of men we called "cannon cockers." No sooner had we swallowed this latest crumb than the door slammed open once again. As if given a command in close-order drill, the entire class turned in their seats in unison. In strutted the now all-too-familiar sergeant major.

"Excuse me, Sergeant Lewis," he said, once more telling, more than asking, our instructor to stand down. Up came his clipboard once again, and he began reading off names again—too many, on a list I thought was never going to end. No need to ask what unit these men were from. They had to be infantry.

"Report back to your units immediately," he ordered. "Move out, Marines!" There was that word again, but this time it was plural.

Whatever was going on, clearly it involved all the infantry units of the 5th Marine Division.

The classroom became a lot noisier, as forty people began to gather their personal belongings. With each man's hasty exit, the little room seemed to grow that much larger.

That latest list of names had liberally oiled the rumor mill. Up until then, we had been oblivious to noise outside the building, but now suddenly it magnified in volume. Our classroom was near the main road that circumnavigated the entire base. As people left, opening and closing the door like a camera's shutter, we glimpsed snapshots of trucks and more trucks as they roared by, each one laden with troops.

Those of us not on the sergeant major's list could only look at one another in bewilderment. The departure of half the class so disrupted the rest of us that the befuddled Staff Sergeant Lewis told us to take a fifteen-minute break. We bolted for the door.

Filing outside, we lit up cigarettes and watched the departure of our ex-classmates, each with his sea bag on one shoulder, heading for the main road to catch the base bus. Then the buzz began.

"What the hell is going on?" we asked one another.

Following a short lull in the road traffic, another convoy of trucks roared by, most towing howitzers behind them. Something was definitely in the wind. "Whatever it is, the cannon cockers are involved too," said one corporal as he pointed to the artillery pieces in tow behind the trucks.

We all knew that the Marine Corps didn't move artillery pieces around on a whim, but we were clueless as to why. The tension among us rose, and with each passing truck, we grew more apprehensive. You could feel the electric anticipation in the air. Who would be called out next?

Then one of our classmates observed the first piece of solid information. "Hey!" The corporal next to me pointed at the umpteenth truck full of Marines as it disappeared around the bend in the road, "I know that guy. He's with the Twenty-seventh Marines."

The 27th was one of three infantry regiments that made up the 5th Marine Division (the 26th and 28th being the other two, each with about four thousand men). The 26th Marines had deployed to Vietnam the year before and, at that very moment, was entering Marine Corps lore with its heroic stand, halfway around the world, at a surrounded remote fire base called Khe Sanh.

Even more unsettling was that everyone sitting in the entire convoy of trucks had on his helmet and flak jacket. They were holding onto M16 rifles between their legs, the muzzles pointed up. The trucks and the men inside them looked like they meant business. This was no training exercise! They were loaded for bear, packed full of men and equipment. A major infantry unit was definitely mounting out—but where? And more important, why? What had happened in the world that we weren't yet unaware of?

As the last truck drove out of sight, the rumor machine began hitting on all eight cylinders. What would warrant such a rapid deployment of America's best? You had to be dead not to feel the hairs tingling on the backs of our necks. We tried to evaluate everything we knew. The most mundane occurrences had us looking for profound implications.

In 1968, the world situation was a potential tinderbox, and rumors ran rampant. Speculations had those loaded trucks being shipped out on forays to all sorts of destinations, each with its own logical justification. Only two weeks earlier, North Korea had seized the USS *Pueblo*. The Tet Offensive in South Vietnam had just begun. Television footage had shown us fighting inside the U.S. embassy in Saigon. Another rumor had us going up to Los Angeles to put down riots in Watts, but this was the wrong time of year for that sort of thing. Other little hot spots, all around the world, could flare up in a heartbeat: Korea, Cuba, and Quemoy and Matsu, two islands off the Chinese mainland that were sporadically shelled by the Red Chinese. And of course, there was NATO and its Iron Curtain nemesis, the Warsaw Pact, and the always-volatile Middle East.

Our speculations were brought back to earth when we were ordered to return to class. Just as we started inside, a Marine whom none of us knew walked past and gave us a tidbit that shook us to the bone.

"The base has been closed to all outgoing traffic!" he said. "I just got that from an SP!"

"They can't close it," someone said in disbelief. "There's too many Marines and civilians living off base!"

"They're rounding up anyone on liberty in Oceanside," the stranger volunteered, "telling them to get back to their units immediately!"

Oceanside was the town just outside Camp Pendleton. For many of us, it was often the first stop on a weekend pass, our first link to the sanity of the outside civilian world, and it was now off limits! He said the SPs—the Shore Patrol—were cruising the streets, entering every bar and eatery, sending anyone with crewcuts (remember, this was the long-haired 1960s) back to the base and to their units, on the double.

What had begun as a cold morning was warming up in more ways than one. As soon as we got back in the classroom, we shared this latest scuttlebutt with Staff Sergeant Lewis. "Pendleton is closed," he confirmed. "I just heard it from my office people."

Our first question was, "When was the last time they closed the base?" We hoped the practice wasn't unusual. Secretly, of course, we all knew better.

"I've never heard of it being closed except during the mount-out for Korea, back in nineteen-fifty. Speaking of Korea," he added, trying to retreat into his history lesson, "Who said, 'Retreat? Hell, no! We're just attacking in another direction!'?"

Nobody heard him. We were all someplace else again, busy processing his latest morsel: The last time they shut down the base was Korea. So whatever was going down must be of a similar magnitude. Who had been invaded? Who needed rescuing? We were desperate for a radio or any communication with the outside world.

We didn't get too long to wonder about it. We all jumped in our seats to a sound that should have been familiar by then and turned to see the sergeant major making another grand entrance, clipboard in hand.

Staff Sergeant Lewis silently stepped aside.

Uppermost in our minds were two questions: Who's next? and Will it be me? If not in that order. A small part of me wanted to be on the sergeant major's clipboard, just to find out what was going on. On the other hand, maybe staying in Southern California wasn't such a bad deal after all. I slid down in my seat.

He called off three names. We were all tank crewmen. I was now caught up in whatever it was that was going down.

In some way, it was a relief. Now maybe I could get a few answers to the thousand questions on my mind.

The three of us packed our gear and waited for the base bus to take us back to Las Flores and the 5th Tank Battalion. As soon as we climbed the steps of the bus, we asked the driver what was going on. He had nothing to tell us, but he did confirm that the entire base was in a state of more hectic activity than he'd ever seen.

We glued our faces to the windows, looking for any clue as to what was going on. Traffic on the road was unusually heavy, with all sorts of vehicles, including civilian tractor-trailers—an uncommon sight.

The bus let us off and pulled away in a cloud of dust. For a full minute we stood in disbelief, trying to take it all in.

There in front of us was Las Flores, swarming like an ant farm with people and trucks, military and civilian. The heaviest activity was at the rear of the base, up on the ramp where all the tanks were located.

"Whatever it is," said one of my classmates, "tanks are definitely part of it!"

Spread out before us was a sea of activity, with every individual apparently on his own mission. Civilian trucks were lined up on the road that led up to the tank park. Men were crawling over, in, and out of the seventy tanks that made up 5th Tank Battalion.

A tank park, more commonly referred to as "the ramp," was a huge expanse of concrete for all the battalion's tanks. Fifth Tank Battalion was made up of five companies. Four were gun-tank companies, and the fifth was a headquarters company. Each gun-tank company was made up of three platoons, each of which fielded five tanks.

The tanks sat in neatly ordered rows, all precisely aligned. They were always spotless, and their insides even cleaner—which I thought strange, because there was no way to hide dirt in the white-painted interior of the dirtiest dirt-making combat vehicle in the whole Marine Corps. I knew people who wouldn't buy a car with a white interior because it required too much upkeep. Keeping a tank clean was a full-time job.

Alpha Company had shipped out for Okinawa the year before, but Bravo, Charlie, and Delta Companies were still at Las Flores. Alpha, Bravo, and Charlie were medium gun-tank companies equipped with the M48A3 Patton tank. Delta Company was made up of heavy tanks—M103s. Large as they were useless, they were often called "ramp queens," because they seldom left the tank ramp. I had been in Charlie Company for the past thirteen months, ever since the day I left Tank School. I loved my job and was very good at it.

Crossing even the roughest of terrain, the 52-ton Patton tank rode every bit as easily as a Cadillac. It was powered by a Continental V-12 turbo-charged diesel engine that developed 750 horsepower. There was nothing like being able to drive something anywhere, over and through anything. For a young kid into cars and performance, it was the ultimate machine. Luckily, diesel fuel was free, because the M48 chugged a hefty two gallons per mile.

The first time I got in the driver's seat I discovered it had a steering wheel and an automatic transmission; I had been expecting it to drive like a bulldozer, with levers. There wasn't anywhere we couldn't go—or so we thought until we heard the stories of returning Vietnam veterans.

Tanks are large vehicles manned by four crewmen, three of them in the fighting compartment. The driver is isolated in his own compartment, right up front, in the center of the vehicle. The three other jobs were the loader, whose job it was to keep the .30-caliber machine gun fed and the 90mm main gun loaded with its four-foot long rounds; the gunner, who aimed and fired the weapons and never saw the outside world except through his periscope and gun sights; and the tank commander, the man in charge of the vehicle who also had his own mini-turret, which housed a .50-caliber machine gun. I loved any job around the beasts, but driving was everybody's favorite.

After getting off the bus and staring in disbelief at all the activity that lay before us, we crossed the road and headed to our barracks, closer to all the commotion up on the ramp. Each tank had its tarp spread out in front of it, with all its equipment neatly placed on top. By itself, this was no unusual sight. Every three months, each tank's tools, equipment, and crew were inventoried and inspected.

"Is this what it's all about?" I wondered aloud. "Just a silly inspection?"

A classmate offered the first good explanation I'd heard all day: "Maybe it's part of our readiness response test." He was referring to a test that occurred once a year, at random, to check how well prepared we were.

Carrying our sea bags into the barracks, we asked the first man we saw what was going on?"

"Bravo Company's mounting out," he said. "The Twenty-seventh Marines are boarding planes right now!"

We looked at him in disbelief. "Where are they going?"

"Rumor has it, to rescue the crew of the *Pueblo*."

Even in Los Flores, the rumor machine was alive and well, I thought. When it became obvious that we hadn't brought any new information with us, the Marine dropped us as quickly as an ugly girl on a blind date.

Then I bumped into John Cash, whom we all called Johnny, because he played country guitar just like his musical namesake. "What gives?" I asked.

"Nobody's saying, but rumors are that Bravo Company's going to The Nam—tanks and all!"

That was the second time someone had mentioned Bravo Company. I breathed a sigh of relief, hoping my billet with Charlie Company would keep me out of whatever was going down. But Bravo Company couldn't possibly be going to Vietnam. It was made up of recently returned Nam veterans, who were assured a year in the States before they could be rotated back to Indochina. At least that's what we liked to think. The truth was, they could send you anywhere they liked, except Vietnam. Your "year away" could mean a six-month stay at

Guantanamo Bay in Cuba, followed by a six-month Mediterranean cruise, then back to The Nam. Therefore, using flawless logic, Bravo Company was obviously going somewhere, but it wasn't RVN (Republic of South Vietnam).

Another thing didn't sound right. This was 1968, and already there was so much equipment in Vietnam that everyone flew there; no one went with his tank. It was common knowledge that once you flew to Vietnam you would be assigned to either the 1st or the 3rd Tank Battalion. Both had been in-country since 1965. Getting orders for Vietnam always brought fear to any tanker or other supporting-arms Marine, because there was no guarantee you'd end up in a tank unit. If they were desperate to fill grunt positions, you could be snoopin' and poopin' in the grass and never see a tank except from your foxhole. That was not the travel package any tanker wanted!

I didn't know that this scenario, in a slightly different form, had taken place prior to my getting back to Las Flores. I was about to learn what I had been lucky enough to miss.

I quickly got to my barracks, unpacked my stuff, stowed it in my locker, and sought out my tank commander. I had been told that Sergeant Molocko was up on the ramp, so I started the short walk past the other barracks. Even the mess hall was a flurry of activity. Metal carts piled with sandwiches, along with several large drink dispensers and other foodstuffs, were making their way to the ramp.

This was the first time I had ever seen food brought to the men. Something really big was in the air. The closer I got to the ramp, the more nervous and inquisitive I got.

Most tanks were parked behind the battalion's maintenance building. When I passed the building, I saw two civilian tractor-trailers. One was disgorging the new-style searchlights we had been a waiting for more than a year to get. Now, magically, they were here. The other truck was unloading large wooden crates, one of which a forklift was delivering to each Bravo Company tank.

I immediately recognized them as fording kits. Used only for amphibious landings, they allowed a tank to cross deep water safely, so long as the water didn't reach over the top of the tank's turret. This was a sure sign something major was in the works. I thanked my lucky stars that I was in Charlie Company, where there wasn't much activity going on.

I walked down to the Bravo Company tanks, where I bumped into Sergeant Molocko. He seemed overly glad to see me, and I assumed he was visiting friends who were part of the mount-out. "Where've you been the last two weeks?" he asked.

"NCO school. But enough chitchat. Does anybody know what's going on?"

"Well, about twenty tankers were shipped off to the Twenty-seventh Marines early this morning, to become grunts. They're boarding planes. Is that enough for you?"

Holy shit! I thought. Maybe I'd been lucky to be away at NCO school.

Molocko explained that all the tank crews had been reassigned within the battalion. Most of our Charlie Company platoon had been transferred to Bravo Company. "Bet you didn't know you were in Bravo Company now, did ya?"

"I'm part of this after all!" I gasped.

"Yes, we are," he said sarcastically. "I've already done one goddamned tour in Nam, and only six months to go before I get out. I don't like this shit!"

"So, where are we going?"

"Nobody's saying, but I'd bet Vietnam."

On the ramp I noticed a lot of men I didn't recognize. Most were just standing around with their hands in their pockets.

"Who are all these strange faces?"

"Fuckin' amtrackers!" was Molocko's disgusted reply. I soon discovered that they had been sent over from the 5th Amtrac Battalion to fill vacancies left by the tankers now boarding planes as grunts! Well, that explained why so many were just standing around like lepers in a nudist colony. What military genius had decided to break up a well-trained tank unit—and then thought they could be replaced with amtrac crewmen?

It defied explanation. An amtrac, or amphibious tractor, was officially known as a Landing Vehicle, Tracked—LVT for short. They were designed to carry about twenty Marine grunts ship-to-shore in an amphibious assault. They were huge, lumbering aluminum boxes about the size of a bus that could waddle through the ocean and drive up onto a beach.

About the only thing amtracs and tanks had in common was that both shared the same .30-caliber machine gun. The idea that LVT crewmen could easily transfer over to a tank must have been dreamed up in division headquarters by some idiot with no knowledge of either vehicle's capabilities and limitations. His absurdly unfortunate decision would come back to haunt us two months later. Why hadn't they simply taken the amtrac crewmen for the grunts?

People were scurrying all over the ramp. New equipment was arriving all the time, and what didn't arrive fast enough was robbed off my former Charlie Company tanks. About the only good news Molocko had heard was that our platoon sergeant, Robert Embesi, wasn't going to change.

I never met anyone in the Corps who knew more about tanks than twenty-seven-year-old Staff Sergeant Embesi. He was the only platoon sergeant I'd ever had in my short Marine career with 5th Tanks, and I had more respect for him than any officer I ever encountered. Robert Embesi could have been a recruiter's poster Marine. Always sharply turned out, he expected the same of his people. I had never seen him in a fight, but everybody knew you didn't want to mess with him.

I think he took a liking to me because I had never been assigned to any of the countless shit details that were always available. Also, he gave me the opportunity to attend NCO School and NBC—Nuclear, Biological, and Chemical—School. I respected him as a leader and never wanted to do anything to disappoint him.

I was in awe of him. He pulled off countless little tricks, shortcuts, and miracles that never appeared in any tank manual, freely sharing his knowledge with anyone who showed an interest. All the other platoon sergeants looked up to him, deferring to him whenever a question came up that they couldn't answer. Embesi was a superb leader and the acknowledged tank expert within the battalion. His remarkable knowledge of the tank's weapons systems was responsible for my coming to love the TC's .50-caliber machine gun—a most misunderstood weapon, and the scourge of most tank commanders. Later on, another of his .50-caliber lessons would make me an instant hero.

Whenever someone asked a puzzling question, the usual reply was, "Ask Embesi."

I had been assigned as gunner to a tank in the 2nd Platoon. When I heard that its number was B-24—the platoon sergeant's tank—I knew immediately that Embesi had a hand in my assignment.

My new tank commander was Sergeant Hearn, a tough Irishman who was proud to show how he could remove the front teeth from his mouth. I had no reason to doubt what he told everyone, that his original ones had been knocked out in a bar fight. When I learned the real story—which was much scarier—it convinced me I had been assigned the right tank commander.

Hearn had been on Operation Starlite, America's first large-scale operation of the war, and one of its most successful. It had been a true Marine-type operation, with amphibious landings and simultaneous helicopter assaults that enveloped the enemy's rear and resulted in more than a thousand enemy dead. Sometime during Starlite, a detachment of tanks and amtracs was sent out on a resupply run and was ambushed. The flamethrower tank that Hearn was commanding was hit by 57mm recoilless rifle fire and RPGs—rocket-propelled grenades. One of the recoilless rounds penetrated the TC's side of the turret, taking off Hearn's belt buckle and nearly cutting him in half.

Fearing that the huge napalm bottle inside the tank might blow, he and his crew abandoned their burning vehicle. Hearn had the foresight to take the tank's .30-caliber machine gun with him and continued to fight off the enemy.

He was wounded in five different places. One bullet had entered his cheek and exited his mouth, explaining his removable front teeth. His crew fought alongside him, armed only with pistols, and they were all wounded. With his entire column wiped out, Hearn hid in the brush and managed to evade and avoid enemy patrols until a Marine patrol rescued him the next day. For his heroism, he was awarded a Silver Star and a Purple Heart.

Two months later, I would discover just how the terrifying experience had affected him. Hearn would be my tank commander unless the 2nd Platoon was deployed in force. If so, Embesi would take over the TC's position, leaving Hearn free to select the crew position he wanted.

Going by the book, the next job down was the gunner, followed by the driver, and then the loader. Few men wanted to be the gunner, because he was the only crewman without a hatch to stick his head out of. On field operations, a gunner never saw the sky or breathed fresh air. Most men preferred the risk of getting their heads shot off by a sniper than being confined inside a hot, cramped tank all day. But the gunner's job suited me just fine.

After I introduced myself, Sergeant Hearn told me that a couple of the amtrac people had been made TCs because they outranked some of the tankers. Rank alone was enough justification for you to be assigned a leadership job, whether you were qualified or not.

It was downright dangerous to place men's lives in the hands of an ill-trained, incompetent TC. I had yet to serve in Nam, but I knew that any tanker with thirteen months' training was a lot more valuable then a rookie sergeant from amtracs. I was lucky that Embesi wasn't about to put any rookies on his crew.

After I saw the new Bravo Company roster, one thing seemed certain: The newly reorganized unit had too many Vietnam veterans. Some had done their tour of duty, been in the States a year, and were waiting for their discharge in six months. Most weren't career Marines. There was no way we could possibly be going to Vietnam with so many short-timers.

There was also a hefty number of career Marines, "lifers." Most had been to Vietnam at least once, if not twice—which fueled the rumors even more. What was our final destination going to be? Everyone had his own guess. North Korea was at the top of the list, and that idea just felt good. Being part of rescuing a Navy crew had an appealing dash of glory to it. But everyone was discussing Vietnam.

Two days later we mounted the fording kits and new hardware; we packed up our gear and stowed it on the tanks as well. Our sea bags were full of our nonessential and noncombat gear, so we turned them in, to be held for us until we got back from wherever we were going. All we knew for sure was we would be making a beach landing somewhere in the world. We just didn't know which Berlitz language course to buy.

The twenty tanks of Bravo Company were driven to the embarkation point on the beaches of Camp Pendleton. Anchored a mile offshore was the USS *Thomaston*—a Landing Ship, Dock, or LSD. From her stern came two Mike boats—Landing Craft, Mediums, or LCMs, ferrying three tanks and their crews out to the mother ship at a time, which took most of the afternoon. This kind of loading was always a slow job, no thanks to a landing craft's ramp, which was exactly twelve feet wide. A tank's width measured eleven feet, eleven inches. Squeezing fifty-two tons through, with only half an inch on either side, was tricky and tedious.

We loaded onto one of the LCMs and it motored out to the *Thomaston's* stern. Slowly we entered the LSD's cavernous well deck, and the Mike boat beached herself inside. After our boat dropped its ramp on the well deck, each tank carefully inched its way off and was guided by Navy personnel to a pre-assigned location. We were surprised to see that ours weren't the only vehicles on the ship. Packed well forward in the LSD's hold were several cranes, bulldozers, and other large noncombat military vehicles.

Each tank crew was responsible for chaining—or in Navyspeak, "dogging down"—its vehicle to the well deck, which required four large, heavy chains.

What made it even harder was the lack of room between vehicles. The Navy sure knew how to use every square inch of available space, but that severely limited our working area. The tanks were packed asshole-to-elbow, with only eighteen inches between them. What could have been a ten-minute job took two hours.

Once Bravo Company was aboard and dogged down, the LSD raised its stern, pumped out the water, and we got underway. Only then was our destination finally, officially announced over the ship's PA system. Our destination was the port facility of Da Nang, Republic of South Vietnam.

The impossible had happened! Some Nam veterans who hadn't been back in the States for even a year yet had been caught up in the mount-out and were going back again. You could hear jaws dropping all over the ship.

Sergeant Hearn, who had only a few months left to serve in the Corps, was one of the most pissed-off. The perceived wrong only magnified the seriousness of our rapid deployment. The enemy's Tet Offensive, then in full stride, had touched every city and hamlet throughout Vietnam. Someone had desperate need of us, and we were on our way.

Suddenly the veterans started treating us first-timers like second-class citizens. Even though we were all figuratively (and literally) in the same boat, they despised us because "we" hadn't yet done our part, yet here they were, going back over for a second time—some for a third. I could sympathize, but I hated their strange and unfair rationalization and the way they took their anger out on us.

The USS *Thomaston* was to be our home for the next three weeks. She was fourteen years old—considered new by Navy standards and a tub by us Marines. Everyone gathered on the fantail and watched as the California coast sank beneath the horizon.

Few spoke as we watched the land disappear. We wouldn't see the States again for thirteen months. The reality of what was happening began to set in, along with the uncertainty of what lay ahead.

I thought about my father and his similar departure to a war in the Pacific in 1944. Now his son, a Marine just like him, was shipping out, twenty-four years later.

It was announced that we would be stopping in Guam for refueling in about twelve days. Guam was in the Marianas, the same island chain containing Saipan and Tinian, the two islands where my dad fought. He had survived three landings and served in his war for three years, until its conclusion. Marines of the Old Corps had served for their war's duration, waiting to be either victors or casualties. Right then, I couldn't understand how any of them had managed to survive.

Thinking about it, I realized I had it a lot easier, having to survive for only a year before I returned home. But at that moment, it seemed like an impossible goal. Eternity was staring me in the face.

Chapter 2

Crossing the Pond

As the shock of learning our destination wore off, we looked to find our assigned berthing areas. They assigned a swabbie to lead our 2nd Platoon's five tank crews to the berthing area, where we would sleep during the next three weeks.

All passageways look alike aboard a Navy ship, so he tried to explain how to find our way around using a numbering system painted on every bulkhead throughout the vessel. The system was more confusing than the ship itself, impossible for any Marine to interpret, but the swabbie assured us that we would know our way around in just a short time.

As we soon found out, that—along with anything and everything the Navy told us—was a bold-faced lie. Actually, it took something close to two weeks before we got the hang of it, which meant many hours of wandering a frustrating myriad of corridors—"passageways."

Our first days at sea found Marines bumping into each other throughout the bowels of the ship. A conversation would start out, "Do you know how to get to the ship's mess?"

"No. Do you know how to get to the showers?"

But for some of us, those three weeks were a blessing. Many inexperienced amtrackers had to assimilate what was normally an eight-week Tank Crewman School without the benefit of land for practice. They had no experience driving a tank, much less firing any of its systems. But, hey, aren't tanks and amtracs just about the same thing? In some idiot's mind, they were.

Twice a day news was posted on a bulletin board outside the ship's radio room—once we could find our way there. Each subsequent posting fed us a little more information as to why we had been pulled out of California so abruptly. We were part of a response to the Tet Offensive, which had caught Army Gen. William Westmoreland's Military Advisory Command, Vietnam (MACV), totally off guard.

Only days before our own departure, the 27th Marines had left California by plane and were already in the field in Vietnam. Some ex-tankers were humpin' the boonies as grunts. We didn't ignore our luck. We were a lot safer aboard ship than in the field with the mud and the bugs. Luckier still, our three-week voyage would count against our thirteen-month tour of duty. God must have meant for me to be a tanker!

But, just like our own tanks, we were crammed into a berthing area efficiently designed to pack as many people into as little space as the Navy was willing to provide. Our compartment, straight out of every World War II movie I'd ever seen, consisted of a free-standing row of bunks, stacked four-high down the middle of the compartment. Down each side of this center island ran aisles only two feet wide. Against each bulkhead were more bunks, also stacked four-high. The ship was one giant sardine tin, with us as the sardines.

Shipboard life brought us into direct contact with our Navy brothers. I say "brothers" because the Marine Corps is actually part of the Department of the Navy. We had no problem with this arrangement because we considered the Navy to be like a giant department store— and we Marines were its men's department. We often bragged how the Corps built the Navy so that we could get around.

In short, the two services weren't particularly fond of one another; and the squids—as we called Navy personnel—loved to pull practical jokes on us unsuspecting landlubbers. Squids always liked to make us Marines look stupid, which wasn't always hard to do. After all, we were strangers in an alien environment. A little showmanship and convincing lines made many a Marine into an easy mark.

We had been at sea for only a couple of days when one squid visited a hapless Marine around 3 a.m. and told him, "Wake up. It's your turn for mail buoy watch."

Being awakened for a two-hour watch was hardly unusual; every outfit always had some kind of watch going on. At three in the morning, a groggy Marine didn't ask too many questions. Conditioned to obey orders automatically, he would do whatever was asked of him—provided it was delivered with enough authority.

"What's mail buoy watch?" he might think to ask.

"For the next two hours," the squid would explain, "it's your turn to stand watch on the ship's bow and watch for the mail buoy."

"What's a mail buoy?"

"All the forwarded mail for you Marines gets flown out ahead of the ship and dropped in a bright-colored buoy. Your job is to look out for it."

To the half-awake brain, this sounded more than halfway plausible. Much as the tanker craved sleep, he sure didn't want to be the guy everybody resented for missing their letters and packages from home! For the remainder of our cruise to Da Nang, it wasn't unusual to see one lone Marine standing on the bow, cigarette in hand, scanning the horizon for letters from home.

Wouldn't victims of this prank band together and warn their comrades? Quite the contrary, because the sucker, embarrassed by his own gullibility, wouldn't breathe a word. Sometimes, he would even aid and abet the Navy pranksters' next attempt, helping lead his fellow Marines to the slaughter. Each new sacrificial lamb helped restore the previous victims' self-respect, reassuring them that they weren't that dumb after all.

Our days weren't free by any means. During the voyage, we maintained normal working hours. Amtrackers attended class while we worked on the tanks. Something on those complex mechanical beasts always required attention. One day, which will stay with me forever, I saw my brief life flash before my eyes.

Sergeant Hearn ordered me to disassemble and clean the main gun's breechblock assembly. This was the solid steel block that slammed home after a round was loaded into the chamber. It closed with enough force and authority to intimidate any new tanker. Disassembling and cleaning the breechblock had to be done from inside the tank. It involved hooking a chain hoist to the top of the turret to lift the very heavy block out of the gun.

One of several tricks to expedite its removal involved elevating the gun instead of jacking the chain hoist. I hooked up the hoist and began elevating the gun, which meant that the breech, inside the tank, was going down. As it did, it slowly pulled the block out of the breech. I had elevated the gun almost to maximum when I heard a soft muffled pop.

What the hell was that? Immediately I stopped and lowered the gun to investigate when a strong smell hit my nose. I thought it was some kind of solvent, but then a small amber river began to meander along the turret's floor. I recognized the smell of Scotch!

I was already guilty of violating the rules. To elevate the main gun, I had used the TC's override handle, which engaged powerful hydraulic pumps. Officially, the book stated that any movement of the turret or gun in a confined area must be done by hand, in order to avoid damage to the turret's hydraulic motor should the gun abruptly bump into an obstacle. But because turning the turret or elevating the main gun manually was very time-consuming, many of us paid little attention to the rule. We just made sure that our platoon sergeant or platoon leader wasn't around when we did it.

I followed the little river of liquid to its source and found a Scotch-soaked canvas AWOL bag that had been stuffed way under the main gun. To see whose bottle I had just broken, I looked for some name or identifying mark on the bag. When I turned it over, the name hit me with the force of a prizefighter's blow: SSGT. ROBERT EMBESI.

All I could say was, "Oh, shit!"

Suddenly queasy, I broke out in a sweat. Please, God, anybody but Embesi! I'd rather have been stripped of my rank—rather have eaten that broken bottle—than tell Embesi I broke it. Where could I hide until we got to Da Nang? Getting rid of the bag was impossible—the smell permeated the entire tank. And the Navy had very strict rules; having alcohol aboard ship was a court-martial offense.

What was I going to do? Could I run fast enough and long enough to outrun him? Suddenly the *Thomaston* had shrunk to the size of a small dinghy, and swimming suddenly seemed like a very serious option.

Embesi wasn't around, which may well have saved my face from being permanently rearranged. My two fellow crewmen, working on the tank's exterior, followed their noses and peered down into the turret from the two hatches above me.

"What the hell's that smell?" they asked with Cheshire Cat–like grins, assuming that I—sitting on the turret floor, about to be nauseous—had been holding out on them. But when I explained what had just happened, they both looked at each other, then back at me, their eyes big as saucers.

"You broke Embesi's bottle?" they asked in unison. "Embesi's bottle?"

"Oh shit, man!" said one. "You're dead!"

"No shit!" I replied. "Tell me something I don't know!"

Some people just love to see others squirm in a difficult situation. "Are you a strong swimmer?" the other guy asked with a half-giggle.

"I don't suppose either of you has a bottle, do you?" I pleaded.

"On a Navy ship?" they both said, feigning shock that I would even dream of their breaking such a rule.

Now I dreaded having to tell Embesi what I'd done. The last thing I wanted to do was disappoint him, because he had been very good to me. I was only a twenty-year-old "snuffy" still wet behind the ears, less than two years out of boot camp, with no combat experience.

I cleaned up the mess and gave serious thought as to how I should approach Embesi about his secret bottle. I dismissed the thought of playing dumb—the inside of that turret reeked of Scotch and there was no way to get rid of the smell. But while cleaning up, I came up with a great idea. When I explained what had happened, I'd use the word "we," thereby deflecting some of the wrath that I knew was sure to follow.

I walked through the bowels of the ship, scared to death and rehearsing my lines, while trying to find his quarters. Eventually I found the staff sergeant's quarters and approached Embesi. He was in the midst of a Pinochle game with three other staff sergeants.

Gathering up my courage, I asked, "Can I talk with you a minute? We have a little problem on the tank."

He had just called trump after winning the bid. "What is it?" he wanted to know.

"I can't say right here."

Unintentionally, with his fellow staff sergeants sitting right there, he made it even more difficult. "Whatever you got to tell me can be said here. What's the problem?"

"We were cleaning the breechblock," I began, "when we raised the gun to . . ."

"Don't you even fuckin' tell me!" he shouted.

"It was a mistake. We didn't see . . ." Again I had no chance to finish, but I thought the *we* part was working well.

"That was a thirty-dollar bottle of Glenlevit! What fuckin' idiot raised the gun using power? Didn't anybody bother looking underneath the fuckin' gun?"

Out of first-person plurals, I looked down at the deck. "Sergeant Embesi, it was me."

The small room broke into catcalls. Half of them began needling Embesi about having a bottle of booze on board a Navy ship and not sharing it with his fellow staff sergeants. The others asked me, "Do you know how short your life expectancy just became?" and "Did you pass your drown-proofing test?"—a type of training all Marines go through in case we're stranded in the ocean for any period of time.

"You dumb son-of-a-bitch!" Embesi yelled. "I was saving that bottle for . . . get the fuck out of my sight!"

He didn't have to ask me twice. I went back to the tank to hide out and count my blessings—and my teeth. I felt unbelievably lucky I hadn't been given a personal one-on-one karate demonstration.

The next morning, Embesi climbed in the tank's turret. I heard him inhale deeply, and he looked at me like someone who had just lost his best friend. "God," he said, "I love that smell!"

To his credit, he never mentioned the incident again.

Until I put this story down on paper, I didn't realize that the bottle of Scotch—broken or not—was a court-martial offense for its owner, not me. I could have just as easily said, "Sergeant Embesi, why'd you hide that contraband under the gun of my tank? Don't you realize you could go to the brig for that?" But I was far too young and naïve.

That night, I wrote my mother a letter, pleading with her to break all U.S. postal laws and send me a replacement bottle. Of course, my letter wouldn't get mailed until we had landed in Vietnam, and her bottle could never reach me fast enough.

BY THIS TIME, our voyage was beginning to get old. The squids had enjoyed messing with us, playing one long mind-fucking game after another, until we found their weak spot. We disliked C rations, but they loved them. Because each of our tanks carried several cases of twelve meals each, we soon realized we had some major negotiating power.

Embesi's experience—nine years in tanks and a previous tour in Vietnam—proved invaluable. One tip he shared with us was how handy thick nylon rope could be. It was very strong, far more flexible, much lighter and easier to work with than our issue tow cables, which were stiff, unwieldy, and hard to get on and off a tank. "Try to borrow, swap, or steal some from the Navy," he told us. That became my job.

Of the very little I had learned about the Navy, I knew that if you wanted to procure anything aboard ship, you sought out a boatswain's mate. With that in mind and a case of C rations under my arm, I sought out a petty officer first class—in the Navy, a rank equivalent to that of a staff sergeant like Embesi. "I'm looking for rope," I told the squid. "And for the right kind I'm willing to trade a case of C rats."

To my surprise, that got his immediate attention. "How much do you need?" he asked. "What diameter?"

"Fifty feet of three-inch rope should do the trick."

He looked at me like I was a complete idiot. "Why do you need such thick rope?"

I explained how we would use it in the field, instead of our stiff heavy tow cables.

"You sure that's what you want?"

"Yes," I replied, naïve enough to think I was dealing with an honest seaman—sort of like assuming I'd found an honest lawyer.

"Where do you want it?" he asked. "Ya know, ya can't leave it sitting out, or we'll both get in trouble." He added that the thickest rope available on ship was only two inches in diameter.

"No problem." I said. Doubled up, the thinner-diameter rope would still be much easier to use than our heavy cables. "Just make it a hundred feet then. I'll leave the tank's hatch unlocked, so you can drop it inside the turret."

He confirmed my order. "Ya want two-inch rope, right? Ya know, it ain't gonna fit inside."

One hundred feet of rope would fit inside a tank's turret with room to spare. His last statement should have set off a warning bell in my head, but I was too caught up in making the deal.

Before I could say anything, he nodded. "I'll just put it on the back of the tank and throw your tarp over it."

"Okay," I replied. "No problem."

He smiled. "I'll arrange for the delivery tonight. But I'll take the C rats now." I handed him the case, proud of the good deal I'd just negotiated.

Next morning, we were eating breakfast in the ship's mess when Embesi walked over to me. "What's that pile of crap on the back of the tank?" he asked.

Knowing how much he wanted the rope, I told him what a great job I'd done and all the details of the trade.

He just started to laugh. "Go down to the well deck and check out the tank."

I finished eating and went below, squeezing my way between the rows of tanks until I got to ours. When I climbed up on its back, I was confronted by our tarp hiding a truly voluminous mass. Hell, I could supply all of Bravo Company with all the rope I had here. That Navy guy had really outdone himself!

I pulled back the tarp, and my jaw dropped. Lying there before me—knee-high, nearly four feet in diameter—was a gigantic coil of the thickest, heaviest steel cable I'd ever seen. It weighed at least a thousand pounds!

I stood there, stunned. What the fuck was going on here? I proceeded to scour the ship, looking to track down the dumb squid who didn't know nylon rope from steel cable. When our eyes finally met, he smiled—as if he'd been expecting me!

"Why the hell'd you leave me all that goddamn cable, instead of the rope I asked for?" I demanded. "I couldn't even budge that pile of shit!"

"No," he replied, "I don't suppose you could. I had to use the ship's crane to get it up there."

I was really pissed. "Look, I asked you for one hundred feet of two-inch-diameter rope. What do you call that pile of steel cable on the back of my tank?"

"I call it rope, son," he said in a condescending tone. "Maybe what you really wanted was line."

That was my first lesson in seamanship: What we Marines called rope, the Navy called line; and what we called cable, they called rope!

He had kept his end of the bargain and was sticking by it, knowing I didn't have much choice. "Of course," he volunteered, "if you want me to replace it with line, it'll cost ya' another case of C rats."

I certainly couldn't leave a half-ton of cable sitting on the back of my tank, so—shrewdly—I negotiated for him to remove the rope and replace it with the line I wanted.

He just smiled. "Been nice doin' business with ya, son, but I'll take the C rats now."

After being taken like that, I really hated the Navy. My revenge would come later, but right then, I couldn't imagine how.

As OUR DAYS AT SEA became longer and longer, the ship seemed to get smaller and smaller. Several of us were so bored we broke into one of the frozen-food lockers. Over the ship's intercom, our angry captain demanded that the guilty parties come forward. Of course, we didn't. But at least he got a lesson in the kind of tools that tankers carried with them—a Marine bolt cutter goes through a Navy padlock with no trouble at all.

We ate our fill of ice cream that night. But try as we might, we couldn't empty three five-gallon containers. After a couple of hours, we had to dispose of the evidence before we had a mess on our hands. At 2 a.m., three faint splashes could barely be heard on the port side of the *Thomaston* as we shared our leftover dessert with the fish.

Well into our second week, we sighted our first landmass, Guam. I was surprised at the island's size and its degree of civilization. Except for the tropical palms and the jungle we passed on the way into the harbor, it could easily have passed for a base back in the States, with its streets of houses with cars, telephone poles, and streetlights.

The six-hour layover gave us all a chance to get off the *Thomaston*. It was easy to spot landlubbers who had just spent twelve days on the high seas. We were the ones experiencing the strange symptoms of what the squids called sea legs, weaving from side to side as if the island itself was rolling—or so it felt.

Refueling went way too fast, and we were ordered back aboard.

We spent our days down in the well deck going over our chariots, cleaning, inspecting, and returning every part that was humanly reachable.

A tank's most vulnerable component was its very heart: six very large 24-volt batteries, accessible through a hinged door on the turret floor. Only two batteries could be reached at any one time, and you had to rotate the turret to get to the next pair under the floor. Their contacts and connector cables required frequent cleaning, especially in the salty air. For a rookie tanker, the job could be hazardous. By definition, a tank's 24-volt battery discharged a mere twenty-four volts, but it also delivered the enormous amperage needed to turn over the M48's twelve-cylinder diesel engine.

And so, when working around these large batteries, great caution was necessary. First you removed your watch and any rings—especially rings!—because any metal tool making contact between a battery post and any part of the turret caused an immediate arc.

If a wrench ever slipped out of someone's hands, bouncing against a terminal and the turret floor at the same time, the resulting crack! of amperage and shower of sparks could make the calmest man jump. There wasn't a tanker alive who hadn't experienced this at least six times in his career.

Sometimes, the wrench didn't simply bounce away; it actually welded itself to the points of contact. When that happened, you had to act fast and break the contact—with the blow from a hammer or a swift kick from a boot. If you didn't react quickly enough, the wrench would quickly glow red-hot and make the battery explode. I had never seen this recipe for disaster until one morning, down in the Thomaston's well deck, when one of us got a shocking initiation to one of the many differences between tanks and amtracs.

Getting at the batteries was always a tight fit, and the rolling of the ship didn't make the job any easier. Along with many of the other tank crews, I was sitting on top of the turret, cleaning the copper fittings that screwed each leg together to create the long aerials we used. I happened to be looking in the right direction when, suddenly, a blue-white flash, as if someone was using an arc welder, lit up the well deck. It was immediately followed by a loud CRACK! Every veteran tanker recognized the sound.

A banshee-like scream immediately followed. A solitary ring of blue smoke rose from the turret where the arc of light appeared.

None of us moved. We knew what had happened and we just smiled at the tank silently, looking for the rookie who had made the mistake. Five seconds later, up out of the turret came the head of Corporal Washington, an ex-amtracker. Smoke seeped from his hair like steam rising off asphalt after a summer rain. His eyes were as wide as I'd ever seen on a man. Looking around, he realized that twenty pairs of eyes were centered on him. His expression changed to that of a kid caught with his hand in the cookie jar. Smoke was still coming off his head when he uttered what became the immortal words of the cruise: "Them bat-trees is sure much bigger then them amtrac bat-trees!"

Washington's larger-than-life grin brought the house down. The entire well deck broke out in a roar of laughter followed by a few cat-calls. "Hey, Sparky! Workin' on them batteries, are ya?" Then, with an embarrassed grin, even Corporal Washington started laughing.

THE RELATIONSHIP BETWEEN the Marines and our Navy hosts became strained. One afternoon we ran into a major storm that pushed the ten-uous Navy-Marine relationship to the breaking point. As the seas grew increasingly rough, we quit work and went back to our berthing areas. Scores of queasy men showed signs of seasickness. Then the PA system barked, "All Marines go below and dog down your tanks."

On a rolling ship, a loose fifty-two-ton object becomes a serious threat. Fearing that the tanks might shift around in the well deck, the Navy wanted us to add additional chains, the better to secure them. We put on our foul-weather gear and reported onto the main deck, into the teeth of a driving rain. The *Thomaston* seemed to be rocking more than you would expect for a ship of her size. Later I learned that an LSD has a flat bottom, denying her the ability to right herself as she took on ocean swells, thus accentuating the ship's movement.

All the tank crews were bent over the rail, staring down into the ship's cavernous middle. Not one of us moved. Fifty feet below, our tanks swayed with each swell, straining against the chains. Suddenly—as if one had fired a main gun—a chain exploded and went flying across the well deck.

We all looked at each other, waiting for somebody to make the first move to go below. No one was that stupid.

A minute later, another chain below us let go. "All Marine personnel, go below," the PA system repeated the same announcement, "and dog down your tanks immediately!"

Another chain flew across the well deck. Twenty tank crews looked down into the mayhem, then back at each other. No one budged.

Our commanding officer, Captain Morris, came out among us. "What's the problem?" he wanted to know. "Why aren't you going down as ordered?" Then he saw why. "Stay put," he told us and strutted off toward the ship's bridge.

Five minutes later, we saw dozens of the ship's crew running through the well deck, dragging heavy chains behind them.

Later, we learned that our CO and the ship's captain hadn't seen eye-to-eye about whose responsibility it was to secure the tanks. The Navy captain—equivalent in rank to a Marine colonel—demanded that the Marines go below to tend to the tanks because his ship was in danger. The Marine CO countered that he wasn't sending any of his men down there, that the Navy was responsible for chaining down its cargo. Fortunately, no sailor was injured down there that stormy afternoon—if the Navy didn't hate us before, they sure did now.

Even so, evenings aboard ship were filled with monotony. Writing letters didn't make much sense because they wouldn't be mailed until we reached Vietnam—and no one had yet sighted the mail buoy! We were getting restless. We wanted this cruise to end.

Did I say "cruise"? What a ludicrous, misleading naval term for a floating jail, with us as its prisoners! With boredom coming out of our asses, we couldn't understand how the squids could stand living on a ship. All they seemed to do was chip paint. Twenty or more squids would stand shoulder-to-shoulder, hammers in hand, banging on the side of a bulkhead knocking off the paint. Then someone would come along and paint the bulkhead again. When the squids weren't chipping paint, they were tying pretty rope designs around the hand railings to afford a better grip. We Marines saw that for what it really was—busy work.

Some evenings, they showed a movie in the mess hall, which held only about eighty people—a fraction of those on board. Two weeks of boredom made for pushing and shoving as men tried to get in. By the third week, though, we were bored enough to just listen to the movie without seeing a single frame. What's more, we came away satisfied!

Those Marines not listening to the movie gathered on the *Thomaston's* stern to have a cigarette, because smoking below decks was forbidden. Still others got lost staring at the turquoise trail of phosphorescent foam stretching for miles behind the ship. It was the most peaceful time of day, and it gave us a chance to check on Heckle and Jeckle, who we'd picked up on our third day out of California.

It was the first time most of us saw an albatross. What was so remarkable was their effortless ability to fly without flapping their long, thin wings. The graceful U-2's of the bird world, Heckle and Jeckle cruised about a hundred feet behind us—catching the air currents as the ship plowed through the sea—for the entire voyage. I don't think either bird flapped its wings more than six times across the entire Pacific Ocean.

I wished I had actually read "The Rime of the Ancient Mariner," one of my many missed assignments in high school English. All I could remember was that a seaman killed an albatross and had to wear it around his neck forever. For what purpose, I couldn't remember, nor could I recall what made the bird in the poem so special—but according to the squids, albatrosses were a good omen.

We were only a couple of days from our destination—just as well, because this "cruise" had gone on way too long. Another tanker—I'll call him Joe—and I planned a last act of defiance, to leave our mark forever etched on the *Thomaston*. We went down to the well deck, dipped into my tank's tool kit, and found an open-end wrench of just the right size. For several days now, I had been eyeing the ship's bell. I thought it would make a great souvenir of our three-week imprisonment at sea. Tonight, I decided, was the best time to liberate it.

It was 0200 on our last morning on the prison ship. Joe and I crept forward to the area outside the ship's bridge where the bell hung. The bridge was manned continually, but its windows were waist-high, which allowed us to sneak around the outside without being spotted. Below the window was the ship's bell, a sixteen-inch brass forging, held out from the bulkhead by a bracket with a single bolt—for which we carried just the right size wrench.

While Joe held the bell's clapper to keep it silent, I unscrewed the bolt. It all took less than three minutes. We then stuffed the bell into an AWOL bag and took it down to the well deck. I wrapped it up in our tarp and placed the whole package in my tank's bustle rack on the rear of the turret.

At daybreak, the shit hit the fan. Not only was the ship's captain pissed off, the Marine CO was equally irate. Both of them demanded that if the perpetrators didn't come forward and return the bell, the whole ship would be turned inside out until it was found.

Afraid that the captain would follow through with his threat, I ran down to the well deck. In a heartbeat, I was on my tank. I grabbed the bundle and threw it down on the deck between the rows of tanks. I quickly unwrapped the bundle and pulled out the bell. Where could I hide it where it wouldn't tie me to the crime? Then I was struck with a brilliant idea!

Twenty-one days after leaving California, our "cruise" was finally coming to an end. We couldn't wait to get back on the land that we saw beginning to grow from the horizon—even if it was Vietnam. Around mid-morning the ship dropped anchor. We started to unchain the tanks, getting them ready to disembark. I kept one eye on the bell, which I had wedged beneath the track of the tank ahead of mine. Yes, the Navy would get its bell back, but it would have a slightly different ring to it—a flatter sound, if you will.

All the crews sat atop their tanks, eagerly waiting to unload. Joe was acting as a ground guide, the guy who walks ahead of the tank and gives hand signals to guide the driver over to the waiting Mike boat. He and I were the only ones who knew about the bell. I wasn't about to tell Embesi, because I wasn't sure how he might take it.

Slowly the stern of the ship was lowered, letting seawater slosh into the well deck, up to where the tanks were located. A few minutes later, a Mike boat motored into the cavernous hold and dropped its ramp on the dry deck. The last tank to be loaded in California was now the first to slowly board the Mike boat for its run to the shore.

Finally it was the turn of the tank right in front of ours. Joe gave its driver the signal to move ahead. The engine revved, straining as its treads tried to overcome the unseen wheel chock of solid brass. Joe, pretending to be frustrated, motioned the driver to hurry. He, in turn, added more throttle.

No Navy bell could hold back 750 horsepower and fifty-two tons! Even so, the tank leaned slightly to the left as its right track passed over the obstacle before proceeding effortlessly toward the Mike boat. As the tank vacated the space in front of us, I tapped Embesi on the shoulder and pointed to what looked like a brass manhole cover lying on the well deck. He looked at me without realizing what I was pointing at. It was our turn to move, and he was preoccupied with talking our driver over to the Mike boat.

Goodbye to the Navy and the three longest weeks of my life!

Chapter 3

The Debut

After twenty-one days at sea, we made the kind of entrance rarely seen this late in the war. Here was an entire company of twenty Marine tanks, together with their crews, landing at the docks of Da Nang. Nothing like this had happened since the Marines first arrived three years earlier, in 1965.

As if we had been beamed down from some unseen starship, we left one world and suddenly materialized on another. I didn't realize how often we'd use the term "world" when referring to back home in the United States, as in, "I can't wait to get back to The World." All who served in Vietnam understood that universal term, for it was as much a truism as any description you could ever provide. Nam wasn't so much a world away, as it was a journey back in time. It was as if we had emerged in the Stone Age, different from anything with which we were familiar.

As we came ashore, it wasn't the heat that made the first impression upon me, but rather the aromas. We had been isolated for three weeks from anything but the ocean's salty air, occasionally mixed with a whiff of the *Thomaston's* smoke. Now, suddenly, our noses were overloaded with all sorts of smells, some of which I would never get used to and would permeate everything in the coming year. Along with the usual dockside odors, there was another dank aroma that smelled of dirt and decay that had a sweet, almost nauseating flavor. Part of that smell, I would later discover, was that of burning diesel fuel and human excrement—the ubiquitous fragrances issued by every American outpost in Vietnam. You smelled an American base long before you ever laid eyes on it. Mid-mornings, you could identify the location of an American base from miles away by the telltale columns of black smoke from the burning shitters. No exit off the northern New Jersey Turnpike was more offensive to the nose.

Second most noticeable were the heat and humidity. Having abruptly lost the artificial wind created by the ship, we found ourselves in the very uncomfortable mid-eighties with a humidity index that only a sauna could challenge. Added to all of this was the infrequent and random punctuation of very distant booms, like far-off thunder. But this thunder had a much sharper report, like very distant fireworks. We had heard this sound before, back on the artillery ranges of Camp Pendleton.

Reality began to set in. All at once, thirteen months seemed like a life sentence, totally unattainable. I'll never get out of here, I thought. Some of us wouldn't.

From the Mike boats that ferried us from the *Thomaston*, we drove the tanks up a dirt road and waited for the rest of the company to disembark. We just sat there, taking it all in. I noticed that we were parked next to a fenced-in holding pen containing military vehicles of every description. All were in a horrible state—heavy battle damage, mostly due to mines. The eerie sight of these vehicles was my first visible proof of the unhealthy environment that lay ahead. They were waiting to go back to The World, and after having arrived only a few minutes ago, I wished I could go with them.

Out of this lot of wounded and victimized vehicles, it was easy to spot the lone Marine tank simply because of its size. Our tank crew of four, sitting on top of our turret, naturally became curious as to how one of our own had won a return passage back to The World. More importantly, maybe we could get it to reveal the fate of its crew.

We climbed the fence and approached the tank on our wobbly sea legs, each of us commenting on how it felt like the earth was moving beneath us. As we got closer, our eyes scanned the vehicle, looking for any outward sign of why it had earned a ticket to go home. Unlike most of the other vehicles, it was definitely not a victim of a mine. We examined it like the crime scene that it was, looking for clues.

But the tank appeared to be fine; its suspension and track were intact. "Maybe it's just a mechanical problem that couldn't be fixed here," I suggested.

As we got closer, Embesi said, "Keep an eye open for anything we can salvage." His motives were totally different than ours: We wanted to know the past, and he was thinking of the future.

Embesi's experienced eye spotted it first. On the far side of the turret was a small hole, about half an inch in diameter, surrounded by burn marks, as if someone had tried to use a blowtorch to cut a hole through the metal. We all recognized the hole as that made by a shaped charge. Tanks fired a similar—albeit larger—projectile that left the same type of marks. What astonished us most was the angle at which it struck the tank's turret wall. We guessed it to be about 75 degrees off perpendicular. At such an oblique angle, it should have ricocheted.

"That's an RPG hole," Embesi said. An RPG-7, or rocket-propelled grenade, was the enemy's equivalent of our bazooka—except that it penetrated ten times better. When striking a target with a contoured surface it seldom ricocheted—something a bazooka would do, all too frequently.

This little hole didn't look all that menacing and was far smaller than the hole that one of our HEAT (high explosive anti-tank) rounds would make. Apparently its glancing blow had managed to penetrate through four inches of solid steel.

So this is what an RPG does? I wondered. While stationed in California we had all heard about RPGs from returning veterans, who talked about them only with the utmost respect. We had all heard stories of just how effective their shaped-charge warheads were against even the thickest areas on a tank. Now I was witnessing their capability first hand.

"Find me a piece of wire so I can check this out," said Embesi.

The driver and I scoured the ground, looking for a piece of wire—for what, we had no idea. Finally the driver discovered a one-foot-long piece. Embesi straightened it out, inserted it into the little hole, and then pushed it all the way in. It met no resistance, confirming that the RPG had penetrated the turret wall.

It wasn't hard to imagine the rest of the scenario. Without looking, we could visualize what lay on the other side of Embesi's wire. Inside the turret, where the hole came in, was the ready rack—where the first and most accessible rounds of main gun ammunition were stored.

An RPG-7 is a Russian- or Chinese-made shoulder-launched, unguided missile that was fired from a handheld tube. The missile had fins on the end; it looked too similar to our own bazooka rocket. But unlike the bazooka, the RPG missile was not launched from inside a tube that might have increased its accuracy. Instead, it was stuck on the end of a launcher that had a trigger handle halfway down its length.

Later, I would learn just how fast a well-hidden enemy could jump up and fire one. In two short months, we would see for ourselves that thirteen inches of solid steel was equally vulnerable. An RPG could enter at almost any point and spray the inside of the vehicle with a jet of molten steel.

Like any weapon it also had its limitations; fortunately for us, it was highly inaccurate. To ensure a hit, the shooter had to position himself very close to his target. Fortunately, too, most RPG hits were not lethal, provided a crewman wasn't directly in its path when it punched its way inside the vehicle. But it was catastrophic if the molten jet came in contact with any of our four-foot-long 90mm main gun rounds—of which there were sixty-two stowed inside the tank. Therefore, a hit from an RPG was a crewman's worst nightmare.

Now I was more curious than ever about the fate of the crew. A million questions ran through my mind. What had happened on the inside? Did the crew get out in time? Was the gunner spared? The three of us hoped to satisfy our morbid curiosity by looking inside. We climbed up on the tank and opened the loader's hatch.

"Holy shit!" we said in unison as we looked into each other's awestruck faces. We had opened the door to a crematory whose smell overpowered us. We jerked our heads back, trying not to gag.

None of us was prepared for the unbelievable sight. The inside, once white, was now jet black. The radios had been melted into an unrecognizable pile of scrap, and the plastic control handles at the gunner's station had melted away. Each of us dwelled a little longer on the spot where his own crew position would have been.

We sat back up to catch our breath with another gulp of fresh air. From the ground, Embesi reminded us to see where his wire entered the turret.

The three of us held our breath again and looked back inside. As we had suspected, it came in right next to where one of the 90mm rounds would have been stowed. Obviously the RPG had detonated the projectile sitting there.

Probably curious as to our reaction, Sergeant Embesi climbed up on the tank and looked inside the loader's hatch. Unfazed, he said, "Now there's an oversight on somebody's part, leaving the .30 in there. Somebody go down and pull that gun out. We can always use another machine gun."

Leave it to Embesi to make lemonade out of lemons, but I couldn't believe what he was asking us to do. Had it been anyone else, I'd have said, "If you want it so bad, you go down there and get it." It was one of those orders directed at no one in particular but meant for either the driver or me. We wanted no part of climbing into someone else's coffin.

He and I just looked at each other, hoping the other would make the first move.

Sergeant Hearn sensed our hesitation and lowered himself through the loader's hatch. He tried to remove the machine gun, but it wouldn't budge. Welded in place by the intense heat of the explosion, it was as worthless as the rest of the tank. That was fine with me, because I felt taking it would be like stealing from the dead.

Embesi's initial observation had been right. The RPG had detonated the first round it came in contact with, and then the rest of them. No crewman could have survived such an unlucky hit. Embesi was quick to explain to us that this was a perfect example of infantry not working with the tanks. Little did I realize that this would be a constant struggle throughout my entire coming year. It was natural for the grunts to want to stay behind such a large, solid object as a tank; they thought of us as being invulnerable. They didn't realize just how much we needed them to flush out the enemy RPG teams ahead of us.

Well, I thought to myself, that was a hell of a welcome to Vietnam. I had just been splashed in the face with a cold bucket of reality. Suddenly, for the first time since becoming a tanker, I felt vulnerable. The fingernails of my subconscious dragged across the blackboard of my consciousness, sending shivers down my spine. My suspicions were suddenly confirmed: I was not going to like this place. And the already unfathomable next twelve months seemed more like twenty years.

Thoughts of that blackened tank and its crew stayed with me for several months. In hindsight, that burned-out shell of a tank could have been the worst example to show an FNG (fuckin' new guy). For me, it was the best example. That charred interior galvanized in my mind the vitally necessary cooperation between tanks and infantry.

IT TOOK THE REST OF OUR COMPANY another two hours to get ashore, then we got underway. We must have made an impressive sight—twenty tanks moving out in one long column. Next to flattening the *Thomaston's* bell, it was the best part of my day.

We traveled through the outskirts of Da Nang into the countryside, still traveling on a dirt road. The road was on an earthen berm, elevated about five feet above the ground. I looked around, expecting shell craters and burned-out vehicles along the way. I never saw even the faintest suggestion of a war, except for the constant amount of military traffic. But it was the amount of civilian traffic that surprised me most of all.

We passed several troop-laden vehicles heading in the opposite direction. The passengers turned their heads to gawk and point at us, then laughed. The more trucks we passed, the more obvious it became, until I was sure we were on the outside of an inside joke. At first I thought it was the large mass of armor that was drawing everyone's attention our way. I supposed it wasn't every day that one saw twenty tanks traveling in a column in The Nam, as if out on a Sunday drive. It never crossed my mind that *we* might be the joke. All those passing veterans saw were twenty brand-new tanks with crews in clean stateside uniforms traveling as if on parade, as if the circus had just come to town. In their eyes, we were instantly branded FNGs. It must have been embarrassing for the returning veterans in our company, some of whom were back for a third visit.

We began passing some of the ubiquitous rice paddies that make up the lowlands throughout all of Vietnam. It was the first time I saw people working their sunken plots or was treated to the common Vietnamese practice of squatting in a paddy to relieve one's self, right in plain sight, followed with a whip of the hand to dispose of what had been gathered from the barehanded wipe. They were their own source of fertilizer and didn't mind sharing the view with us.

"Jesus!" I moaned out loud without taking my eyes off the woman in the calf-deep muddy water who had just wiped and flung. Embesi and Hearn laughed at my typical FNG reaction, but I made a mental note to never eat Vietnamese rice for the duration of my tour.

We turned onto a side road, which led up a steep grade and into a combat base. Our grand and noisy entrance brought all activity inside the base to a standstill. We were subjected to incredulous stares. As we pulled into the tank park of 1st Tank Battalion, I got my first glimpse of what real tanks looked like—after serving in the field a little too long. After thirteen months of stateside tank duty, I could only stare in disbelief at their beat up, disheveled condition.

Four or five of them were being worked on. Most were undergoing a PM (preventative maintenance) procedure—a glorified oil change that all tanks receive every three months. These were fighting tanks that had been in-country for years and thus showed their wear, tear, and mistreatment. All of them were missing their headlights. Most were missing one or more fenders and had homemade replacements of corrugated roofing material. Their infantry phones on the rear fender had been ripped off long ago, and only one or two tanks still had searchlights. These veteran tanks had been in combat longer than any World War II tank had ever served.

Common to all were the sections of track bolted along the outside of their turrets to afford extra protection against RPGs. In front of the driver's position, welded homemade brackets holding a dozen sandbags gave him a little more protection. Several tanks had their .50-caliber machine guns mounted outside and on top of the TC's cupola, in a configuration called a sky mount—their solution to the jamming problems associated with the .50. It looked cool, but I knew it was foolish. Embesi agreed with me that a sky mount required the tank commander to stand far too high out of the turret to operate the gun.

Finally, I realized why we were the object of so many flabbergasted stares, why the sight of our twenty brand-new stateside tanks drew nothing but laughs and guffaws. We were the new guys pulling into the veterans' tank park with our glistening chariots. In the Marine Corps, you never wanted to look like an FNG, because that immediately singled you out for any shit detail when someone needed a warm body.

Back when I was first assigned to Tank School in California, I had just finished Advanced Infantry Training at Camp Lejuene, North Carolina, and had been in the Corps fewer than five months. Our brand-new green utility uniforms, or work clothes, had yet to fade like those of veteran Marines. Some of us would go into town to an Army/Navy store to buy used, faded uniforms so as not to look like the rookies we really were. Now, sitting in this "real" tank park, I wished I could buy a used, faded tank!

One of the veteran vehicles had a noticeable list to one side, and I went over to investigate why. It was obviously the victim of a large mine; most of its roadwheels were missing on the far side. The name painted on its gun tube—Mother's Worry—reflected the concern of somebody back in The World. From the looks of this tank, Mom had every right to be worried. Was her boy okay? I hoped so.

Looking around in the park, I saw that all the veteran gun tanks had names on their gun tubes. There were also two flame tanks, sometimes called Zippos after the cigarette lighter manufacturer, capable of shooting a stream of napalm several hundred feet. Flame tanks all had one thing in common—they always had great names. Thirty years later, I can still recall some of them: Looks Like Jelly, Burns Like Hell, Crispy Critters, Dante's Inferno, Devil's Disciple, and Baby Burners.

I decided we had to come up with a name of our own. After securing the tank, we got our stuff together and were led to temporary living quarters—tents stretched over wooden frames. But they did have wooden floors and were up off the ground, plus the compound had electricity, hot showers, and hot food.

Our driver came into the hooch and said, "You ain't gonna believe this, but they got movies too!"

"A movie?" I asked in total surprise. "In The Nam?" Maybe this wasn't going to be so bad after all!

Once we got situated and unpacked, we walked around to get the lay of the land and stumbled across an enlisted man's club where beer was served after working hours. Things were really looking up for us. I found the mess hall and planned on eating dinner that night. Overall, I was feeling pretty good about my first day in-country.

Next day we worked on the tanks, had a warm lunch, and worked some more. That evening, after chow, I grabbed an early seat for the movie. I still couldn't believe we were going to watch an outdoor movie in The Nam! Hell, I thought, I just might be able to do this year thing standing on my head, no problem at all!

The movie theater was an open area with rows of benches; the screen was a building with one side painted white. That evening turned out to be as surrealistic as any I would ever experience in Vietnam. It felt like we were at a drive-in movie, but without the cars. Odder still was the random and distant rumble of very distant artillery; the war would continue as we watched the movie. I found it quite disconcerting, as I sat in the open with a large group of people, that I couldn't help thinking that one lucky incoming mortar or rocket could take out the entire crowd of people. How could this kind of entertainment go on at night in the middle of a war zone? At that moment, we were all certain that the war was nearby. After all, we could hear it and see its flashes on the horizon. Little did any of us FNGs realize just how far we were "in the rear with the gear."

The most ludicrous thing about the entire evening was the movie itself. A more absurd film could not have been shown to a group of Marines. John Wayne's *The Green Berets* brought ninety minutes of non-stop catcalls and laughter at Hollywood's interpretation of the very war in which we were now immersed. The fact that it was an Army story made it even funnier. But we FNGs totally missed the highlight of the evening. One of the last scenes of the film brought a cacophony of out-bursts, finally drowned out by a hysterical laughter that grew in intensity. But I didn't understand the joke.

There was John Wayne, standing on a beach somewhere in Vietnam, watching the sun slowly set on the ocean's horizon—an impossibility unless the Earth changed the way it turned! In front of me, once I was clued in, was a gross error made by Hollywood. That scene later con-firmed to me just how little anyone back home understood this war.

We remained in the tank park to load ammunition off numerous supply trucks. It was hot work and took two entire days. The 90mm ammunition came in wooden boxes, two rounds per box. Each crew had to carry thirty-two boxes to its tank, cut the metal bands, and take out each projectile, which was enclosed in its own cardboard tube. Then we had to break the seal around the tube and pull off the very tight top, much like a large mailing tube, and carefully slide the round out.

Each 90mm round was actually a giant rifle bullet four feet long and weighing around thirty-five pounds. On the bottom of the round's base was the primer, just as you would find on a bullet, only much larger. It was the primer that, when struck by the firing pin, would detonate the powder in the shell casing. It required only twelve pounds of pressure to set it off. Needless to say, you didn't stand the projectile on its base. You always held rounds with one hand over the base to protect the primer as you carefully loaded them into the tank. It was slow work that took all four crewmen. Two of us on the ground broke open the boxes and passed each round up to a man standing on the fender next to the turret. He then passed each round down through the loader's hatch to the loader himself, whose job was to store the ammo.

There were several different types of main gun ammunition and each was suited for a specific job. Canister was our favorite for its shotgun-like properties that threw out a wall of 1,100 quarter-inch diameter chopped steel rod, each of which was about a half-inch long. It was extremely effective out to 300 meters and would lay a swath through the thickest of grasses—or masses of people. The next most common round we carried was high explosive or HE, which was an artillery-like projectile that would throw shrapnel in all directions at the point of impact. It was good against people when they were beyond the reach of canister. HE's best feature, however, was the delay setting that could easily be made by the loader that permitted the round to penetrate a structure before detonating. It was excellent against bunkers.

A new round had just been introduced into the tank arsenal called flechette, more commonly referred to as beehive. What made this round unique was that it had a plastic dial on the nose of the projectile. It was the loader's job to turn the dial to the range of the target, which the tank commander would give him. Beehive was an antipersonnel round that was full of 4,400 one-and-a-half-inch long nails that had fins on the back of them; they looked like miniature darts. When the round left the gun tube, it would explode at the preset range and set up a wall of darts 100 meters in front of the target. It was a good round against massed enemy troops in the open, which wasn't a common occurrence. Its one drawback was that it didn't have any "knock-down" effect. An enemy soldier could be hit by several darts that served only to really piss him off. Close in, canister was, by far, the better round.

We also carried white phosphorus, or "Willy Peter," which was just like an HE round except that it was loaded with phosphorus that burned on contact with the air. It was very effective against bunkers, but was used more often for marking purposes to show aircraft where a target was located. Most tanks hated to carry the stuff for fear that it could ignite inside the tank if hit by an RPG. There was another main gun round that was being phased out that we sometimes came across called high explosive plastic (HEP). The projectile was made up of soft C4 plastic explosive that flattened out against the target before it detonated; it was actually an antitank round that was marginally okay against bunkers but did not have the penetration capability of HE nor its deadly shrapnel. The last type of round we carried was high explosive antitank (HEAT), which was excellent against armor or steel-reinforced bunkers. It was not the round of choice in 1st Tank Battalion's TAOR, but was the number one round in 3rd Tank Battalion tanks. This was due to the enemy armor threat that was purported to be up north along the DMZ. It was up to the tank commander to decide the mix of ammunition he wanted and where and how it would be stored.

We also unloaded case after case of machine gun ammunition. Typically we carried 10,000 rounds of .30-caliber ammo and 2,000 rounds of .50-caliber machine gun ammo. It all had to be broken open, spliced together, and laid in the huge ammo boxes inside the turret. The remainder was packed on the back of the bustle rack. You could never carry enough .30!

Twenty tanks would require almost seven hundred cases of main gun ammo, eight hundred cases of .30, two hundred cases of .50, and several cases of .45-caliber pistol and submachine gun ammunition. It was an enormous, backbreaking effort, and the hot March sun didn't make it any easier. Anytime an FNG complained about the heat, the veterans chuckled among themselves and told him, "This ain't shit. . . . Wait until July."

We also scrounged up as many pieces of spare track as we could find lying around the tank park and bolted it to the sides of the turret, but spare track was in very short supply. Slowly we began to look like a vehicle ready for combat.

A few days later a Captain Johnstone, who had been in-country a few months, replaced our company CO. We then moved out as a full tank company, taking all twenty vehicles to a firing "range"—actually an area that bordered on a free-fire zone. These were zones designated as being "open season, all season" for anything caught moving within them. It meant that you could shoot with no questions asked, for anything found inside these areas was the enemy. There was no reason for anyone to be in those areas, and all the locals knew it.

The area we were going into was actually the entrance to a wide preserve called Happy Valley. According to the veterans in our unit, some of whom had previous first-hand experience in the valley, it was anything but happy.

The reason given for our little excursion was to "sight-in the guns," the most ridiculous excuse ever given to a bunch of men. After all, these tanks had just come from Pendleton, the perfect environment for setting up guns and sighting systems. No, the real reason for our jaunt was to give a little training to the amtrackers. They had never so much as seen a tank fire, let alone driven one. They were totally unaware of the complex ballet that goes on within the turret during live fire.

We traveled a dirt road through an area covered by scrub and low bushes. It was hot, dry, and dusty. A column of dust trailed behind us as twenty tanks churned up the dry earth. Our tank, B-24, was in the middle of the long column.

We had been on the road for only twenty minutes when the column came to a halt. Over the radio we heard that somehow the lead tank had become mired in a mud bog. Just where the mud came from was anybody's guess.

The rest of the tanks formed a large defensive perimeter around what looked like a prehistoric beast stuck in a tar pit. Embesi and Hearn jumped down and took our Navy line with them. Embesi told me to get up and man the TC's position and keep watch on our side of the perimeter. I traversed the main gun to cover an area dense with scrub and brush. The driver remained in his position, keeping an eye out as well. He and I talked over the intercom as I kept him abreast of the rescue mission to our rear.

Between talking with the driver, watching the perimeter, monitoring the radios, and occasionally glancing over my shoulder at the progress being made on the stuck tank, I failed to notice that our tank was . . . moving. It was imperceptible to both the driver and me, but it was, nonetheless, moving. At some point, something just didn't look right.

We both noticed it and even commented upon it, but neither one of us could put a finger on it.

Looking over at one of the other tanks manning the perimeter security, I noticed immediately that it had settled about a foot into the ground, halfway up to its roadwheels—and then it hit me! Our tank was also slowly sinking into what looked like dry, dusty ground!

I jumped out of the turret and onto the fender to take a closer look at our situation. We had sunk further than the tanks on either side of us, but my first thought was that Embesi was going to kill me!

"Pull up!" I yelled to the driver, "Pull ahead! We're sinking!"

The driver overreacted, added too much power, and caused us to sit down even further in the quagmire until the tank's hull was sitting on the ground!

The noise we made by revving the engine had drawn everyone's attention, causing Embesi to run back to the tank. I was afraid he would be really pissed and blame me for the situation I had gotten us into—and he wouldn't have been wrong. At the same time, all the other TCs ran back to their own tanks as soon as they discovered that they had the same problem too; most had sunk at least a foot or more. It had quickly become a scene where the rescuers might be the ones in need of rescuing—a giant cluster fuck; it later became known as Johnstone's Folly.

Our tank was hopelessly mired. Embesi ran to the other tanks of his platoon, warning them of the danger of applying too much power and allowing the tracks to spin and dig themselves into a deeper hole, as we had done. By applying a slow and steady amount of power, all the tanks were able to extricate themselves from the mud. Embesi then backed one of the freed tanks up to ours, hooked up the tow cables, and with a lot of difficulty, finally pulled us out.

Once free of the mud, the tanks had to keep moving in order to avoid sinking again. That day, the driver and I both learned something vital that would come in handy time and again, during the coming months: Never take anything for granted, not even dry dusty ground!

Embesi never said a word to me. He knew that I had just learned a lot from that little incident. Nevertheless, as we started to move out of the area, he did say, "That was the damnedest ground I've ever seen" and warned me later to be more observant.

Jesus Christ! I thought. I had to watch the bushes, check all the potential avenues of approach for an enemy I was certain was out there, and monitor the radios. I also had to keep an eye on how they were doing with the mired tank, make certain we didn't run down our batteries—and I was supposed to watch our height above the ground too?

This was going to be one very long year!

Chapter 4

Welcome to Eye Corps

The military had divided South Vietnam into four geographical areas called military regions—I, II, III, and IV. U.S. Marine units operated in the northernmost area, Military Region I, which was overseen by the ARVN and thus called "I Corps." South of that was II Corps, then III Corps, and the southernmost IV Corps. All of these corps areas were referred to by their numeral designations, except for I Corps—One Corps was universally called "Eye Corps."

At the northern border of I Corps was the Ben Hai River, which separated North from South Vietnam. On each side of the river was a 3,000-meter buffer zone, set up by a United Nations mandate in the mid-1950s. This neutral area was called the Demilitarized Zone—the DMZ—or simply, "the Z." It should have been called the Militarized Zone, because it was anything but demilitarized. Our side bent over backward to honor the neutrality, but somehow the North Vietnamese never got the word. The DMZ became a Communist sanctuary, even on the southern side of the river. It fell within the TAOR (tactical area of responsibility) of the 3rd Marine Division, headquartered in Quang Tri.

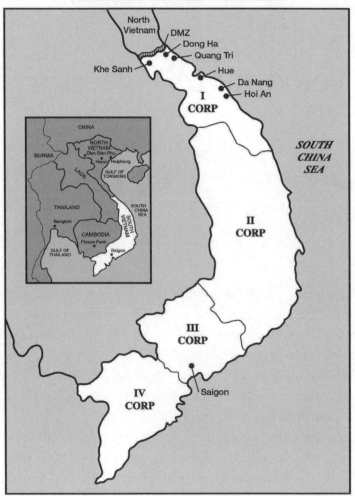

THE FOUR MILITARY CORPS AREAS OF SOUTH VIETNAM

One hundred and seventy miles south of the DMZ lay the large coastal city of Da Nang, home of the other Marine division operating in Vietnam, our own 1st Marine Division. When it came to the type of war each division was fighting, the 170 miles separating the two might as well have been 1,700 miles. The North Vietnamese Army troops along the DMZ were extremely well equipped, being in such close proximity of their supply bases. Third Marine Division troops didn't have to worry themselves about flinging away an empty C ration can, but in the Da Nang TAOR, you didn't dare throw anything away. Once Charlie got hold of it, yesterday's empty tin can could become tomorrow's homemade mine.

The fighting wasn't any harder in one area than in another, just totally different. I didn't know it yet, but in the bloody year of 1968 I would be one of the few Marines to fight with both the 1st and 3rd Marine divisions. Both divisions were facing the same enemy: hardcore NVA regulars reinforced by full-and part-time Viet Cong guerrillas. The major difference was that 3rd MarDiv (as it was also called) had to contend with North Vietnamese heavy artillery from the north side of the Ben Hai River. Their large-caliber guns—mainly 130mm and 152mm—shelled all the Marine fire bases at will, as far south as ten miles below the DMZ. One day in 1967, for example, Con Thien—an isolated fire-base overlooking the DMZ—received more than 1,200 rounds of enemy artillery. Up north, it was closer to the kind of combat experienced in Europe during World War II than in any other part of Vietnam.

Outside Da Nang, 170 miles to the south, the NVA was far more resourceful and relied on psychological warfare by the placement of thousands of booby traps. They played a real head game on anyone who had to walk for a living; a grunt never knew if his foot would still be attached with each step he took. Tankers had to tie down their aerials so as not to snag booby traps placed up in the trees that were designed to kill the unwary tank commander.

FOLLOWING THE GIANT cluster fuck of the sinking tanks in Happy Valley, Bravo Company received orders assigning its tank platoons to different combat bases southwest of Da Nang. All five tanks in our platoon were sent to support 2/27 (pronounced "two-twenty-seven," which stood for 2nd Battalion, 27th Marine Regiment). They were part of the 5th Marine Division and had arrived in-country just weeks earlier; they were part of the same stateside reaction force to the Tet Offensive that we were.

We packed up our gear for a trip that took us past Hill 55 to 2/27's newly established fire base. Fire bases were common to the Vietnam War and consisted of a defensive position that had at least a battery of artillery set up inside of it. Artillery's role was to support the patrols that went out beyond the fire base as well as other fire bases within range.

Weaving throughout the Da Nang TAOR were countless numbers of rivers, which meant lots of bridges. If there was one truism in I Corps, it was that bridges always came in pairs. There was the wooden one you actually used, and the steel one that had been blown up a decade or so before. It seemed that the French hadn't done a very good job of guarding the steel bridges. But that was another war, and besides, they lost theirs—something that we, early in 1968, couldn't imagine ourselves doing.

The French influence was obvious throughout all of Vietnam, which was sometimes a little disconcerting in view of what we all knew became of them. But their most frequent souvenirs were the concrete bunkers— or what was left of them—usually found at both ends of most steel bridges.

Our platoon was assigned an area within the fire base. The base was about two hundred meters in diameter, with plenty of room for our two large tents and our cots. Not bad, I thought. At least we wouldn't be sleeping on the ground. Little did I know that we would almost never sleep on the cots. Once set up, we had to build an ammo bunker for storing extra tank ammunition. That hot, nasty job required the filling and stacking of thousands of sandbags. The temperature was still cool by Vietnamese standards—meaning that during the afternoon it was in the low 90s. As for the humidity, I was sure it could have been assigned a measure of viscosity.

It took us three days to build the ammo bunker and another day to unload and stack the spare ammunition that was brought in by truck. For that first week, we were still together as a complete tank platoon, but slowly we were introduced into the routine of Vietnam. At night, we always stood watch in our tanks on the battalion's perimeter, and soon we began to accompany the morning road-sweep teams as a security force.

Every morning, all over The Nam, road sweeps took place at the same time—about an hour after sunrise. They consisted of two men waving mine detectors back and forth, seeking out little gifts that Charlie might have planted during the night. It was a slow process that required the presence of a security force to protect the sweepers. Generally, two tanks moved along fifty feet behind, their turrets pointing at opposite sides of the road in anticipation of an ambush. Following behind the tanks would be two or three trucks carrying additional grunts as a reaction force should we be ambushed.

Nights at the fire base were spent on the tank, usually assigned to one of several slots around the battalion's perimeter. An earthen berm made up the fire base's perimeter; each slot was a revetment into which a tank could drive, leaving only its turret exposed level with the berm. Occasionally, if all the platoon's tanks were inside the perimeter for the night, we kept one tank next to our living area as a reaction unit, just in case it had to be summoned elsewhere on the perimeter. Embesi rotated the crews through that enviable reaction job. That meant that every fifth night I got to sleep on a cot and didn't have to stand watch. In The Nam, you didn't often get a full night's sleep unless you were an officer or a senior NCO.

Occasionally, G-2, the division intelligence section, alerted the battalion to expect a possible attack on a given night. Such warnings guaranteed two things: first, that we'd get only four hours' sleep because half the crew would have to be up and ready all through the night; and, second, that we wouldn't get hit at all! G-2 was not known for its reliable intelligence.

There were hot showers within a short walking distance of our tents, and the mess tent was nearby too. We had left behind the luxury of the movies and the NCO Club, but—naïvely—I began to think this wasn't so bad, that I could handle the twelve months that lay ahead. I had no idea how lucky we had been so far.

The first day of our arrival at the fire base, several men sought us out to say hello. These were ex-tankers who had been plucked from 5th Tanks at Camp Pendleton to fill grunt positions. They immediately recognized the presence of several strange faces in our platoon. When we told them these were amtrackers who had taken their place, they became justifiably enraged. Who could blame them?

One of these former tankers was a friend of mine—I'd been best man at his wedding only three months earlier—who gave me some first-hand scoop on just how bad it was to be a grunt. "The worst things are the booby traps," he said. They had already lost several men since arriving in-country a month earlier. He was afraid that as a grunt he would never make it out alive, that the odds were stacked against him. "It's only a matter of time," he told me. Like all the other ex-tankers, he wanted to get back into a tank outfit in the worst way. Several months later, I learned that he didn't make it after all. His story read like a script from a cheap Hollywood war movie, where the guy just knows he's going to get it—and does.

During the day, there was an endless list of details you could get assigned to, but I never got stuck with any of them. True to form, I owed my "luck" to Embesi. He was watching out for me; my getting assigned to the platoon sergeant's tank wasn't just a stroke of luck, after all. Embesi usually saved the really bad chores, like burning the shitters or mess duty, for disciplinary cases. Burning the shitters was a morning routine all over Vietnam. It meant dragging the collection cans from the outhouses, adding diesel fuel, and lighting the contents. Just what the purpose was is still a mystery to me today; the practice continues, even through the war in Iraq.

Embesi called the group of troublemakers his "shit-birds," men who always seemed to be on the edge, trying to see what they could get away with, getting into some kind of trouble and waiting for Embesi to bail them out. He stood behind his men but made them pay for it later with the lousy jobs.

At the head of the list for platoon troublemaker was Cpl. Gary Gibson, a round peg looking for a square hole. Gary was a really good guy, dependable under fire; he knew what he was doing but was always trying to see what he could get away with. His mouth and Irish temper often got him into trouble.

Gary had served with Embesi during a previous tour in The Nam. One night, while standing watch in the field, Embesi told me a story about Gibson and another guy stealing some food from the mess hall, late one night.

The two men had managed to sneak inside and put together quite a stash before the mess hall's gunnery sergeant caught them. Fuming and wanting justice, the gunny demanded to know what unit they were from, then asked for their platoon sergeant to be summoned to the mess hall.

When Embesi arrived, he acted surprised and disgusted, and verbally dressed the two men down. Then he told the gunny that he'd like to punish the men right then and there. Would the gunny stand outside the mess hall door and keep a look out for any officers? The gunny was from the Old Corps, so he watched Embesi roll up his sleeves; he knew exactly what this young sergeant had in mind. That suited the gunny just fine—those two deserved a good ass-whipping.

Embesi grabbed the two men by their collars, flung them into the mess hall, and snarled, "I'm gonna make sure you don't do this again!" The gunny just smiled and stood guard in front of the door, listening to the gratifying sounds of a full-blown brawl. Embesi was beating the tar out of them. Chairs were thrown, fists connected with flesh, bodies crashed on the mess hall deck. Against Embesi, a multi-degreed black belt in karate, they didn't stand a chance.

It was all over in a few minutes. Embesi dragged the moaning figures out of the mess hall; they were holding their faces in their hands. "They won't be doing that again!" he promised the gunny, as he took the two in tow. Satisfied with their punishment, the gunny dropped the charges against the pair that had violated his mess hall. Unbeknownst to him, Embesi never laid a hand on his men; he just bailed them out the best way he knew how. He staged the entire fight!

You had to like a guy like that. He didn't let any outsider impact the men under his command. You didn't get away with anything and the administration of any discipline stayed within the platoon.

BUILDING THE AMMO BUNKER was exhausting work. At lunchtime it was too damned hot to eat, and several of us preferred to rack out. About six of us were lying on our cots when Corporal Gibson dreamed up a prank to pull on our new lieutenant (LT). We had picked him up when we left 1st Tank Battalion, and nobody had much respect for him. After all, he was a second lieutenant and didn't know diddly squat about tanks or The Nam.

Gary got hold of the LT's poncho liner. These liners were relatively new to Vietnam. Made of a soft nylon material with a camouflage pattern, they also served as blankets and were prized by everyone. Gary filled a small cup with battery acid and, as if it was Holy Water, sprinkled it all over the liner. Once he finished blessing the blanket, he folded it up and put it back at the head of the LT's cot, right where he found it.

That night, the crews were all out on the berm with their tanks. Several days later, I heard the rest of the story from Embesi.

After playing cards, Embesi and the lieutenant decided to turn in. The lieutenant's cot lay near the entrance to the tent. A single lightbulb hung from the tent's center beam. Facing the light, the LT shook open his blanket. The shadowed side of the blanket was pierced by dozens of beams of light streaming in from the bare bulb.

The LT stood there, dumbfounded, looking at what appeared to be a giant slice of camouflaged Swiss cheese. "S-s-s-ergeant Embesi!" he stuttered, "What happened to my poncho liner?"

Embesi knew what—the LT's blanket had fallen victim to an old tanker's practical joke. "Moths, sir?" he asked.

"Moths that eat nylon?" The lieutenant was really pissed; he knew somebody had messed with his blanket. "There's a chemical smell to it, but I can't tell what it is."

Embesi took a sniff to confirm his own suspicion—but he never shared it with the LT. He also had a pretty good idea who the culprit was, because he had supplied Gary with the battery acid earlier that afternoon for his tank. But he kept that to himself. He simply promised the whiny lieutenant that he would get him a new blanket.

Gary Gibson had made Embesi's shit list once again.

Chapter 5

First Rites

Every war has its own nickname for the infantryman. World War I had its Doughboys. World War II had its GIs. "Grunt" was my generation's term for the combat infantryman. No better term could have been found for this war, in this ungodly hot country where men in the field had to pack eighty to one hundred pounds of gear on their backs. "Grunt" said it all.

For any new man in The Nam, the first thirty days was a make-it-or-break-it situation. In order to survive, you had to digest—quickly—an overwhelming amount of information never mentioned in training. A grunt, in particular, could not afford to be a slow learner, nor would his comrades tolerate it.

There was an endless list of things to learn:

• Upon arriving in Vietnam, the first thing you learned was not to wear both dog tags around your neck. You removed one and tied it in the laces of your boot. The reason behind this practice wasn't very reassuring to anyone who just arrived in The Nam. Its purpose was to increase the likelihood of identifying your body if you got obliterated by an explosion.

• A green star cluster—a pen-sized device that shot up colored fireworks—meant that a patrol was coming in. A red star cluster signaled an enemy ground attack.

• Take one white malaria pill every day, and the big red one on Sunday.

• Take your salt pills four times a day.

• Don't aim the tank's main gun over the driver's head. In case your tank hits a mine, he won't split his head open on the gun tube.

• When you hear a flare pop in the night sky, cover one eye. That way, you can retain night vision in the other eye.

• Never use the word "repeat" over the radio. It's an artillery term that means "Keep firing until told to stop." Rumor had it an entire company had been wiped out by someone's misuse of the word over the radio. Supposedly, the unit moved into an area that had just been heavily shelled by artillery. A radio operator with the grunts was having trouble understanding a garbled message and said, "Repeat your last."

Unfortunately, the artillery unit that had just done the fire mission was monitoring the same channel. What they heard was a request to repeat their fire mission. We all doubted the story, but we never used "repeat."

• Before inserting your rifle magazine into your weapon, tap it against your helmet, so that the bullets don't jam as they feed into the rifle.

• The first P-38 can opener you find, attach it to the chain with the dog tag around your neck. A P-38 was the only tool that could open a can of C rations.

• Never go on a night ambush with a canteen not filled to the very brim. Anything less than full would slosh and make noise.

• Before starting the tank's engine, shut off all radios to avoid blowing their fuses.

• Before shutting down the tank, turn off the radios—for the same reason.

• If the enemy is close by and you can't talk over the radio, one click of the radio's handset means "Yes" and two clicks, "No."

• Tape down the spoon on every grenade in the tank, in case a pin should rattle loose and set one off.

• Keep more tension on the tank's track than in the States to discourage it from coming off.

And so on, ad infinitum. There was so much to remember and so little time in which to learn it, that—especially if you were a grunt—you only hoped you got it all before it got you.

DURING LONG OPERATIONS, Marine grunts were beasts of burden, inhumanely loaded down with equipment either in, or on, their 782 gear. The Marine Corps called its antiquated ex-Army packs 782 gear; it was used to hump a grunt's basic living essentials into the field. Nonessential items were limited to what you were willing to carry in the hundred-plus-degree heat. Needless to say, personal effects were kept to a minimum.

On extended operations, packs usually contained extra pairs of socks, two or three meals of C rats, an extra canteen of water, salt pills, and a few personal items such as a toothbrush and maybe a razor, depending on how strict your CO was. Troops shaving in the field was a sign of a unit with discipline.

I remember thinking that shaving in the field was an officer trying to impress his superiors by demonstrating his authority at the expense of his men and their morale. Every man bitched about keeping his chin clean, but today I can appreciate the method behind the madness. Something as mundane and senseless as shaving provides a traditional reminder of the normal world. It helps maintain discipline in the midst of insanity. More importantly, it instills pride and self-respect.

Every grunt's pack contained the last letter from home, along with a spare bottle of "bug juice." All Army and Marine grunts wore their primary bottle of insect repellent on their helmets, held in place by a thick black rubber band.

It was also common practice to secure the plastic poncho to the outside of the backpack to make room for extra C rats, Claymore mines, and trip flares to be hauled out each evening to set up night defensive positions in the boonies. The poncho not only kept the rain off, but doubled as a makeshift stretcher, with a Marine at each corner to carry its owner to the rear—and hopefully to medical attention. Its last job was to act as a body bag, a drape to cover the dead in the field. Contrary to Hollywood, regular body bags were used only in the rear areas; they were never brought to the field.

Attached to the pack was an entrenching tool used to dig foxholes, although not everyone carried one. The infantry carried other items too, in a collaborative group effort toward their mutual survival. You could see some men hauling a couple of 81mm mortar rounds, while others carried extra belts of machine gun ammunition. Both mortars and machine guns devoured large quantities of ammo, and when the shit hit the fan, running out of ammo could spell instant extinction. So everyone carried as much ammo as he could.

Hung on the packs' shoulder straps were other items such as flashlights, hand grenades, and usually a knife unique to Marines called a Ka-Bar. Officers and senior NCOs also had a compass and map case hanging from their belts.

No matter what his job, every man wore around his waist a web belt, attached to the shoulder straps on his backpack, which helped defer some of the weight. Like the pack, the belt was loaded down with several items—always at least two canteens of water, sometimes three or four. There was also a medical kit and possibly, but not usually, a gas mask. Under the pack, everyone wore the ten-pound flak jacket that was mandatory in the field. Each grunt wore a heavy steel helmet on his head, plus an inner helmet liner. To top it all off, each rifleman had to carry at least two bandoleers full of loaded M16 magazines slung over his head and shoulders. Along with this enormous load, a few men needed to carry a couple of Light Antitank Assault Weapons (LAAWs) that were effective against enemy bunkers. A total load of eighty pounds was commonplace, but many were often far heavier.

Some men, such as the M60 machine gunner and radioman, carried even greater loads. The radio was a heavy, back-mounted box with a large appetite for batteries; extras always had to be humped into the field. The machine gunner had to be part pack mule to carry all of his gear, ammo, and the bulky weapon. To make their plight even worse, radiomen and machine gunners sustained the highest casualty rates. Due to their effectiveness, they were the NVA's first targets. After the opening shot in a firefight, their life expectancy was purported to be eight seconds. That high casualty rate was no surprise because they were so easy to locate. The radioman had an antenna sticking up from his back like a neon sign screaming, "Here I am! And the guy next to me is the commanding officer!" The machine gunner was slightly more fortunate. He didn't draw attention to himself until his gun opened fire—at which moment, the M60's distinctive sound and rate of fire instantly revealed its location. Unlike the little 5.56mm (.223-caliber) rifle bullet that the M16 used, the M60 was the only weapon on the battlefield that fired the heavier 7.62mm (.308-caliber), which had tremendous penetrating capability and wasn't deflected by grass or light obstacles. When an M-60 opened fire, the enemy would immediately direct all their fire at the indispensably deadly weapon.

Grunts were the centerpiece of any Marine operation. They certainly had every tanker's respect, and we thanked God for not being assigned as one. Odd as it seemed, every grunt I ever talked to was glad not to be in tanks!

The heart of the Marine Corps philosophy was that we were all infantrymen, first and foremost. Anything else we did was a secondary job, and all other jobs existed only to support the infantry. That meant that all pieces of heavy equipment, from tanks to jet fighters, were referred to as "supporting arms."

The marriage between tanks and grunts was essential, yet often difficult—a real yin-yang relationship. We needed them to provide us with close-in protection, and they needed us bulletproof tankers for our ability to take on a dug-in enemy. Grunts either hated us or loved us, depending upon the moment. Often they begrudgingly tolerated our presence. Seeing us as a magnet for enemy fire, they naturally wanted to distance themselves from us or get directly behind us. The tank commander had to know where the grunts were at all times. If he let them get too far away, his tank would be exposed to enemy RPG teams. We also depended on the grunts to keep Charlie from overrunning us and getting on top of a tank. If they did, the crew's life expectancy could be quickly curtailed, because the enemy needed only to lob a grenade down an open hatch.

True, we drew a lot of fire, but the grunts seldom realized it was fire no longer aimed at them. They objected to our tanks' noise and the occasional breakdowns that would hold them up, forcing them to stay with an injured vehicle until it could be repaired. Also, they felt natural resentment toward anyone who rode while they walked, who had food and water when they didn't, and who didn't have to carry supplies on his back. But once the shit hit the fan—when the cry of "Tanks up!" went out and a unit of pinned-down grunts saw the mix of accurate and devastating firepower we could provide—suddenly they loved us.

There were drawbacks to being a supporting arm. We were totally subservient to the infantry, which meant our tanks were often misused in unimaginative ways. The infantry's concept of armor was born of ignorance and lack of experience, compounded by the constant turnover of grunt officers. For some strange reason, officers were rotated out of the field after only six months in-country, which added to the already high turnover of new, hastily trained junior officers who became casualties to their own inexperience.

This policy also created resentment toward officers. If they didn't have to spend their entire thirteen-month tour in combat, why should we? It seemed grossly unfair. More importantly, just as an officer who survived long enough became proficient in the field, he was relieved, often saddling the unit with another FNG officer—and it was FNGs who got men killed.

The grunts' lack of tank experience doomed us to being viewed as mobile pillboxes or bunkers on tracks. The uninitiated grunt officer often made several false assumptions about tanks. The most common was our perceived invulnerability, followed closely by ignorance of our capabilities and the type of terrain we could (and couldn't) negotiate. Consequently, we often found ourselves delegated to the static, mundane jobs of protecting bridges and fire base perimeters, which nullified our two strongest assets: mobility and shock effect. Grunt units rotated in and out of bridge security jobs while we were condemned to sit there, day after day after day, in our perpetual role as bridge protectors. Boredom became an enemy and familiarity a cause for sloppiness—and it was sloppiness that Charlie looked for when he planned an attack.

Shifts of night watch became less critical with the passing of each uneventful night. For the first month we seemed doomed to play the role of immobile artillery. We settled into the boredom of filling sandbags and complaining about the awful heat and the constant upkeep that tanks required. And when we were done complaining, we could bitch about the heat some more.

While sitting at a bridge site, sometimes we would play games on the grunts. During the long days, when we had a lot of spare time, we would sometimes get visits from curious grunts who wanted to see a tank up close. We developed a little routine to play with them and to make it appear they really missed out not being a tanker.

Sometimes it was downright scary some of the borderline idiots we ran across. I never again wondered why we Marines are known as Jarheads.

Some of their questions were ludicrous, like, "Y'all got air condishonen?"

"Hey," I'd call down to the loader in the turret, "turn on the air conditioning!" That was the opening line for a well-rehearsed play, with our tank's entire crew as part of the cast.

First, the loader would turn on our air-extraction motor. To some people, I guess, the air that it blew out of the turret convinced them that we had air conditioning; they never asked why the blower motor was so loud. But that was only half the routine. Seconds later, the loader would pop out of the turret with a can of beer in his hand and ask if the grunt wanted a sip. Of course, we were sorry it wasn't chilled, "but our refrigerator is out."

A beer materializing out of nowhere was unusual enough, but an apology for its being warm usually freaked the grunt out. He would go away convinced we had it way too easy.

The most memorable prank we ever pulled on a grunt—another of Dixie's finest—only convinced me that the draft was still on and was accepting anybody who showed up.

We had already pulled the beer skit when the grunt wanted to know more stuff about the tank. He pointed to the searchlight over the main gun.

"What's the box for?" he wanted to know. "It looks just like a TeeVee!"

Well, that was all I needed! "It is a TV," I told him. "It's to entertain the troops in the field."

"Y'all gotta TeeVee?" he asked, incredulous. We could tell he thought he had stumbled on a real secret and had made quite the find. "Well, what'cha y'all git, with that there Tee Vee?"

"We get AFVN-TV," I replied, using the call letters of the radio station we all listened to. "What time you got?"

"It be six-forty-five."

"Hey, Bonanza is on in fifteen minutes. Let me know when it's close, and we'll all watch it."

However unlikely you might think this is, let me assure you that it really did happen. At almost 7 p.m., he called up to me, "It's almost 7 o'clock, Mr. Tank Man."

I turned the turret completely around to the back of the tank, so that the main gun was over the engine. Then I lowered the gun so that it was sitting on the armor plate. I signaled for him to go sit on the gun tube: "It's the best seat in the house."

Once the country bumpkin climbed up the back of the tank, I had him move farther back so that he was precariously straddling the gun tube near the edge of the tank. I had the loader take off the stiff canvas cover protecting the glass front of the searchlight. The grunt was all ready for his personal viewing pleasure. He was staring into the searchlight's silvery mirrorlike reflector, which he still believed was a television's picture tube.

I couldn't believe anyone could be so dumb. Surely any minute he would realize he had been duped.

"Hey," I called down from the cupola, "you want a beer while you're waiting?"

I thought he was going to die of delight when I handed him a warm can of beer, "Sorry it's warm, but the refrigerator . . ."

His mouth dropped as he took the warm beer. I worried that our loader was going to give away the ruse because he was about ready to bust a gut. I couldn't blame him, for we had never taken the joke this far before; we were making it up as we went. I told him to go below and turn on the air conditioner. He was thankful for that, because the sound of the blower motor covered his stifled laughter coming out of the turret.

"Damn!" our guest exclaimed. "Y'all got everythin'. I wish I was a tank man." He glanced at his watch.

I had all I could do to keep a straight face. "We don't want to waste our batteries. Tell me when it's exactly 7 p.m."

A minute later he said, "It's time!"

"Okay!" I reached for the switch that turned on the searchlight from the TC's position. Suddenly, Bonanza and every other TV show he had ever seen hit him right between the eyes with 75-million candlepower. He flung up his hands, lost his balance, and fell off the back of the tank.

All four of us were in hysterics at the victim's unusual exit. We walked over to the back of the tank. "You okay?" we asked. He was holding his hands over his eyes, moaning that he couldn't see.

That night, the country boy's lieutenant and corpsman came over to give Hearn and me one hell of an ass-chewing: "If that man's sight isn't back by tomorrow, you're up for a court martial!" the LT told me.

Our victim had gone blind? The corpsman hoped it would be only temporary.

Happily, the next day proved him right. But meanwhile, I spent a long night worried that I had permanently damaged someone's eyes. But still, how dumb can you be?

WE DECIDED TO GIVE our tank a name. The crew got together and spent several weeks mulling over possibilities. I was hoping for something humorous and different, having seen too many tanks named after some tank commander's girlfriend back in The World. We threw out name after name until we finally settled on one I'd proposed.

At the time, Dow Chemical Company used an advertising slogan, "Better Living Through Chemistry." I suggested changing the last word to "Canister," the type of antipersonnel ammunition we used most often.

Canister was the tank's equivalent of a giant shotgun shell, a nasty and very effective projectile against "soft targets," the military's term for people. Immediately upon leaving the gun tube, a wall of 1,200 half-inch-long, quarter-inch chopped-steel rods would spread out and remained extremely effective for up to 300 meters. Our tank would be forever known as Better Living Thru Canister, and I was given the task of painting the name on the gun tube.

None of us could have ever imagined just how prophetic a name it would become. In just a few short weeks, a canister-like round fired at us by another tank would save our lives.

During late afternoons we tried to sleep, but usually wound up sitting around listening to AFVN radio. The only English-speaking station in the whole country, it started each day with "G-o-o-o-o-d Morning, Vietnam!" later made famous by the Robin Williams movie of the same name. Other than mail from home, it was our only link back to The World and the sanity we had left behind.

Upon arrival, I was totally surprised to find out that we had our own radio station in-country. I still remember a few radio personalities like Chris Noel, whose voice I fell in love with. I wrote to her, and to my delighted amazement she responded, enclosing a couple of photos to prove she really was the fox she sounded like. I also wrote to Vicki Lawrence, an unknown at the time who did some radio work; she too wrote me back and sent her picture too.

Certain songs, when played today, immediately take me back to the Cao Do or Ha Dong bridges, where we sat around, bored out of our minds. The Animals had the greatest song of the war, the perfect sing-along for anyone near a radio. Everybody joined in, as loud as they could, on the refrain: "We got to get out of this place, if it's the last thing we e-ver do!" God, how we loved that song! Half a mile outside any American fire base, you knew whenever it came on the radio because you could hear everyone belting it out.

Bobby Goldsboro's "Honey" always reminded me of my fiancée, Michele, a lab technician back in The World on Long Island. Among my favorites were the Mommas and the Papas' "This Is Dedicated to the One I Love," along with Otis Redding's "Sittin' On the Dock of the Bay," and the Turtles' "So Happy Together." During late 1968 and early 1969, we turned up anything by the Doors.

Two or three times a week, we slipped down the muddy banks to bathe in whatever river flowed under whichever bridge we were guarding. Refreshing as the water was, I always felt uncomfortable doing this. Even with my clothes on, I felt naked; I didn't like being away from my flak jacket and steel helmet. Moreover, I didn't like being away from the tank. I washed quickly and got out while others fooled around, grab-assing and having water fights as if they were back in The World. Heck, I had seen how the Vietnamese fertilized their crops! Who knew what was floating in that water? And why would I want to swim in it?

WE OFTEN PROVIDED SECURITY for the morning's road-sweep team. That meant travel—from the bridge we were protecting to the next bridge or fire base down the road, or until we were met by another sweep team coming in the opposite direction. Our tank moved at a deathly slow pace, behind a grunt on foot who was fanning a mine detector from side to side. When it came to planting mines with prodigious ability, Charlie was a regular Johnny Appleseed. During one such routine, in April, our boredom was punctuated with raw adrenaline.

Our tank was following fifty feet behind two minesweepers and a squad of grunts spread out behind them. Another fifty feet behind us trailed a second tank, and behind that were several trucks loaded with armed men crouched down behind the trucks' low metal sides.

To avoid running over an undiscovered mine, you always kept your vehicle in the tracks left by the vehicle directly ahead. Because mine detectors were nothing but glorified metal detectors, it was easy for them to miss the homemade mines encased in wood that Charlie planted. So even if a road had been swept, drivers adhered to the tracks of the vehicle in front. But any truck following a tank was faced with a dilemma. Because tanks were so much wider than trucks, a truck driver could keep only one pair of his wheels in the tank's tracks. That meant the left side of a truck would stay in the tank's tracks because no truck driver was going to risk running over a mine on his side of the vehicle.

One April morning, our tank was nearing the halfway point of our road-sweep when a truck behind us was lifted off the ground by a large explosion.

I was sitting in the gunner's seat; I could feel the concussion through the tank's hull. "What the fuck was that?" I asked over the intercom. My answer came, not from my tank commander, but from dozens of ChiCom AK-47 rifles.

I had the main gun trained on a tree line on the right side of the road when I saw Christmas lights twinkling throughout the undergrowth. Seconds later, enemy mortars began dropping rounds all around us. I could hear their crack! crack! and feel each impact through the hull.

I already had our main gun pointed in the direction of the tree line—as with defensive driving, you always anticipated the most logical place an ambush could start. I immediately returned fire, unleashing the .30-caliber machine gun against the tree line. Tracers from the other tank's machine gun joined mine, impacting along the same area.

Over the intercom, Sergeant Hearn issued a fire command: "Gunner. Canister. Tree line." I heard the loader, a few feet from me, wrestling a round into the breech. Then came the resounding ka-chung! as the breech slammed home.

I had already picked out my target and was waiting only for the loader's signal.

"Up!" he yelled, to tell the crew that the main gun was ready.

Several RPGs whooshed out of the tree line, so I laid the gun on the source. "On the way!" I shouted to give the loader a split second to get out of the way of the gun's breech. Then I squeezed the electric triggers in the control handles that I had in both hands. The main gun kicked back two feet. The tank rocked with the gun's recoil, and the canister round immediately defoliated a portion of the tree line. Within it, I noticed, there were suddenly fewer flashes of AK-47 fire. But not few enough.

A three-foot-high embankment along the road's edge meant we couldn't assault the enemy position. Our tank could have climbed it easily, but that would have exposed our thin underside to the enemy RPGs issuing relentlessly from out of the tree line. Charlie had picked the only spot on the road at which a tank wouldn't dare turn to assault his position. The NVA were slightly above and shooting down on us— a good vantage point.

Ka-chung! Two seconds after I fired, our loader had another canister round in the chamber. I had already switched over to the machine gun and was laying down a deadly swath of .30-caliber fire. Tracers ripped into the tree line, some ricocheting off the ground and flying wildly into the air. From my gunner's seat, it looked like somebody had strung the trees with twinkling Christmas lights.

"On the way!" Another 90mm canister round swept over the tree line, catching one of the enemy RPG teams.

Hearn's voice came over the intercom: "Watch out for the grunts, they're assaulting the tree line. Use the thirty!" He meant the .30-caliber machine gun.

I followed with one more "On the way!" and let fly another canister round that pruned the trees a little more, instantly eliminating twigs and branches. I heard Hearn open up with the .50, though I couldn't see what he was shooting at. Suddenly his gun stopped and the turret was taken out of my control. The tank commander had grabbed his override handle and was turning the turret to the left. I could only watch as scenery slid by my sights.

"The gooks are running into a temple!" he yelled as he gave me back control of the turret after I yelled, "Identified!"

I saw what he was talking about—a small stone structure with kind of a red brick roof. Three NVA with their distinctive pith helmets ran into the structure. I turned to the loader and yelled, "Gimme an HE on delay!"

It took him a few seconds to set the fuse on the High Explosive round. The breech slammed shut. "Up!" he yelled.

"On the way!" I replied as I squeezed the electric triggers again. The main gun kicked back and dropped another hot shell casing on the turret floor. I watched the red tracer on the back of the projectile as it punched its way right into the temple.

Because of the short delay we put on the projectile's fuse, it didn't detonate against the stone wall, as it would normally have. Instead, the ensuing explosion took place inside the temple, making it far more effective. The roof went straight up, and the walls blew out. Stones, mortar, and body parts flew in all directions. Yet, still standing where the temple once stood was a gook, AK-47 in hand. He spun around on wobbly legs like he was drunk until he keeled over. We had just gotten our first sure kills!

The two tanks overwhelmed the enemy fire, and the grunts were able to advance against the enemy position. The fight was over, just as the other road-sweep team arrived from the opposite direction. The grunts policed the area of weapons, equipment, ammunition, and bodies—theirs and ours. The loader threw out the huge brass shells that had piled up on the turret floor while I kept sweeping the turret back and forth, peering into the tree line, looking for any signs of Charlie. But things had pretty much quieted down.

The air inside the turret was thick with fumes from the expended shells and the smoke from the machine gun. I felt like I had been down there all morning and thought I would go crazy without a breath of fresh air. I begged Hearn to let me take a breather for just a few minutes, and he said, "Okay."

I stood up, halfway out of the loader's hatch, grateful for the fresh air. I could have sworn it was afternoon. But when I looked at my watch, only fifteen minutes had elapsed! It was my first firefight, but as I stood there, sucking in deep breaths, I was about to get another first-ever sight.

Every FNG arrived in-country with some trepidation of how he would react under fire, and a morbid curiosity to see his first enemy dead. I had been trained to kill the enemy, but no one prepared me for the sight of my first dead and wounded Marines.

Coming toward our tank were four grunts, each holding one corner of a rain poncho, carrying one of their own to the truck at the rear of the column. As they drew closer, I couldn't help but stare. The boy lay face-up, his head hanging over the poncho's edge and bobbing with each stride of his bearers. His eyes were closed, but his mouth was open, as if frozen in a yawn. With his bright blond hair, almost like a surfer's and far too long for any Marine I had ever seen, he seemed especially young. The only hint of his demise was a trickle of blood that ran down his cheek. Had it not been for his uniform, I could have imagined him straight off a farm in Kansas, a teenager dressed in Army clothes, play-ing at war. He looked too young to be here, too young to be dead—and then it suddenly hit me. We were all teenagers, and this was no training exercise. I had just gone through the real thing. For the first time in my life, targets had shot back!

The all-too-real, short little firefight was the difference between living the war vicariously through news reports and returning veterans stories, and having actually participated in it. Even now, I'm amazed at how naïve I was. Of course I knew we would suffer casualties, but the finality of death on display sent a chill down my back. As one of the the poncho bearers walked past, he looked up at me and made eye contact. He had caught me watching. I quickly turned my head; I felt as if I had broken some unwritten law.

I never recalled that boy's face, only his blond hair waving like wheat in a gentle summer breeze. My eyes welled up for this total stranger, alive only seconds earlier. I never learned his name.

Trailing behind the four bearers, a corpsman helped a wounded Marine along. They brought him up to sit on the back of our tank. Where his cheek should have been was a hole about the size of a quarter. Blood flowed freely from his mouth, and within the wound. I could make out his teeth and jawbone. I had seen enough. I slid back down into the turret and got back in my seat. I no longer felt the heat; a chill went through me that lasted quite some time.

I rested my head against the gunner's sight. Its narrow field of vision had shielded me from the reality of the outside world, which was now catching up to me. The hot minutes of the firefight had seemed more like a drill with no consequences—no different than the thirteen months of practice war games back in The World at Camp Pendleton. The twinkling lights in the tree line looked exactly the same as the blanks fired at us in mock ambushes in California. Only these weren't blanks.

I came up for another breath of air. Our loader was helping some of the grunts—whose truck had been blown up—climb up on our tank. Now we would provide their transportation. Glancing around, I spotted several grunts out by the tree line, dragging dead NVA by their ankles. The sight of these dead bodies was deeply satisfying. We hated the inhuman little bastards. No Marine I ever met turned away from looking at dead North Vietnamese.

One of the grunts came up on the tank carrying an NVA pith helmet and pack. Going through the pack, he came across the photograph of a young woman. Charlie had a girlfriend? I couldn't believe it. Suddenly Mr. Charles seemed a little more human—but not nearly enough.

Adrenaline from the ambush was still pumping through our veins when we got back to the bridge. All of us agreed: That morning's firefight had been exhilarating. Even though I would witness more ambushes over the coming year it was satisfying to have that first one behind me. I performed my job and was still among the living! Every new guy, in the back of his mind, harbored doubts about his performance under fire. Now, at least a few of mine were laid to rest.

Shortly after the engagement, we all suffered from the same malady—the shakes. As we discussed the day's events, sharing our perspective of the firefight, the reality of it all began to sink in. That morning's fight had been strictly the kind of mindless, knee-jerk reaction embedded in us by our training back at Pendleton. Fear showed itself only when we had time to realize what we had just gone through and how close we might have come to being hit.

Cigarettes shook from our lips as we tried to light them. Shaking hands kept chasing the moving cigarettes. We were now combat-veteran Marines.

The Dirty Two Dozen, 2nd Platoon, Bravo Company, 5th Tanks at 2/27's firebase. (Back left is SSgt. Robert Embesi standing next to Lieutenant Gilliam. Author is on far right with no hat. Gary Gibson middle of front row with hands clasped. Sergeant Hearn kneeling in front of author. Taken a few days before Operation Allen Brook.)

Mother's Worry at 1st Tank Battalion's Tank Park. Welcome to Vietnam.

Better Living Thru Canister sinking into what appeared to be dry ground outside Da Nang during what became known as Johnstone's Folly.

The author after completing the paint job on the gun tube.

The crew of Better Living Thru Canister during Allen Brook. (Left to right standing: author, SSgt. Bob Embesi and Sergeant Hearn. Richards, the driver, is sitting on tank.)

Forty-two and still counting on Better Living Thru Canister. (Author and Richards)

The author wearing Korean Marine utilities after his fell apart.

The fire control tower where spotters for the USS *New Jersey* would call in fire from her huge 16-inch diameter guns.

Pray for Slack on top of the dune with gun facing due west.

One of two Army M42 Dusters at Oceanview.

A grenade clears off the scum of the swimming hole.

The pool cleaning
bomb takes care of all
the dud grenades.

The crew of *Pray For Slack* (Standing: Bob Steele, Bob Truitt; Driver, and author on the tank.)

Tank hits mine inside the perimeter at Oceanview.

North Vietnamese 152mm artillery round lands near author's tent at tank park in Dong Ha.

Author's prized fireman boots cut in half by shrapnel; it could have been the author!

Chapter 6

Time

There were two types of time in The Nam—"long" and "slow." Long time was what you experienced, day in and day out. The worst kind of long time was standing watch at night. You peered relentlessly into the darkness, alert for any sight or sounds of Charlie. That was the kind of time that never moved, time that made you look at your wristwatch once every hour, to find that only five minutes had passed since you last checked it. A two-hour watch was the longest two hours you'd ever spend in The Nam—and you got to do it every single night, for more than a year.

SLOW TIME, THE OTHER KIND, could turn seconds into minutes, and several minutes into half a day—as I'd experienced in my first firefight. It was like throwing the slow-motion switch on a movie projector. Speech became slurred. Volume went down. The world moved at the pace of cold honey pouring out of a bottle. For me, firefights always occurred in slow time. But my strangest experience with slow time wasn't during combat and was mysteriously shared with a fellow crewman.

We were one of two tanks guarding the Ha Dong Bridge, each on opposite sides of the river. Our tank was positioned just off the side of the road, where the southbound traffic had to bear right and go down the embankment to the pontoon wooden bridge. We rarely visited the other tank crew. It wasn't the distance that kept us from socializing with them, it was the heat. It was too damned hot to walk, so why bother if we didn't have to? Plus I had my own mantra: *Never* get off the tank. The farther I ventured from its safety, the more uneasy I felt.

Behind us lay the river and the remains of an old French railroad bridge of box-truss construction, similar to its many counterparts back in The World. Like all the metal bridges in this country, its back had been broken by an explosion in somebody else's war, fifteen years earlier, its steel spans now half-submerged in the middle of the water, its railroad ties and tracks now long gone. But for its trestles, still connected at both ends of the river, we'd have never guessed that this well-traveled, busy road had been a railroad line in a previous life.

We had been sitting at this bridge for more than a month, so bored that we actually looked forward to the morning road sweeps, just for the chance to do something. A tank crew lived on its tank, ate meals on its tank, slept on its tank, and stood watch on its tank. About the only times we ever got off was to perform routine maintenance on the suspension system, take a bath, or relieve ourselves. During the day we watched the traffic but not, as you might expect, for security reasons—that was the grunts' job. We just watched the hundreds of six-bys (the ubiquitous truck used by all of America's military) hoping to recognize somebody from home. There was also a lot of civilian traffic as well, made up of mopeds, minibuses, and bicycles. And, of course, we always had a radio.

On this typical just-another-hot-humid day, a new grunt unit was moving in to relieve the infantry platoon that had sat with us for the past two weeks. Our tanks never budged, but the grunts rotated in and out every two weeks like clockwork. Accompanying them was their platoon leader, a Marine lieutenant.

If this war had a glossary of self-evident axioms, number one would be: The most dangerous thing in the Marine Corps is a lieutenant with a map.

No matter what anybody says, map reading is an art form. A lot of additional training was wasted on those who couldn't understand that a military topographical map is a two-dimensional, spatial, and mathe-matical relationship of the three-dimensional world around them. In my experience, either you grasped that, or you didn't.

When picking up a map, you first oriented it with landmarks around you, so that the map's north was aligned with magnetic north. Only then could you establish your position and record your coordinates. The next step was finding the location and associated coordinates of your target—which could be anything from a true military objective to simply someplace you wanted to wind up.

When the shit hit the fan, it wasn't unheard of for someone under lots of pressure to get his coordinates mixed up. I don't mean mixed up, as in the wrong order. I mean that the guy on the radio might give his own grid coordinates instead of the target's. You can guess where the first round landed! Well, on this particular day at the Ha Dong Bridge, we saw one of the Corps' finest do exactly that.

None of us suspected that this incoming unit was any different than all the others that had passed through before. The platoon's leader was a second lieutenant—the lowest kind of officer there is. Worse yet, he was a boot, a rookie, an FNG. Had any of us known that, we would have taken different precautions. Whenever a grunt unit was setting up in a new position, it was SOP—standard operating procedure—to register the supporting artillery unit's guns.

Supporting artillery was often at a fire base miles away, but it could spell the difference between life and death during an enemy attack. Reg-istering the guns was a way of getting artillery to respond on target during the hectic moments of battle; it was particularly valuable at night. The process involved the firing of a smoke round safely out in front of friendly lines from coordinates provided by the infantry leader.

The artillery battery recorded the setting on the guns after they fired the smoke round. Both parties—the infantry commander and the artillery battery—now had a reference point from which the infantry commander could direct the guns during an attack.

Little did we know that Axiom Number One had gone into effect. The lieutenant was standing on top of his CP (command post) about a hundred feet to our rear, at the base of the old steel bridge. Through his handset, he gave a set of coordinates to the gun battery back at 2/27's fire base.

Everyone around the perimeter was alerted to expect an artillery round to come cruising overhead in a few minutes. Richards, the driver on our tank, and I climbed up and sat cross-legged on top of the turret to watch. It was always fun to see how good someone was when requesting an "arty" mission. (I did mention how bored we were, didn't I?)

We were looking out into the field in front of us, waiting for the show to start. We heard the distant report of a 105mm howitzer from 2/27's fire base. "Round out!" yelled the lieutenant, alerting everyone that a friendly round of artillery was on its way.

Richards and I waited for the sound of the shell cruising overhead just before impact. But we never got to hear it. Instead, from directly behind us came a startling explosion—Crack!—followed by what sounded like the largest, low-frequency Chinese gong ever heard: Thwong-g-g-g-g-g-g-g-g!

The noise jerked our heads around. A cloud of white smoke showered over the still vibrating bridge. People were diving for cover including the LT, who had given the guns his own coordinates instead of those far out in the field. Fortunately for him, the shell had landed short—scarcely seventy-five feet behind him, but short nonetheless!

Richards and I were sitting about three feet apart. As we looked over our shoulders at the cloud above the bridge, we both said, "Holy shit!" We couldn't believe we had just hit our own bridge! At the same instant, from out of the smoke, a large piece of black steel came whirling through the air, turning slowly on its own axis.

Already my brain had entered slow time; my real-life movie had suddenly switched into slow motion. As I watched the approach of the six-foot lawnmower blade, I could see that it was a huge piece of angle iron that must have easily weighed 150 pounds. We were directly in its path—about to be decapitated!

Yet in slow time, it was rotating ever so leisurely, spinning so tediously slow. Time had slowed so drastically, in fact, that I began to realize that it wasn't going to hit us. Its flat spin appeared perfectly timed to pass harmlessly through the three-foot space between us! Richards and I wouldn't need to budge an inch.

And so it came to pass. Neither of us ducked or so much as flinched as that enormous piece of angle iron whirled harmlessly between us. We just turned our heads to follow its flight for another hundred feet until it finally hit the ground, skidding along the road and raising a cloud of dust.

Slowly Richards and I locked eyes with each other. For the second time, we both uttered, "Holy shit!" in unison. Then, it was just like someone threw a switch. The movie projector's speed went back to normal. I couldn't believe that we had come within inches of becoming headless.

Stranger still was the way we each recollected the event. As Richards and I recounted what had just happened, it suddenly became obvious that we had both seen it happen the same way, in slow time!

Several grunts ran over to our tank. "Hey, are you guys all right? You coulda been killed! Why didn't you duck?"

"We didn't have to," was our reply.

Our shocked audience left, shaking their heads. I turned to Richards. "Why didn't you duck?" I asked.

As I suspected, his answer was the same as mine, "I didn't have to. It wasn't going to hit us!"

The grunts couldn't believe how calm, cool, and collected we were. Or appeared to be, at least. Seconds later, both of us got the shakes and—as if a wave had just crashed over us—began laughing like schoolgirls as we started to shiver. It felt like the air temperature had suddenly dropped thirty degrees. It was our brains' subconscious half trying to tell its conscious side that we had just felt Death's scythe breeze by.

Over the next few weeks, Richards and I shared our experience with several other men. They listened to us but couldn't understand, except for a couple of guys who had experienced terrible car accidents back in The World. They confirmed our recall of the slow-motion experience. Each of their accidents seemingly took forever to play out, and they witnessed it more than experienced it. All these victims confirmed that during the entire accident they were totally helpless—as if they were just along for the ride, as if the outcome was already certain. But Richards and I never experienced helplessness. Time had slowed for both of us, yet we were absolutely convinced we weren't going to be hit, certain that we were in no danger.

Yet in the back of our minds, Richards and I had a nagging question we never shared with anyone else. If we had realized the metal was going to hit us, could we have moved to avoid it? Neither of us was really sure. At that split second it wasn't even a consideration. But could we, if we had had to? It gnawed at us for months.

There were several ways to measure long time in The Nam. Many grunts wrote their rotation date on their helmets. Sometimes they listed all thirteen months on the side and put an X through the months served, like notches on a gun. Tanks afforded a lot more space to display the time remaining for a short-timer—anyone with less than one hundred days left on his tour. If the crew included a short-timer you could probably find his calendar posted on the inside wall of the turret, a proclamation taped to the steel, like the ninety-five theses that Martin Luther nailed to the church door, for the rest of the crew to witness. A tank crew always knew who their "shortest" guy was. The shorter he got, the farther they often tried to distance themselves from him. Short people could drive you crazy.

The most common design for a short-timer's calendar was the picture of a nude girl, divided up into ninety-nine areas or boxes, with each one numbered. The junction of her thighs was reserved for the final box—number zero, his rotation date. The short-timer began coloring in the boxes, one day at a time, starting ninety-nine days out. It gave him a way to measure his time left in the insanity that was Vietnam. I only wished I had a hundred days left; I was still looking at 300-plus days. In-country, that was a lifetime.

How could you tell how long a tank commander had been in-country? Simply by observing him out in the field. If you saw only his head sticking out of his hatch (or cupola, as it was called), he was an FNG. If you saw only his eyes sticking above the cupola, he was a short-timer.

But you can't lead effectively if you're hiding down in the turret. So between those two extremes—or for about nine months of his tour—you would find him chest-high, exposed and doing his job.

By AND LARGE, we spent the huge majority of our time in utter boredom. Time was something we had plenty of, and in the Marine Corps, that meant busy work. You often got burdened with mind-numbing work like filling sandbags or, if you were unlucky enough, disgusting work like collecting drums from the shitters. Time also came in unequal increments. It never passed swiftly except on R&R, when it flew by all too fast.

My time in personal hell was about to end. Not with a ticket home, but when my mother's rescue package arrived.

I don't remember why, but our platoon found itself back together again, inside the perimeter of 2/27's fire base. The mailbag came to us by truck every few days with other supplies, and the latest one had just reached us. Before handing out the letters, Embesi removed several small packages from inside the bag and set them on his cot.

One box jumped out at me, because it bore my mother's distinctive handwriting.

To say we lived for mail would have been a gross understatement. Letters were something we could never get enough of. A package, how-ever, was a gift from God, appreciated by everyone. Because tank crews shared everything among themselves, we all enjoyed the arrival of a box. But I wasn't about to share the contents of this particular box because Mom had done the impossible. Inside, I knew, lay my long-awaited bottle of twenty-year-old Glenlevit Scotch.

I had received some letters too, which I tore open and dove into, keeping one eye on Embesi all the while. When he finished reading his mail, I went over and sat down on the cot across from his, keeping one hand behind my back.

He looked at me, sharing an easy smile. "How's it been out at them damned bridges?"

"Sergeant Embesi," I asked, "if you could have one thing right now, what would it be?"

His smile grew wider, and his eyes twinkled to life. "A piece of round-eyed pussy!" he instantly replied, flashing a big white grin from beneath his black mustache.

Why had I bothered to ask such a dumb question? "Can't help you there," I said, presenting the bottle from behind my back, "but I may have the next best thing."

His eyes focused on the bottle's label in disbelief. Speechless, as his grin got even bigger as he comprehended the two-month-old debt he never expected, much less asked me, to repay.

Whatever special occasion Embesi had planned for that first bottle of his, it was lost forever that day. Cracking open the seal, he removed the cap and simply inhaled its fragrance.

"God, I love that smell! Go get your canteen cup."

He poured a couple of shots into my cup, then shared it with Lieutenant Gilliam, who was sitting on a cot on the other side of him. We all clicked cups and chugged in one swallow.

"I'd written that bottle off," Embesi laughed. "Never expected I'd ever see another one. Not here, at least." Tickled to death to get his replacement, he couldn't believe my mother had gotten it through the mail unharmed, much less undiscovered. But he didn't know my mother.

There's more to this story that begs to be told. Knowing that my mother had gotten one bottle through the mail successfully, I implored her to send another one to my friend, John Wear. He and I first met in tank school and upon graduation were both assigned to Charlie Company, 5th Tank Battalion. John went to 1st Platoon, and I went to 3rd. Four weeks before the mount-out of Bravo Company he received his orders for Vietnam and like ninety-five percent of all those who served in Vietnam, he flew across the Pacific. Only on his arrival was he assigned to a unit. That was always a risky affair because you were never sure that once you got there you'd end up doing what you were trained for. If they needed grunts—hell, you've already seen how that worked.

But John's luck held. He was assigned to 3rd Tank Battalion. You might argue that wasn't luck at all, for it meant that he was up north, on the DMZ. So while I was sitting on a bridge outside Da Nang, bored to death, John was in a flame tank on the outskirts of Hue while the Tet Offensive was still going on. He was supporting the 5th Marines, who were retaking the city, one block at a time, just as the Allies had in Europe during World War II.

In any war, street fighting is the worst and deadliest kind of combat, generating the most horrific casualties. During the Vietnam War, it was only seen during Tet in Saigon and Hue City, where it lasted several weeks. It was house-to-house, block-by-block—the worst scenario for a tank to be in. Several tank commanders were killed by snipers from windows and rooftops. Marines all over Vietnam were aware of what was going on, and for a short time the media's coverage of Hue almost eclipsed the siege at Khe Sanh. Down around Da Nang, where we were, rumors had it that we were about to be drawn into Hue as well.

So if anybody could have used a bottle of Scotch, I thought it was John. Once more, I implored my mother to send a bottle through the mail. John never got the bottle, but to understand the rest of the story, you have to see the war through a mother's eyes.

The year 1968 was the bloodiest year of the entire war, when the number of Americans killed easily exceeded two hundred a week. Today, it sickens us to hear of six deaths in Afghanistan or twenty-two in Iraq. But back then, the six o'clock news was crammed with film of the war. And once Tet got started, none of it was very good. Hue was still going on, as was the siege of Khe Sanh. On the DMZ, Con Thien had taken a heavy pounding. Fighting also picked up around Da Nang. Marines were taking substantial casualties.

Mothers of Marines lived as harrowing a year as their sons. These women were usually surrounded by oblivious strangers who went about their everyday routines, caring little about the war. Many sons were attending college or had draft deferments; a few had fled to Canada. But mothers of Marines in the field never knew what news lay around the corner. They dreaded the ring of the telephone or the contents of their mailbox.

One morning, a plain-colored car drove up my mother's long narrow driveway. Looking through the curtained windows she saw that it had white government license plates. When she saw a uniformed man exit the car, she was certain that he was an officer bringing her news that I had been killed in action. Her knees almost gave way as tears filled the proud woman's eyes as she tried to face the news.

Maybe I was only wounded, she hoped, knowing only too well that this wasn't how families were told about WIAs. She could barely bring herself to open the door.

"Mrs. Peavey?" he asked.

"Yes," was all she could muster as she held onto the door for support.

"Did you send a bottle of liquor through the mail?" he demanded.

She didn't understand this question at all. "What?" was all she could ask.

"I'm an inspector for the United States Postal Service. We have a box with your return address on it that contained a broken bottle of liquor. You do know it's a Federal offense to send alcohol through the U.S. Mail, don't you?"

"What?" she repeated.

"Mrs. Peavey," he persisted. "Do you understand why I'm here?"

Then it began to dawn on her. This wasn't about me! Suddenly the gravity of federal charges meant nothing at all. She started to laugh as if he had just told her the funniest possible joke.

He had no idea why this woman was laughing in his face. After all, these were very serious charges! Finally she explained why she thought he had come.

He realized what he had just put this woman through, which made him feel like an idiot. Excusing himself, he awkwardly left her at the door with a polite warning.

Later, through the mail, I pleaded for her to try again, suggesting that she pour the Scotch into plastic baby bottles that wouldn't break. Understandably, she was reluctant—for several months. But that's a later story.

To this day, more than thirty years later, Embesi still breaks into a broad grin when he recalls the moment in which I replaced his bottle. Our drinking Scotch from a tin cup is one of his fondest memories of both of his tours in Vietnam.

But that pleasant moment was soon followed by a sobering one. The very next morning brought us the call: A Marine unit had stepped into a hornet's nest and was calling for tank support.

At first, it didn't seem to be all that significant; we would be gone longer than anyone guessed, and we would see far more than any of us ever wanted to see.

Chapter 7

Allen Brook

We didn't realize it, but we were entering the first week of what would become the bloodiest month of the Vietnam War. May 1968 began the start of the second phase of the enemy's Tet Offensive, which was later referred to as Mini-Tet. Like its predecessor, this offensive would prove to be devastating to the North Vietnamese, but with it came a high cost of American casualties, much higher than February's Tet Offensive.

It routinely reached 100 degrees Fahrenheit around noon, and I couldn't help but wonder what July would be like. May 4 was the beginning of another hot day. After standing watch on the perimeter of 2/27's fire base, we came off the line. Most of us had spent too many days on nameless bridges eating C rations, so we took advantage of a hot breakfast in the mess tent. Later, we sat around reading yesterday's mail for the fifth or sixth time.

It was a real treat to be back at the fire base again, where the cool showers were rivaled only by the hot meals. Our living area remained unchanged, except that, because of the heat, the tent flaps had been rolled up. Compared to bridge duty, this was really living.

Rumors that abounded said we would be pulled into the fighting up north. So when Staff Sergeant Embesi and the lieutenant were summoned to a meeting at the battalion CP, we all waited in anticipation. Something was in the air.

They returned an hour later. "Want to join me on a helicopter ride?" Embesi asked me.

"Sure!" I agreed. "Where are we going?"

"We're being assigned to an operation. We're going to make an aerial recon of an area, to see if tanks can go into where they want us."

I was flattered that he had asked me, of all people! And a helicopter ride sounded like fun. If nothing else, it meant a break from the boredom. But, as I threw a few things together, I couldn't help but wonder why a staff sergeant asked a lowly corporal to accompany him. It would have made more sense for Embesi to ask one of the five tank commanders instead. But my feeling of pride that Embesi had asked me overrode any common sense I had gained in two months in-country. In hindsight, I realize Embesi must have known the answer any veteran tank commander would have given him—and he figured right.

But this was my first helicopter ride, and I was still naïve. I thought I could snap some great photos from the air, so I grabbed my camera, helmet, and flak jacket and headed off to grab the submachine gun we carried inside Better Living Thru Canister. I wasn't taking any chances in case some mechanical problem caused us to unexpectedly have to set down. I hadn't been in-country long enough to learn that mechanical problems weren't what I should have been concerned about.

Sitting on the LZ—the landing zone within the base's perimeter— was a vintage Korean War H-34 helicopter, powered by a gasoline radial engine. It was one of those flying antiques that made up the bulk of the Marine's chopper force, a helicopter the Army had done away with years earlier. By this time, the Army was using jet-powered Hueys, which were quieter, faster, and far more powerful. But that was the Marine Corps for you—making due with whatever the Army threw away.

As we approached, I heard the chopper's engine running, but as we got on, its blades were standing idle. Later, I wondered if this was a well-planned deception to lure the unsuspecting fly into the spider's web, for when the engine's RPMs dropped way down and the blades began turning slowly, I started to doubt my eagerness to take this joyride.

The faster its blades turned, the more the giant eggbeater vibrated like a car's tire that sorely needed balancing. The vehicle shook faster and faster, vibrating and gyrating like a machine gone mad—and it was still sitting on the ground! I realized now that I had probably made a serious mistake. But it was too late. I was committed.

I could feel it trying to leave the ground as it strained, bent on flailing itself to death, as its rpm increased. Was some unseen anchor holding us down? Finally, painfully, slowly, the machine began to win its fight with gravity and to lift itself off the ground at a rate I could have measured in inches per minute.

My immediate thought was that we were seriously overloaded. My eyes darted around the chopper's interior, looking for the source of the engine's strain—but Embesi and I were its only cargo. The door gunner looked very nonchalant, not worried in the least. That eased my apprehensions. Years later, I learned that the H-34 was seriously underpowered, especially in high heat, and what we were experiencing was considered its "normal flight characteristics."

A cacophony of noise consumed us. We climbed slowly. Cupping both hands in front of my mouth, I screamed, "Sergeant Embesi, where do you think the Corps got these things?"

"I don't know," he replied. "But they sure got took, didn't they?"

We flew over an area that seemed to interest him, although it was beyond me how Embesi could read a map in this flying cocktail shaker. ("Flying" was a gross misuse of the word when used in context with the H-34.) I was only along for the ride, if you called the harmonic rattling of your guts and brain a ride.

Embesi and I wore our pistols, but the thought of our chopper being shot down never crossed my mind. My education about the numerous shortcomings of helicopters would come in just a few days, under the very spot we were passing over.

In my hands was our tank's submachine gun, an example of American firearm design at its worst. Every Marine tank had an M3 "grease gun." It cost Uncle Sam only $15 to manufacture, and rumor had it they really were made by Mattel. I could never stop imagining grease guns coming off the same assembly line as Barbies. My guess was, they'd designed the M3 as an accessory for Ken, but he refused to be seen carrying it, so they gave it to us Marines.

Eventually our giant Cuisinart made its way back to the fire base. I managed to snap a couple of pictures, even though I was certain nothing would come out. I didn't think the fastest shutter speed on my camera could disguise the vibrations of our ride. Embesi reported his observations to the lieutenant. I already knew what his verdict was: We were going in.

No sooner had I stowed the M3 back on our tank than Embesi summoned three tank crews. "Get your stuff together and be prepared to mount out in thirty minutes. Pack enough for three days. We're joining a sweep already in progress, on a place called Goi Noi Island."

At the announcement that we were going to an island, I thought he'd lost it. Our chopper ride stayed at least ten miles from the nearest coastline. So while everyone was getting busy, I walked over to ask him. "Island? We didn't fly over any islands!"

He looked surprised. "Didn't you see the rivers around that huge chunk of real estate?"

"No," I half-kidded. "I was too busy getting homogenized by that goddamned whirling blender to see much of anything. But do me a favor? Don't ask me to come on any more helicopter rides."

Embesi only smiled.

Just as he had described it, Goi Noi Island was bordered by two large rivers and a smaller one. It was a large chunk of uncontested ground that Charlie and his rich uncle, Mr. Charles, had owned for years. "Mr. Charles" was the term of respect we used to differentiate the hardcore North Vietnamese Army regulars from "Charlie," or the local Viet Cong.

The day before, 2/7—Second Battalion, Seventh Marine Regiment—had set feet on the island and stepped into a whirlwind. Resistance was so fierce that we were part of a reaction force to bolster the Marines' presence on the island along with 3/7, another Marine battalion. We soon found out that Ben Green, a tank commander from 1st Tank Battalion, had been killed in the engagement.

Embesi told the crews we would be gone for three days, but we were ordered to take several extra five-gallon cans of water. That was more than we usually carried, but with Embesi you didn't ask why, you just did it. Also, he had us load up five days' worth of C rats and all the machine gun ammo we could store in our gypsy rack. Did he know something he wasn't telling us?

The gypsy rack was technically called the bustle rack—the open area on the back of the turret, where we stashed personal gear, extra ammo, and anything else we didn't want cluttering up the inside. Every tank I ever saw had as much junk stuffed into this external area as possible. No one ever called it the bustle rack, and because it made every tank look like a gypsy wagon the name stuck. It was even more fitting because we operated like gypsies, with no permanent home, never longer than a week or two with any one grunt unit, shuffled continually between one unit and another.

It was mid-morning by the time we packed everything up and exited the fire base. We were to join up with other units of 2/7 and several tanks from 1st Tank Battalion under Lieutenant Scott. They would be waiting for us at Phu Loc 6, near Liberty Bridge. To get there, we had to make a long road march past Hill 55, down past Hill 42, through the Dodge City area, and past Hill 37. Liberty Bridge was a major landmark in the Da Nang area. We had all heard about it, but I had never seen it. None of us realized that it was no longer in service.

We arrived to find what had once been a very high wooden bridge, several stories tall in fact. It was a charred skeleton that extended only halfway into the river. We soon learned that during Tet, two months earlier, the bridge had been set ablaze during an enemy attack—by Marine artillery that had accidentally hit it. Was a Marine lieutenant

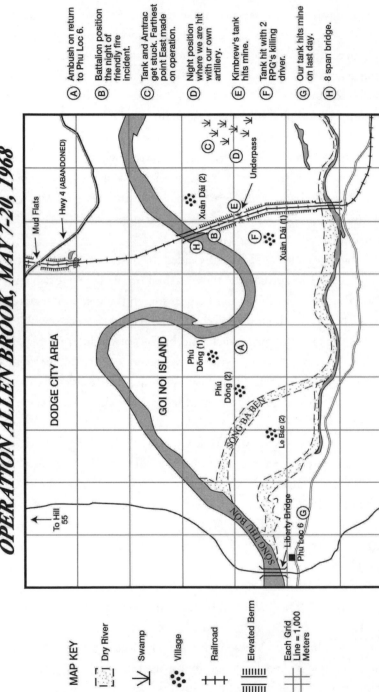

OPERATION ALLEN BROOK, MAY 7-20, 1968

Ⓐ Ambush on return to Phu Loc 6.

Ⓑ Battalion position the night of friendly fire incident.

Ⓒ Tank and Amtrac get stuck. Farthest point East made on operation.

Ⓓ Night position where we are hit with our own artillery.

Ⓔ Kimbrew's tank hits mine.

Ⓕ Tank hit with 2 RPG's killing driver.

Ⓖ Our tank hits mine on last day.

Ⓗ 8 span bridge.

DODGE CITY AREA

GOI NOI ISLAND

Mud Flats

Hwy 4 (ABANDONED)

To Hill 55

Xuân Dài (2)

Xuân Dài (1)

Underpass

Phú Đông (1)

Phú Đông (2)

SONG BA BEN

Le Bac (2)

SONG THU BON

Liberty Bridge

Phu Loc 6 Ⓖ

MAP KEY

Dry River

Swamp

Village

Railroad

Elevated Berm

Each Grid Line = 1,000 Meters

involved? Someone must have gotten his ass chewed out pretty good over that one.

We were able to ford the Song Thu Bon downstream from the blackened remains and meet up with our infantry and tanks at the little fire base called Phu Loc 6. We would begin our sweep from there onto Goi Noi Island and link up with the Marine unit that had fallen into trouble the day before.

By mid-afternoon our combined relief force departed Phu Loc 6 in search of 2/7. We caught up with it by late afternoon and began a sweep of the western end of the island. We spent two uneventful days trying to locate Charlie, but the only thing we turned up was sporadic sniper fire. It wasn't effective, but it seemed to dog us wherever we went. It was Charlie's way of letting us know that he still cared about us.

On the third day we encountered our first enemy activity about two klicks (a klick, or kilometer, equals 1,000 meters) into the island. The grunts had gotten into a brief skirmish and had taken a few casualties, but none of our tanks was involved. A medevac (medical evacuation helicopter) was called in to take out the wounded. Before long, one of the antique eggbeaters came in to pick them up. With it came a foretaste of the kind of situation we were about to find ourselves in for the duration of the sweep.

At the helicopter's approach, one of the grunts threw a smoke grenade to signal the pilot where to land and indicate the wind direction. As the bird turned and started its steep descent, suddenly the serene afternoon exploded all around us in a maelstrom of heavy and light machine gun fire. We couldn't see the enemy's guns, just their green tracers streaking toward the chopper. The quiet countryside suddenly opened up with heavy machine guns all around us! What shocked us most was the size and astounding quantity of the enemy's .51-caliber Chicom machine guns. These were large crew-served weapons that took lots of effort and manpower to move around. It was suddenly obvious that around us was a large, as yet unseen, enemy force.

The bird made it in, and a few of the wounded were loaded aboard the chopper. "If they ain't dead yet," Embesi said to me, referring to our earlier flying experience, "they soon will be."

The chopper struggled away with its bleeding cargo, dodging the hail of enemy fire. We learned later that the bird was badly shot up and barely made it home.

The helicopter incident magnified the gravity of our situation. Later, other choppers carrying food and much-needed water tried to make it in but were turned back by the intense volume of fire. It was our first indication, though we didn't realize it at the time, that we couldn't count on getting much helicopter support in the coming days. Resupplying a reinforced Marine infantry battalion in the field can be done only by helicopter. Without them, grunts could last only a couple of days before having to head back to a fire base.

Another flight of choppers tried to resupply us with precious water and ammunition just before twilight. This time, they were the newer CH46 Sea Knight helicopters—larger birds with two sets of rotors and a large ramp at the rear that expedited the transport of troops and supplies. But even these capable machines couldn't make it in as the area around us erupted into a maelstrom once more.

After a few daring but unsuccessful attempts to land, they took the hint and flew off. "Fuckin' great!" said one grunt near our vehicle as he watched the birds vanish into the distance.

A few minutes later, the grunts threw several smoke grenades out along one side of the perimeter—we had no idea why. We were near where one of the smoke grenades was burning; the sweep had come to a halt. I was eating a cold can of beans and franks, with my head sticking up out of the loader's hatch. The top of the turret served as my table.

We heard them before we saw them. It was hard to tell where the sounds were coming from, when suddenly three Sea Knights popped over a hill, heading directly parallel to the smoke from the grenades. The helicopters flew low and fast down the battalion's front line, pushing supplies out the back as they skimmed across the ground at ninety miles per hour. The grunts ran out to scavenge everything they could find in what was otherwise a debris field. What was left of the supplies lay in a swath of broken ammo boxes, damaged C ration cases, and scattered bags of mail. Some of the wooden boxes, each holding two rounds of 90mm

tank ammunition, had broken open when they hit the ground, flinging shells all along the wreckage path. But no matter how badly those
ammo crates fared, they still did better than the plastic containers of
water, which mostly ruptured leaving the grunts with a serious water-
shortage problem.

Average daytime temperature hovered between 110 and 120 degrees
and the heat was taking an enormous toll on the grunts. Some were
dropping from heat exhaustion, and several medevacs had to brave heavy
fire to reach the men before they died. Rumors that the thermometer
had reached 130 degrees began taking a toll on morale. Water quickly
became a scarce commodity, worth almost its weight in gold.

That extra drinking water Embesi had us load aboard our tanks was
never meant for us. From his past experience in The Nam, he knew the
value of water. When we began dispensing that precious water, it
endeared us to the grunts closest to our tank, the very troops we
depended on to protect us from enemy RPG teams.

We didn't dispense our water for free. As with another army—the
Salvation Army—the grunts got a sermon before their sustenance. As
we poured water into their waiting cups, helmets, and canteens, we
reminded them that we relied upon them for close-in protection. The
grunts agreed to look out for us, and Embesi's extra water became our
"insurance" policy.

The beginning of the fourth day, the battalion resumed its attempt
to force an engagement with the enemy. We were trying to make Charlie fight on our terms. We knew he was around from the very heavy fire
he directed at our helicopters, although up to now he had pretty much
eluded us. Typically, he fought only at a time and place of his choosing—
unless cornered.

That morning, the battalion CO, a lieutenant colonel, decided to
send a small armored force of three tanks, a couple of amtracs, and a
platoon of infantry back to Phu Loc 6. We were told it was going to be
a milk run, a cakewalk. I was happy that our tank was chosen to lead
the column; it would give us a chance to get off this island for at least
one night.

We gulped down an uncooked breakfast as we kept an eye on the tree line in front of us. You never took your eyes off the tree lines anywhere in Vietnam. Meanwhile, a platoon of grunts climbed on top of two amphibious tractors. As troop carriers, the amtracs, or "tracs" as we usually called them, were slow, ponderous, and ungainly. They were never designed to be land taxis, the way we used them in Vietnam. But they were the only viable way for taking out the dead and not-so-seriously wounded. No one would ask a chopper to risk landing in a hot LZ for any but the most critically wounded or those suffering from heatstroke. More importantly, amtracs could return loaded with food, ammo, and the most critical item of all—water.

A stroke of luck had blessed this operation with an unusually large number of tanks. In this war, such foresight was rare. Someone must have expected serious trouble. Our departure would still leave the battalion with four tanks in support while we made our little jaunt off the island.

The tracs were loaded with the wounded and dead from the fighting the day before. We had barely finished breakfast when the word went out, "Crank 'em up!"

We were anxious to get underway, looking forward to delivering our morose cargo and the chance to shower, eat a can of warmed-up C rations, and get at least six hours of uninterrupted sleep.

The convoy started with our tank in the lead and Sergeant Kimbrew's tank following right behind. Trailing him were two amtracs, and another tank took up the rear. It was a powerful armored column, designed to complete its round trip of exchanging body bags for bags of water.

The grunts always preferred to ride on top of the amtracs. No one in his right mind rode inside a trac except the dead, for the belly of the beast was lined with hundreds of gallons of gasoline. Amtracs were so notorious for "lighting up" after hitting a mine that we often referred to them as Shake 'n' Bakes. Even though sitting outside, with no armor for protection, left the grunts exposed to rifle and mortar fire, they figured it was safer than being turned into charcoal briquettes.

Thirty minutes into our trek we were about to cross our third tree line of the morning. We were retracing the same tracks we left days earlier—a smart move, because in order to plant a mine Charlie needed to disturb the impressions we had left. Embesi kept a careful watch on the tracks in front of him, looking for the slightest disturbance in the old impressions.

As a precautionary measure, our main gun was pointed at the tree line we were approaching. It came at an angle from our left side, and we were about fifty meters from where it crossed our path. As the tank's gunner, my job was to slowly sweep the main gun back and forth, looking for any sign of movement within the trees. I alternated between the gunner's periscope and the powerful telescope mounted alongside the main gun. Through it, I could see nothing in the tree line that made me suspicious.

But when I went back to the periscope's wider field of view, I saw them. They lay ten meters in front of the tree line, in dry grass two feet high; their khaki uniforms blended into the grass. My first thought was that the grunts had gotten way too far ahead of us. Then I realized that each one had an RPG launcher on his shoulder, and they were all pointed at—me!

Immediately, without warning anybody, I opened up with our .30-caliber machine gun. Embesi, who was startled at the unexpected firing, got only one word out of his mouth: "Cease—" before the world to our left front simply exploded. At the same time I wasted the two NVA, seven or eight RPGs whooshed out of the tree line, trailing their characteristic signature of yellow smoke. All were aimed at the two lead tanks. They scored a hit on the tank behind us, and several more RPGs narrowly missed us.

Over the radio came Kimbrew's voice. "I'm hit!"

Kimbrew's gunner, Gary Gibson, keyed his com-helmet so that all the tanks could hear him over the radio. "We're OK. Fire the goddamned fifty!" Gary was letting us know that he was pissed at Kimbrew for not returning fire with the TC's larger machine gun, but at least the tank was still functioning.

A heavy volley of machine gun fire raked the amtracs, and the grunts were swept off the vehicles as if by an invisible scythe. Those who were still alive rolled off to the amtracs' safe side, seeking the safety of their aluminum hulls. Those who fell off the front or remained on top were already dead. Several more grunts sought out the safety of the tanks, desperate to put anything between them and the volcano of smoke and fire erupting from the tree line.

More RPGs gushed wildly from out of the trees, but they missed their intended targets. Our immediate, voluminous return fire kept the NVA from taking good aim. All three M48A3 Patton tanks spit salvo after salvo of canister rounds into the trees and brush, all aimed at those twinkling lights.

We fired a dozen rounds of canister in two minutes. I kept the .30 firing nonstop. The heat and smoke inside the turret became intense; I had never fired so many 90mm rounds in such rapid succession. Hot brass shell casings littered the turret floor. Sergeant Hearn, the loader, kept feeding both the machine gun and main gun. In ten minutes he was knee-deep in three-foot-long hot shell casings that were burning his legs. Normally, the loader threw the brass out of the loader's hatch, but Hearn was having all he could do keeping up with the .30 and the main gun. The 90mm brass casings were slowly filling up the tight space of the turret.

I kept firing the machine gun, saturating the tree line, throwing out the book on "controlled bursts" that kept a machine gun barrel from overheating. Whoever wrote that advice never faced an onslaught like the one we were facing now. Three tanks pounded away at point-blank range, at a dug-in and tenacious enemy. The North Vietnamese stood their ground with maniacal intensity, trading blow-for-blow in a display of relentless firepower and determination.

After fifteen minutes, having gone through all the canister and beehive rounds in the turret that we could reach, we started using HE rounds, only to find that some didn't detonate when they hit the ground. We were too close for the projectiles to arm themselves!

Embesi got on the radio and tried to get the other tanks to maneuver, but they were all pinned in place by grunts clinging to them for cover. Given that torrential onslaught, you couldn't blame the grunts. It was any port in a storm. As we pounded away, the entire length of the tree line, which was two hundred feet long, spewed fire, dust, smoke, and exploding trees—and still RPGs came flying out of the dense vegetation. I didn't think it was possible for anything to live through the deadly volleys the three tanks were pouring out, but the RPGs continued to fly out of the tree line.

I was too busy concentrating on the tree line to pay much attention to anything else. My job was to take out the RPG teams, our primary threats. I continued to lay on the .30, following each yellow trail to the point at which it had exited the tree line, hoping to nail the shooter. But the RPGs still came on, unrelentingly.

After I had fired several thousand rounds of machine gun ammo, the gun became so hot that it began cooking off—that is, it sporadically fired on its own. The heat of the gun set off the bullet sitting in the chamber. In a vain attempt to cool it off, Hearn poured oil all over the gun. That only added more smoke to the already bad air inside the turret.

I fired the machine gun again, going for the last RPG trail. Suddenly, my tracers were flying wildly all over the place—I had shot the rifling out of the barrel. It was something I had only heard about and never experienced. The barrel was now worn smooth providing no spin on the exiting bullets, causing them to fly all over the place.

I got on the intercom. "We gotta change the barrel on the thirty!"

That was the last thing anyone wanted to hear in the middle of a firefight. Taking the .30-caliber machine gun off line was one very serious matter.

It surprises laymen to learn how much we depended upon our .30s. Most tend to think that a tank's long main gun—its most obvious feature—would be its most critical weapon. But in this war of close-in fighting, the .30 was the heart and life of a tank, our key weapon to keep enemy infantry at bay.

Embesi got on the intercom and told Hearn to get ready to change the barrel while he prepared his .50-caliber machine gun with a new tray of ammo. Until the loader got the barrel changed, the .50 would have to do the talking. That would be the longest two minutes of the war so far. I had one round in the main gun, but had to use it judiciously until

Hearn finished with the machine gun. He couldn't tend to two weapons at the same time. The machine gun's barrel was smoking and radiating intense heat, and all of its other parts were almost as hot, making the loader's job very difficult. He had to wear thick asbestos gloves, which made it all the more difficult to handle the small parts of the light machine gun.

Due to our infantry's increasing casualties, their rifle fire now began to wither away. Our close-in protection was slowly dwindling. The few grunts who were still alive were hunkered down behind the vehicles to ride out the storm. It didn't take Charlie long to make the grunts' lives even more miserable. Enemy mortars began to drop on the convoy's far side, searching for the men hiding behind the vehicles.

Of course, when the mortars began to fall, the grunts only huddled lower to the ground. Very few had their heads up to see the tree line. It was then that a small group of NVA soldiers rushed the column. Charlie really had his shit together that morning.

Before Embesi realized it, two NVA were on the back of the tank, over the engine. Each one had an AK-47 and a satchel charge, a large pack loaded with explosive designed to take out an entire bunker. With our main gun perpendicular to the tank's hull, the NVA were able to crouch behind the loader's side of the turret. Embesi immediately pulled out his pistol with one hand and turned the TC's cupola with the other, thereby placing his half-opened hatch between him and the NVA—who had their rifles up but not their heads.

As Embesi later explained it, "The dink or Marine who made the first move to shoot at the other would be a dead man." It was a Mexican standoff on top of our tank.

All of this was transpiring without the rest of the crew's knowledge.

Embesi, cool as ever, got on the radio. "Kimbrew! Scratch my back!"

"Scratch my back" was a term all tankers immediately recognized—and feared, for it meant that enemy infantry had overrun a tank and were on top of the vehicle. Scratching another tank's back was the act of one tank shooting its machine gun at a sister tank in an act of desperation.

It was our good luck that Kimbrew's gunner, Cpl. Gary Gibson, had served with Embesi on a previous tour in Vietnam and instantly recognized Embesi's plea. Suddenly, Embesi saw the turret on the tank behind us whip around until—in less than two seconds—its gun tube was aimed directly at him.

Gary's voice came over the radio: "Embesi! Duck!"

As we found out later, Gary had both hands on the electric trigger grips of the gunner's control handle. He didn't waste time flipping the power switches from main gun to machine gun. He just squeezed the electric triggers to fire the 90mm beehive round in the chamber.

Embesi ducked. An explosion of 4,400 metal darts washed over the tank. A tidal wave of smoke and flame, along with dust and debris, filled the inside of the turret. My first guess was that an RPG had hit us. But I knew I was all right and was focused too intently on the tree line, still spewing out its deadly volume of fire. For only an instant, I turned my head from the periscope to check Sergeant Hearn's progress on changing the machine gun barrel. I needed that .30!

Hearn didn't bother to take the time to investigate the sudden smoke and debris filling the turret. He was too focused on the immediate task of bringing the gun back on line. It could save our lives. In fact, the only man on our crew aware of the two NVA had been Embesi.

Everything in the gypsy rack, along with the two North Vietnamese, had just been turned into shredded wheat.

"Thirty's up!" yelled Hearn. By then he had thrown off those cumbersome asbestos gloves and burned his hands getting the hot gun back in action.

The battalion was still two klicks away, but it was well aware of the fierce firefight going on. Over the radio, they could hear desperate pleas from the few remaining grunts who still hugged our vehicles; the battalion had already turned to come to our rescue.

Inside of thirty minutes we had gone through about forty rounds of our main gun ammunition, or more than two-thirds of it. Preoccupied with keeping the .30 oiled and the main gun fed, Hearn couldn't keep up with the brass expenditure, and the turret floor was covered with thousands of

.30-caliber shell casings and dozens of the three-foot-long 90mm brass shell casings. Suddenly, the turret wouldn't move.

"Turret's jammed!" I yelled.

Embesi's voice pierced through our comm helmets. "Get that fuckin' brass outta here!"

Somewhere in the ocean of brass, a shell had wedged itself between the turret and the tank's hull. I couldn't aim my guns.

Embesi immediately opened up with the .50, giving Hearn a chance to throw the 90mm shell casings overboard. Hearn looked like a sailor bailing out a foundering ship. Three-foot-long casings flew out of the loader's hatch as he searched frantically for the one offending casing. The grunts outside, using us for cover, yelled as the brass shells rained down on them.

After what seemed to take forever, Hearn found the guilty shell. He yanked it free and I was back in business.

Sweat was running off our bodies. The constant deafening chatter of the machine guns was interrupted only by the firing of the main gun. In addition to that, we had the combined voices of three TCs screaming over the radio, making a bedlam of insanity.

Never letting my hands off the triggers, I yelled for the forty-first time, "On the way!" That warned the loader to clear himself from the breech before it kicked back in a two-foot blur and dropped the next hot smoking shell casing on the now-visible floor.

Hearn had already pulled another 90mm round out of its rack and was shoving it into the breech. Ka-chung!—the breech slammed shut. "Up!" he yelled. During that interval of only a few seconds I had switched back to the .30 and was taking the tree line under fire.

With Hearn's yell, I switched back to the main gun.

"On the way!" The tank rocked as our main gun fired for the forty-second time. Another hot brass casing hit the deck, and the process began all over again.

Typically, Mr. Charles's tactics were of a hit-and-run nature. It was unusual for him to stand and fight this long. Later, we found out that the NVA were in steel-reinforced bunkers that allowed them to hang tough against our armored column. We also discovered that the steel in their bunkers was actually the rails that once led to the Ha Dong Bridge!

Why did they put up such a maniacal stand? In hindsight, it should have been obvious—the NVA wanted the infantry battalion to come to our rescue. We were just the unwitting bait for their far larger trap.

Retracing our route, the battalion encountered the same two tree lines we had crossed uneventfully half an hour earlier. They passed through the first and were approaching the second. The eruption that leaped out at them was so loud and intense that we could hear it over the slowing, sporadic gunfire of our own ambush.

They too came up against steel-reinforced bunkers, but these were equipped with .51-caliber Chicom machine guns. As the grunts tried to assault and flank the bunkers, it was carnage. The tanks we had left behind with the battalion took on the bunkers, one by one, with their main guns and eventually swung the tide of the battle. As the sounds of their ambush grew in volume, ours—conversely—began to slacken.

An FO (Marine artillery forward observer) with the battalion called in fire from the big 155mm howitzers several miles away, on Hill 55. He walked the "five-fives" exploding shells along the tree line to give the grunts a chance to maneuver against the bunkers and, finally, assault the enemy position at a cost of many casualties.

Back at the ranch, we were quickly running out of ammunition and still pinned down in our own ambush. But it had slackened off somewhat. Dead and wounded grunts had our tanks pinned in place. We couldn't move if we wanted to, and besides, leaving dead and wounded behind was never an option in the Marine Corps. We had a long and proud tradition that you always came out with all your equipment and men—dead and alive. Nobody got left behind.

Finally, with artillery support, the battalion slowly began to make its way toward our position. It took them what seemed like forever to reach us. They were as shot up and as low on ammo as we were.

It had been an all-day event, or so it had seemed. I was in unimaginable sensory overload, surrounded by varied loud noises, the tank rocking with every squeeze of the trigger, and endless voices screaming through my comm helmet. I was sitting in the turret's intense 130-plus-degree heat, in the confined space of the gunner's position, unable to get a breath of fresh air. Smoke expended from thousands of shells, along with the smoke from the oil Hearn had squirted on the hot machine gun, plus the sharp smell of our own anxious sweat. It was all beginning to overwhelm me. I yelled for the loader to turn on the air extraction blower to vent the choking fumes.

As the battalion reached us, things finally, but slowly, quieted down. There was suddenly nothing for me to do when it dawned on me that I was hungry—very hungry. I had no idea what time it was, but I was certain that it was late afternoon. We had missed lunch, and now, possibly dinner as well.

"Hey, guys," I said over the intercom, now that the firefight had subsided, "How about passing down a box of C's?"

Embesi told Hearn to throw me down a box. "Didn't you eat before we left?" he asked.

"Yeah," I told him. "Of course I did."

"And you're hungry again?"

"Hell, we missed lunch! Aren't you guys hungry too?" I asked.

"Peavey, it's eight o'clock," Embesi's voice came back. "We only ate breakfast ninety minutes ago!"

For me, slow time had been in effect that morning, stretching a forty-five-minute firefight so much that I figured an entire day had passed. Part of the cause for my confusion was not having a hatch to stick my head out of. I had no direct link with the outside world, the sun in particular. Shit! I thought. I had already notched off one day on my mental calendar, and now I was forced to relive it.

The gunner's world was as myopic as my perception of time. A tank's gunner was condemned to wearing a powerful set of binoculars for eyes. He could see far better than anyone else on the tank, but only in a very narrow area and at a great distance. The gunner, just by the nature of his position, never saw the whole picture. If I couldn't see it in my gun sight, it didn't exist. More than once, I climbed out of the turret late in the afternoon, only to be totally surprised by what my surroundings looked like.

Often a gunner becomes so engrossed in his work that he is even unaware of his orientation to the tank itself. Unless he takes his eyes away from the sights to look down at the turret floor, he can easily lose all relationship between the tank's direction and where his gun tube is pointed. More often than not, the tank commander jerks him back to reality by using the TC's override control handle, abruptly taking control out of the gunner's hands. The gunner could sit helplessly, peering through the gun sight, as the turret turns without his input. Then, just as suddenly, the turret stops, and the TC tells the gunner what to look for at some new spot.

The gunner is usually very confused—until the crap hits the fan. During a firefight like the one we had just endured, he has the best seat in the house. He has control over the laying and firing of the guns, and can see the results of his work, up close and personal.

During a firefight, ironically, the loader—who usually rides chest-high out of the turret and can see everything—is the one man in the crew of four who has no idea what is going on. Too busy keeping the machine gun fed and the main gun loaded, he cannot take time to look outside. Also, he can only imagine the results of all his hard work. Meanwhile, all those machine gun cartridges littering the turret floor makes his job that more difficult; it is like walking on marbles in an environment in which he cannot afford to lose his balance. As the gun recoils, he also has to be especially wary of not getting in the way of the breech. If he steps in its path, it will be lethal. Of the whole tank crew, the loader has the most demanding and physically intense job. But for only short periods of time.

Normally, the driver has one of the most desirable jobs. But during a firefight he can contribute nothing and is suddenly the most helpless person on the crew. He can only drop down in his seat, close his hatch, and keep his foot on the brake. His vision is limited to three glass prism blocks, fixed periscopes. Once the shooting starts, he is strictly an observer. He can contribute only an extra pair of eyes, and a pistol is his only defense.

The function of the tank commander (TC) is an entirely different story: He is as busy as the driver isn't. His job is to be aware of the overall situation and the tank's tactical position within it. The TC is responsible for selecting targets, prioritizing their threat potential, and choosing the right type of ammunition to deal with each one. He also has a .50-caliber machine gun that he has to load and fire and he also has to stay in continual contact with other tanks around him and coordinate their fire. He can also stay in communication with the infantry leader on the ground, via the radio or on the tank-infantry phone mounted on the back of the tank—an item that sounded like a great idea, even though it was rarely used.

More than any other crewman, the TC has to keep his head outside the turret, which makes him a popular target of enemy snipers. He is one very busy individual, with a huge responsibility.

THE FIREFIGHT SUBSIDED as soon as the battalion got up to our position. We formed a perimeter, assessed our damage, and licked our wounds. Embesi surveyed all the tanks to see how much total ammo we had. The three tanks involved in the initial ambush were pitifully low. Over our intercom, Embesi told Hearn to run over to the latecomers and borrow some 90mm ammo.

It was just the opportunity I had been waiting for. "Let me go!" I interrupted Embesi. "I need a breath of fresh air down here." I had to get the hell out of there, if only for a few minutes.

"Go ahead," Embesi replied.

I squeezed past the main gun, waited for the loader to get out of the way, climbed up, and stuck out my head. The 120 degree heat outside temperature suddenly felt cool. Drenched in sweat, I took a deep breath, climbed out of the turret, and sat on top of the tank for a minute to get oriented. Now I could see where the ambush had taken place, and it was totally different from what I had imagined.

Embesi pointed out which tanks I was to get ammunition from. He warned me to wear my helmet and flak jacket, which I put on before I jumped down. It felt good to be on my feet again. I quickly walked over to one of the newly arrived tanks and yelled up to the TC, "You got some ninety for me?"

I realized it was Staff Sergeant Siva from 1st Tanks—everyone knew Siva. He was a hard-drinking and hard-fighting American Indian and was famous in Marine tanker lore. You either loved him or hated him and it was a mutual understanding. He said something to his loader down inside the turret, and up out of the loader's hatch came a round of main gun ammunition, followed by the loader himself. Right away, I saw it was a WP round.

"Don't you have any canister?" I asked.

"Beggars can't be choosers," said Siva with a smile. He knew I wanted canister—we all wanted canister!

I made the trip across the perimeter, back to our tank, and yelled up to no one in particular to take the heavy round. Embesi took one look and snarled, "I told that sonnuvabitch I wanted canister. What's he givin' you Willy Peter for?"

It was a rhetorical question. I was just the delivery boy.

Embesi moved his mouthpiece down from his helmet, keyed the radio switch, and shouted something that ended with, "No fuckin' HE, Goddamn it! I want canister! You got extra on the back of your tank, damn it!"

It was true, there were several 90mm ammo boxes tied down on the back of Siva's tank that were left over from a recent supply drop and they were all canister rounds. I made six trips around the perimeter, hitting up all the TCs for extra ammo. More than anything, it was great just being outside. But this would be one volunteer mission where the adage "be careful what you wish for" would suddenly apply.

Three of us, each from a different tank, were going between the newcomers and redividing the main gun ammunition equally. I didn't notice the approaching helicopters until someone threw a smoke grenade into the middle of the perimeter, about one hundred meters from me. Then I realized that a number of wounded had been carried near to where the smoke was billowing.

While I was halfway across the perimeter, carrying a round of HE, the birds started their steep decent. Their landing gear touched the ground and compressed under the full weight of each machine. The men near the noisy choppers couldn't hear the distinct series of bloop! bloop! bloop! noises in the distance, or the shouts of "Incoming!"

Familiar with the sound of enemy mortars by this time, I dropped to the ground on my knees, cradling the four-foot-long round, and laid it carefully on the ground next to me. It was the first time I had ever been caught out in the open, and I was terrified.

Crack! crack! crack! Black puffs followed brief orange flashes as the mortars exploded inside the perimeter. I spread out on the ground, trying to get as flat as I could, as several more rounds crashed into the area. They were landing only seventy-five feet away. Starting with my head, I worked my way down, trying to flatten my body into the earth itself. I flattened my ass, turned my ankles sideways, put my cheek against the earth, and flattened out my fingers on the ground. I could smell the burned powder of the exploding projectiles and hear the pieces of hot shrapnel buzzing through the air on their hunt for human flesh, sounding like the killer bees they surely were.

Unlike the sound made in war movies, an exploding shell's noise was extremely short in duration, a sharp Crack! more like the report during the finale of a fireworks show. A dozen explosions sounded all around me. I thought they would never end.

From those unlucky enough to have been close to the noisy choppers, screams went out: "Corpsman! Corpsman Up!"

A small metal sliver landed harmlessly in front of my hand. Realizing this chunk of metal was of North Vietnamese origin, I wanted it as a souvenir to take back and show the crew just how lucky I had been. I slowly moved my arm, keeping it flat on the ground. I closed my thumb and forefinger around the object.

"Shit!" I screamed. I felt like the idiot I was, and for several days I had the blisters to prove it.

Totally exposed and absolutely scared to death, I went back to trying to melt myself into the ground through osmosis. I wanted to be a drop of water melting into desert sand, but I felt more like an elephant with two burned fingers in a tiny shooting gallery. Now I knew why I was never meant to be a grunt. As I lay there, running through every scheme to make myself smaller, it dawned on me. Jesus Christ, here I was, lying parallel to a 90mm HE round—a brass cylinder filled with twenty pounds of explosive. And it took only twelve pounds of pressure on the right spot to set the damned thing off.

Minutes ago, I was delighted to have it. Now I couldn't distance myself fast enough from the damned thing, but I wasn't about to get up. Then I came up with a brilliant plan. Maybe if I pushed hard enough, I could roll it away from me. Keeping my right hand flat against the ground, I moved it up toward my head, working it between the round and my body.

Crack! Crack! A few more mortars landed nearby, and I waited for the next round to impact. Then I pushed the top of the projectile away from me as hard as I could.

I hadn't given my plan a lot of thought. If I had, its consequence would have been obvious. The long round was like an upside-down ice cream cone, its top narrower than its base. When I shoved the projectile's top away from my head, it simply turned 180 degrees on its wider base and bumped against my leg.

Crack! Another round landed next to its intended target, the helicopters, seventy-five meters away. With my head pressed hard to the ground, the helicopters were directly in my sight. Those whirling machines, loaded with wounded, were just starting to lift off when a mortar went off right beneath one of them. The bird abruptly lost power and crashed ten feet back to earth. The second helicopter was luckier. After straining to lift off, it flew out of the perimeter with its load. I didn't dare turn my head to watch it leave, but as soon as its clatter died away, so did all the firing.

I waited several seconds, then slowly got up, picked up my load, and made it back to our tank. I had to yell several times before Hearn or Embesi opened their hatches. They had waited out the mortar attack from safely inside the tank—where I should have been.

Embesi looked down at me with one of his smiles. "Been out for a walk, have you?"

Over the radio came word from one of the tanks. A tanker running ammo like me had been hit with shrapnel. He had to be medevacked.

That afternoon, I got my second helicopter lesson—the first being, never get aboard one again. Today's lesson was how the NVA would wait for a chopper to land, when it was most vulnerable, to unleash their mortars. Helicopters were flying magnets that drew enemy metal out of nowhere, the way blood draws sharks. You could be on an operation for a week and never see a thing—until a bird came in to land. That was always accompanied by screams of "Incoming!" and "Corpsman!" Then you heard that distinctive bloop! in the distance, meaning you had three or four seconds to find a hole and make love to Mother Earth.

Just like tanks, helicopters had a love-hate relationship with the grunts. Grunts loved what the birds could deliver and bear away, but with their good came the bad—enemy mortars and machine guns. Personally, I hated the damned machines.

The wounded were recovered off the downed helicopter while the crew looked over their wounded bird. We were now fixed to this location; we couldn't abandon the wounded bird. We would have to wait for another, larger chopper to lift it out. In other words, we were going to be here for a while, which was not good news. Meanwhile, Charlie could regroup and marshal all his forces.

We had a tank crew that was short one man, and the wounded crewman was the only trained tanker on the vehicle. Inasmuch as the other three crewmen were all former amtrackers, none of whom knew how to drive a tank, someone had to be taken from another tank crew and reassigned to this vehicle. John Cash was chosen. He left his crewmates and joined the all-amtracker tank as its new driver.

Several hours passed before we heard that a larger chopper was not available. We would spend the night in the same position, having to make it through until daybreak with what little ammo we had.

We made some adjustments to the lines to take advantage of the terrain in order to form a stronger perimeter. Luckily, they allowed us to move back from the tree line, in front of which we had spent our entire morning and afternoon. Lieutenant Scott, our platoon leader, pulled his tank up on line with us, about seventy-five feet to our right. In front of us were several burial mounds, a Vietnamese graveyard. Never mind the grim reminder—we didn't like them because they provided potential cover for would-be attackers.

About an hour before dusk, Embesi and Scott were summoned to attend a sitrep—situation report—with the battalion CO. Gary Gibson came over to our tank. He tried to convince us that during the morning's ambush, NVA had been on top of our tank.

"That's bullshit, Gary. We're not fallin' for that one," I said.

It sounded like a typical Gary Gibson story; he was trying to take credit for our being alive. He was a notorious prankster who couldn't always be trusted with every story he told you. None of us believed Gibson until he noticed Embesi's flak jacket, which sat on top of the cupola. For some odd reason, Embesi had grabbed someone else's flak jacket for his meeting. Gary reached over, grabbed the jacket, and pointed to three flechette darts, one-and-a-half-inch-long metal darts that were packed into a beehive round. Our mouths dropped open. Those darts proved that Embesi hadn't ducked quite far enough. Gary was telling the truth after all!

Better Living Thru Canister had lived up to her name after all. That beehive round from Gary's tank was responsible for us being alive. The three of us looked at one another. All we could say was, "Holy shit!"

For the rest of that evening, Sergeant Embesi's luck stayed with him. He and Lieutenant Scott were walking back to the tank when three RPGs flew out of the tree line behind the burial mounds. The driver and I were standing watch, eating a can of C's, when the RPG streaked right between the two of us, inches above the turret. This was the second time we had been sitting atop the turret when something deadly passed between us. Only this time, it didn't happen in slow motion, and it scared the shit out of us. We didn't know it, but that same rocket continued on and landed between the feet of the returning Sergeant Embesi. With no idea he was approaching our tank, we immediately pumped out two canister rounds in the hopes of getting the shooters. Then, through the glass vision ring of the TC's cupola, I saw Embesi struggling to climb up on the back of the tank.

I opened the TC's hatch. He climbed down inside, obviously in a lot of pain. That's when I noticed his boots and trousers were torn to shreds. Hearn and I took off his boots, expecting to find severe wounds and a lot of blood. To our surprise, we found only two very scratched up ankles and lower-leg abrasions. How he survived was a stroke of luck; how he kept both legs, and his genitalia, was a miracle. In light of his coolness under fire with two NVA on top of the tank and his surviving an RPG between the legs, I knew then that I would follow him anywhere.

Sergeant Embesi could barely stand, but he refused to be medevacked. He didn't want to leave a crew shorthanded, nor turn his platoon over to someone else. We rigged up a board that he was able to sit on and continue his role as TC and platoon sergeant.

That night, we learned that our sweep had been given the operational name of Allen Brook. It was a name that would stay with us for the rest of our lives.

The next twelve hours were some of the most nerve-wracking any of us would spend in Vietnam. And it was only the first of many more scary nights to come. Sergeant Hearn had been a rock all day, under the most difficult conditions. But now he started having flashbacks of his Operation Starlite episode, where he lost his tank and crew and had to survive in the bush for two days. I never saw or heard it, but Hearn started to sob while he and Embesi were standing watch together that night.

As Embesi told me years later, Hearn said he couldn't go through that again. Later that same night, the driver also had words with Embesi. "Sergeant Embesi," he asked, "are we going to die tonight?"

YOU HAD ONLY TO LOOK INSIDE the turret to know we were in a very precarious position. There were only six rounds of main gun ammunition left, and only one of them was a canister round. In other words, just one shotgun round stood between us and the North Vietnamese Army. We all checked our pistols and stretched the magazine springs, making certain they hadn't become weak over the past three months. Contrary to Marine policy, my .45 was cocked and locked, meaning I had a round in the chamber and the hammer back, with the slide safety on. I was certain that I would be using it that night. We all were.

Everyone, grunt and tanker alike, was apprehensive. We were all pitifully low on ammunition. During the morning's ambush we had gone through fifty-four rounds of main gun ammunition, plus the two I fired while Embesi was walking back to the tank. We also were very low on .30-caliber machine gun ammo. And with an LZ as hot as this one was, resupply was out of the question. They weren't about to risk losing any more choppers.

Who could imagine an American unit, in the latter half of the twentieth century, running out of ammunition out in the field? After all, we were the beneficiaries of the largest material buildup since World War II. We had all the latest marvels, the helicopter being just one of them. They wouldn't just leave us out here with nothing to shoot. Would they?

We were all awake. No one could sleep. No one wanted to sleep. The clock moved like the proverbial watched pot that never boils. It seemed like dawn never wanted to show its face. Our main gun, its safety turned off, was loaded with our last canister round. One squeeze of the electric triggers would mow down anything and everyone in front of us. That night, we kept our talk down to brief whispers. All our attention was focused on the area in front of us.

Standing watch at night always began at 10 p.m. The number of men who stood watch at any one time was determined by the threat level, and it was the tank commander who made that assessment. Whoever was on watch always stood in the TC's position, where, through a single handgrip, he had control over the turret and its guns. But this one-man-on-watch arrangement was used only in naturally fortified and fixed positions, like that of a fire base or bridge emplacement. There, the odds of an attack were low, plus the tank was hull-down in a deep manmade trench. That arrangement allowed each crewman six hours of shut-eye.

In the field, standing watch was an entirely different matter. With no revetment or slot to pull into, a tank sat hull-up, high above the ground, rendering it vulnerable to RPGs. In the field, at least two men were always on watch, one wearing his comm helmet in the TC's position, the other—usually without a helmet—in the loader's position, listening for any enemy movement in front of the vehicle.

Having another man on watch next to you helped maintain your sanity. At night, any dark bush often looked like it was moving if you stared at it too long. A second set of eyes gave you someone you could check with, helpful in confirming if the foliage was friend or enemy. In the course of our tour in Vietnam, we killed a lot of friendly bushes.

While in the field at night, the two off-duty crewmen would try to catch some sleep. One sat in the driver's seat, where his sleep was sure to be interrupted. A tank's radios had to be on and monitored, making for a constant drain on the batteries. To recharge them, the engine had to be run once every hour, for about ten minutes. Whoever was trying to sleep in the driver's seat also needed to wear his comm helmet, in case the TC needed to talk to him, and that meant listening to all the radio traffic and static as well. No one in the driver's position ever got much sleep.

The fourth crewman was the only one who would get any semblance of rest in the field. We usually found him curled up on the turret floor. Some men slept on the rear decks of their tanks—which, in the field, was not the smartest place to be. One unlucky mortar round during the night and a sleeping crewman could wind up taking a long snooze inside a zippered bag. When in the field, no good TC ever let his men sleep outside the tank. If the shit hit the fan, the loss of one man jeopardized the rest of the crew. Still, we saw it done. But with Embesi as your TC, it wasn't even an option

With two men standing watch you got only four hours of sleep, providing Charlie didn't play any of his mind-fucking games. He typically caused interruptions all night long by feeling out our position and throwing a grenade now and then. On longer operations, long stretches without sleep took a toll, as it was doing now. Each night left us groggier. After three or four days, we became zombies.

When you stood watch in the field the night air often felt chilly, not so much from the drop in temperature as from the adrenaline that still coursed through your veins. That was especially true on nights just like this one. None of us had any doubt that we were going to be hit. Because the NVA had missed dusk, we knew they would come for us just before dawn. This kind of situation called for everyone to be in his fighting position all night long. That meant virtually no sleep at all.

The North Vietnamese knew we had busted a lot of caps during the day's firefights. They knew, too, that we hadn't been resupplied. Our position was no secret, either, not with seven tanks running their engines every hour. No, Charlie knew damned well where we were. He also knew we weren't about to leave a downed helicopter. What's more, after the day's shelling, his mortars were still zeroed in on our position.

We were easy pickings.

Chapter 8

Angels Flying Too Close to the Ground

The morning began just like the previous six, it was already hot and damp as a sauna, a warm and muggy prelude to the obscene temperatures that soon would follow. Everyone was up before the sun, anticipating an assault that never materialized.

Mr. Charles never hit us that night; our only casualty was the additional loss of sleep. The most sleep any of us got was an hour's worth. The North Vietnamese missed an opportunity that night. An entire Marine battalion—what was left of one—stood a very good chance of being overrun. We could only assume that we had chewed up on Charlie pretty good, leaving both sides with the same dilemma—totally spent, and needing time to regroup. But he wasn't done with us yet, not by a long shot.

Embesi had to sit on the boards we jury-rigged for him, but if we came under fire he couldn't drop lower into the turret. Also, his feet had turned black from toes to mid-calf. It was the worst bruising I had ever seen on the luckiest guy I have ever known. His episode of the previous evening, plus my short foray to collect ammo, formed the basis of the second of Peavey's Axioms: Axiom Number Two: Never, ever, get off the tank.

Six nights of long watches and short naps had left my mind numb. It felt like that annoying feeling you get in those first few dizzy minutes after a carnival ride, while your brain tries to remember which way is up. Except in our case, it never went away. Little sleep made for lethargic eyelids, heavy as the heads behind them. We were functioning on inertia, out of habit instilled in us by years of training.

Everyone suffered from this brain fog, which made for a constant series of little mistakes. A driver over-revved his engine, thinking the transmission was in gear; and a tank commander failed to turn off the radios before the driver started the engine, which threatened to blow the radios. The dull ache in our heads had only two cures: several hours of uninterrupted sleep or a sudden shot of adrenaline—but the later was only temporary. At best, it lasted only a few hours. Then, as with an addict beginning withdrawal, the ache would return, worse than before.

As the sun peeked over the horizon, a collective groan rose from the sleep-deprived grunts around the perimeter. Slowly the ground came to life as camouflaged and tired Marines got ready to face another day on Goi Noi Island. When the grunts realized they had survived the night, they clicked their rifles to the safe position. Nobody spoke. The only sounds came from rifle magazines and hand grenades being gathered up in front of each man's fighting position, along with the rustling of grunts looking through their packs for a cold can of breakfast.

Due to the casualties from the two ambushes and the oppressive heat, our battalion was now numbered forty-four Marines fewer than the day before. Lack of water was also taking its toll. Word went around the perimeter to get ready to move out. It had been decided to leave the H-34 helicopter where it was, a permanent casualty of war. Some back-in-the-rear-with-the-gear genius, probably an officer, had decided that what had been a valuable asset yesterday was now a worthless antique, not worth the tremendous risk of sending another helicopter to salvage it. Someone had realized—correctly—that a large chopper would be a sitting duck as it hovered above the treetops, totally exposed, while cables and slings were hooked up to the downed bird. In Vietnam, there were far too few large helicopters to gamble on the relic we were guarding. It was decided to blow the H-34 in place with C4, a puttylike plastic explosive carried by the combat engineers.

This really pissed off a lot of us who had just spent a most harrowing night. Couldn't they have decided that yesterday? Just chalk it up to military intelligence.

Nevertheless, military intelligence did confirm that we had been engaged by elements of the 2nd NVA Division. That put the odds about five to one in Charlie's favor. Goi Noi Island had been a Viet Minh bastion going back to the days when they had fought the French.

Our battalion left behind a few engineers to plant charges around the chopper and blow it up as soon as we were a safe distance away. We had moved about two hundred meters when the charges went off.

Two infantry companies swept east, and a third protected the battalion's right flank. The Song Thu Bon, about five hundred meters wide, was on our left as we approached an unusually high railroad berm. About twenty-five feet high, it cut across the width of the island in front of us, from the edge of the river on our left to as far as the eye could see on our right.

No sooner had we come within two hundred meters of the berm than we began taking heavy fire from enemy machine guns and rifles, quickly followed by mortars whose rounds tore among the grunts.

The tanks were unaffected by either kind of fire, but we couldn't approach the berm. If we did, we would be forced to shoot up at a dug-in enemy, which would render our fire ineffective. So we stayed back a hundred meters and provided supporting fire while the grunts maneuvered to assault the berm. They made several attempts, but each time a deadly wall of enemy fire drove them back, sometimes just short of the top.

Over the radios we heard the battalion CO pleading for artillery or air support. Finally a battery of 105mm howitzers, or what we called 05s (pronounced "oh-fives"), started raining shells on both sides of the berm. It was impossible to see the effectiveness of shells falling on the far side of the berm, but suddenly the mortars stopped. A few of the artillery rounds hit the top of the berm, but many more impacted on our side, close—too close—to our own troops.

It was getting late, only three or four hours of daylight left. They made another attempt to assault the berm. Some grunts made it, only to be pushed back once again. The dug-in NVA resumed firing their mortars. Behind the safety of the berm the enemy was free to reinforce his position at will. We had no way to flank the berm; pulling back was no option as long as Mr. Charles was shooting down on us. We had to take the berm itself.

Every Marine was asking the same question: Where in hell was our air support? We hadn't received any since this operation began, and we were getting our asses torn up by a tenacious enemy. The heat was intolerable, and the grunts had no incentive to move, having already lost one-quarter of their men over the last three days. Our situation was growing increasingly precarious.

The berm's earthen wall was impenetrable. There was no way around it, except for an underpass about five hundred meters to our right. On our left, the berm ended at the river's edge, where it was replaced by a series of eight very large concrete caissons that marched across the river. Some of them still had their bridge sections intact, but most, true to Vietnam form, were down in the water. These physical barriers had us pinned on two sides and the NVA were making it all work to their advantage. Unless something changed fast, we would soon run out of daylight.

About that time, we witnessed what most of us thought was divine intervention. Had the river parted, it wouldn't have been half as awe-inspiring as those two little Marine A-4 attack jets, called Skyhawks, that appeared from out of nowhere. Where had they come from? How had they heard about our plight? That evening, the atheists among us suddenly found religion.

To us the little planes looked every bit as large as 747 jumbo jets. Skyhawks were small delta-winged attack aircraft that specialized in tactical air-ground support and were notorious for the large bomb loads they could deliver. As they circled overhead, getting the lay of the land, we saw they were fully loaded with ordnance.

Tanks were fortunate to carry three different radios, affording us the benefit of monitoring several different frequencies at the same time. We listened to the grunts on one or two frequencies, plus we had a third one for tank-to-tank communication. So, unlike the average grunt, a tank crewman was usually pretty well informed and had a fine understanding of the overall picture. Now that those two pilots could see our position, it was the only time I ever heard a pilot acknowledge the desperate situation we were in: "You got NVA on the berm, and they're trying to flank your right," came one of the angel's voices. "You boys look like you're having fun down there!" They were talking to the forward air controller (FAC) who was standing near our tank.

"Why don't you come down here, smart ass," I muttered to myself, "and see what a Far East vacation is really like?"

They came in low, parallel to the berm, one ten seconds behind the other. Each was loaded with two napalm bombs and six Snake Eyes—the nickname for 250-pound bombs with speed brakes on the back of them, which gave the airplane that dropped them a chance to get out of range before they went off. They flew over the berm in a continuous circle. As one dropped its ordnance, the other lined up for its attack run. With each pass, the grunts cheered and yelled, "Get some!"

At that point, suddenly, all enemy fire ceased. We got a short breather that gave us time to move ammo around inside the tank and pull more machine gun ammo out of the gypsy rack. It was the quietest part of the day as the Skyhawks made run after run on the berm. They saw the jam that we were in and were well aware of what they had just done for us. Even after they had expended their napalm and Snake Eyes—Nape and Snake—they made several more runs using their 20mm cannons.

The FAC, himself a Marine pilot, and true to Marine Corps philosophy, was supporting the infantrymen in the field with his expertise. He was humpin' it with the grunts in the boonies in order to direct the air support—when and if we got it. I have no idea how the pilots got assigned as FACs, but it made for unparalleled coordination between ground and air. After the bomb run the unlucky FAC knew he wasn't going back to any air-conditioned hooches, hot showers, or warm meals like his brothers overhead. He had to live in the grass with the mud and the bugs, just like us real Marines.

Marine Air made for the finest, most precise air-ground support in the world. During my thirteen-month tour, I was to experience air support from all three services—Air Force, Navy, and Marine. The vast difference between them calls for three more of Peavey's Axioms:

Axiom Number Three: If you're getting air support and you can't tell what kind of plane it is, you're getting it from the Air Force.

Axiom Number Four: If the plane is low enough that you can read NAVY on the side of the plane, you're getting naval air support.

Axiom Number Five: If you can see the color of the pilot's eyes, you're getting Marine air support.

That afternoon, the grunts knew who was delivering this ordnance, because it arrived low and right on top of the berm. Then, having expended all of their heavy ordnance, the Skyhawk pilots kept working the area over with their 20mm cannons while reporting that we had NVA all around us.

After their last gun run, we witnessed a glorious sight none of us had ever seen before. The two Skyhawks came in behind our backs, this time perpendicular to the berm and only fifty feet off the ground. Each announced his departure by pulling up over the berm at a steep angle and putting his plane in a victory roll! The aerials atop the tanks whipped back and forth with the rush of air. The noise was deafening. Everyone loved it. The grunts stood up and cheered!

Their victory roll was an acknowledgment that they understood they had probably saved us. The two angels who appeared out of nowhere continued their climb and dissolved into the sky.

This time, the grunts assaulted the berm and easily took the commanding position. We consolidated our position and began the job of collecting the dead and all the weapons strewn on the battlefield—Charlie's and ours. The number of our wounded overwhelmed the few helicopters that made it in that afternoon. We left it to the tanks and amtracs to carry out the dead.

The tank commanders got together for a coin toss, flipping to see who would get to be the weapons tank and who would be the body tank. It was the fair way of determining which tank would have to carry the bodies. No one wanted to be the body tank. Blood would drip through the grill doors and onto the hot engine, leaving a profound and lasting smell. The tank would reek until its next quarterly preventive maintenance—an oil change every twelve weeks, when the engine was steam-cleaned.

Embesi won the coin toss, making us the weapons tank. It meant that all weapons and packs the grunts found on the field would get stacked on the back of our tank. "Shit!" said the losing TC, "I just got PM'd last week!" He would have to live with the stench for three long months.

Our luck continued; it was nothing short of phenomenal.

Hearn and I began stacking the weapons as the grunts handed them up to us—orphaned rifles, their master's packs, even loose ammunition. We didn't leave anything behind for Charlie. I was kneeling on the back of the tank taking whatever they passed up to me when suddenly I found myself clutching an M14 rifle.

I had thought these were long gone from The Nam by now. All the 7.62mm M14s had been replaced by the notorious 5.56mm M16, except for a few snipers who preferred the M14's longer reach. How this one got handed to me I'll never know because most grunts didn't trust the M16. Well, if nobody else wanted to keep this M14, I did! Quickly I hid it in the gypsy rack. This lone rifle would stay with me for the rest of my tour and save my life six months later.

While we stacked the weapons on our tank, I couldn't help but glance over at the tank handling the bodies. It was like witnessing some bizarre ritual in "The Twilight Zone." Grunts lifted their dead comrades up over their heads and passed them up to the tank crew, as if offering up sacrifices to the Tank God. The crew gently placed each corpse along with the others, four one way, four another. Marine dead were always treated with respect.

I was snapped back to reality when a grunt shouted up, "Hey, man, you gonna take these or what?"

He was holding a half dozen M16s over his head. He looked over at the grisly scene that had gotten my attention, then looked back up at me, realizing that it had affected me.

"Just be glad it ain't you, man," he said. "Don't pay no 'tention to 'em. They be just not as smart as me and you."

"They were not as smart as you and me" would live with me for the rest of my tour. Some of the living found it easier to blame the dead, as if they had caused their own demise. The thinking was, it was always their fault. They had needlessly exposed themselves to enemy fire. Or hadn't seen the trip wire that set off the booby trap. Or should have hunkered down when they heard the mortars fire. That wasn't always true, of course; sometimes it was just the luck of a bad draw or being in the wrong place at the wrong time. But for the living, it was a guilt-absolving way to justify their own continued survival.

I piled the ownerless 782 gear, loose weapons, flak jackets, and empty helmets on the back of the tank. That was the only place we could stack stuff where it wouldn't interfere with the movement of the turret. Right after the air strike, a late helicopter resupply had left us with more tank ammo than we could store inside the tank, so we had four canister rounds already tied down back there. We stacked the battlefield leftovers right on top of them.

A lot of the packs being handed up to me were noticeably light, having been liberated of whatever food and water they had contained. An unwritten law said that except for personal effects, you could take and use anything that the dead or wounded left behind. That liberated food and ammo was often a Marine's last act of generosity toward his comrades.

Embesi was sitting in the TC's cupola on his board, keeping an eye on what was going on among the other tanks. Hearn had gone back down in the turret for some housekeeping, moving the new ammo around inside. I was wrestling with all the gear, glad to be outside for a change—as long as I didn't have to get down off the tank.

I was trying to condense the pile of orphaned equipment when several of us distinctly heard a not-so-loud but very familiar sound. Several heads, including the nearby grunts', immediately jerked in my direction. It was the unmistakable snap! of a hand grenade after the pin is pulled and the safety spoon has released.

"Grenade!" I yelled, along with half a dozen others. Everyone knew that unmistakable snap! when they heard it. For one split second I hesitated, taking one fast glance at the pile of gear where the sound came from, hoping I might find the offending grenade and fling it away before it went off. But in hindsight, I had no place to throw it. We were completely surrounded by infantry.

Embesi, I saw, had already dropped down inside the turret. Only his hand was visible as he pulled the hatch closed. Hearn's head disappeared behind the loader's hatch. I jumped off the side of Better Living Thru Canister and hit the ground running, toward the front of the tank. I wanted to put as much distance and steel between me and that errant grenade, plus the four rounds of main gun ammunition it was sitting on. It was going to be one hell of an explosion!

Five seconds after the snap!, thick scarlet smoke began to billow from the back of the tank. I heard a familiar noise, like the sound of a blowtorch.

"Jesus Christ!" I shouted for everybody to hear. "It's just a fuckin' smoke grenade!"

I climbed back up on the tank. Even though I had reacted properly, I felt like an idiot. Every grunt around the tank was laughing at me, or so I thought, as they got back up off the ground and brushed themselves off. But then I realized they weren't laughing at me at all, simply releasing all their pent-up energy from that afternoon's vicious firefight. It was the first time that day that the grunts had hit the deck needlessly. They had expected deadly shrapnel, and all they got was a harmless cloud of red smoke.

Their giddy laughter died down. The smoke grenade was still emitting its thick, almost liquidlike red smoke as I walked to the back of the tank and confronted the pile of equipment to try to locate the damn thing. I finally found it, tied to some departed Marine's web gear. Like a Roman candle, the grenade was still spitting flame as the red dye within it continued to burn. Only then did I see that the grenade's flame was licking up against one of the canister rounds.

The flame had already burned through the only thing protecting the 90mm round—the thin inner cardboard tube that encapsulated it.

In only a few seconds, the heat would set off the round, along with its three neighbors.

Embesi stuck his head out of the cupola and yelled from behind the safety of the hatch. "Get that fuckin' thing off the tank before it blows!"

Did he think my mother raised an idiot? I gave Embesi a dumb look and hit myself in the head as if to say, "No shit, I never thought of that!" Then I kicked and tore into the pile of gear, trying to reach the pack with the grenade attached.

Hearn shouted more instructions from his position of safety behind the loader's hatch. Each was trying to out-scream the other, rendering them both unintelligible. All the while, the two were standing inside the turret, with only one eye peeking around their respective hatches. Neither volunteered to come to my aid.

Chapter 9

Friendly Fire

One of the terms that came out of the Vietnam War was "friendly fire." One of the most oxymoronic phrases in the military jargon alongside "military intelligence," it was used by U.S. military bureaucrats—who never went into the field—to try and sanitize a heinous, but very real part of twentieth-century warfare.

Except from its point of origin, friendly fire is anything but. It is brother unknowingly killing brother. Today, it's called "fratricide," an even more sanitized term that makes it sound more like some college fraternity hazing that went awry. Killing one of your own is a terrible thing to bear for the rest of your life. We all wanted to believe there was no excuse for it, but nonetheless, it's a reality of the chaos and confusion of combat. During Allen Brook, I witnessed two friendly fire incidents. Regrettably and unwittingly, I took part in one.

After our bloodied attempts to take the railroad berm and the lucky intervention by two Skyhawks, our commanding officer's superiors, back at the division HQ, pressured him to keep the battalion moving farther east. He told them he would try but wasn't going anywhere without his tanks. Now, the only way our tanks could get to the other side of the berm was through an underpass about five hundred meters south of us and to our right. We didn't have to be the sharpest knives in the drawer to realize that Charlie had probably taken steps to make the passage difficult. Embesi suggested to the colonel that along with the next helicopter resupply, they should fly in a team of minesweepers.

The most logical place for Charlie to plant an antitank mine was in the underpass. But the sweepers worked all around the area and came up empty-handed. The engineers proclaimed the area safe. Still, we couldn't believe that Charlie would miss an opportunity like this. Maybe he never imagined that tanks would come this far east on the island. Whatever the reason, seven tanks and two amtracs made it through the underpass in one piece. On the eastern side, the ground was noticeably softer, and it continued to get softer and mushier the farther east we went.

Dusk was beginning to settle when we came to a halt in a large grassy area. There were no tree lines close to our position, and the railroad berm was 750 meters behind us. We all knew that we would be hit tonight— we were long overdue. Consequently, the battalion was pulled into a tight defensive perimeter.

As the sun began to set, Embesi left the tank, limping very badly, to once again attend a sitrep—with the battalion CO. Sergeant Hearn and I stood watch, each trying to keep the other awake while we ate cans of cold dinner. We had on our comm helmets, monitoring the radios, waiting for the NVA ground attack we were sure was coming. The driver was in his seat, eating by himself. No one wanted to be caught out of position.

We were halfway through our meal when a voice over the radio called for a fire mission. The artillery people on the other end of the radio responded, saying that they had five-fives available. The voice proceeded to give them coordinates for a fire mission.

The 155mm howitzers were large artillery pieces with a bore diameter of 155 millimeters, just over six inches. They could throw large projectiles a dozen miles or so, resulting in enormous explosions that threw shrapnel for a hundred meters in all directions. But they weren't mobile enough to be hauled into the field and, consequently, they often served as the centerpieces of some large fire bases.

Hearn and I, standing vigil and listening, wondered who it was that needed a fire mission. The voice at the artillery end of the conversation said, "Round out!" Then we heard a distant, muffled boom from the direction of Hill 55, several miles directly behind us. A few seconds later, we heard the roar of a projectile streaking right over our heads. It crashed and exploded, only one hundred meters in front of us! We dropped our meals at the explosion.

That same voice came back on the radio. "Down one hundred. Fire for effect."

"Roger that" confirmed the artillery battery. "Down one hundred. Fire for effect!"

We looked at each other and muttered, "What the hell?" We'd just heard a radio request for a fire mission, followed by an adjustment after the first shell's impact. Inasmuchas the guns were several miles directly behind us, and their first round had landed directly in front of us, it didn't take a genius to figure out where that adjustment was going to fall. "Down one hundred" meant the next round would fall right in the middle of our perimeter.

What made things worse was the follow-up command of "Fire for effect." That meant, keep firing until I tell you to stop or give you another adjustment.

Several muffled booms sounded in the distance. An entire battery of six 155mm howitzers was firing a salvo of projectiles, all headed our way. Obviously, several "friendly" shells were about to come into our perimeter—several large friendly shells!

"Incoming!" Hearn screamed for everyone on the ground to hear.

Hearn spoke over our intercom, "Everyone button up! Now!" which meant, close all the hatches. "Who's the dumb shit calling in this mission?" he asked no one in particular.

"It's gotta be an FNG lieutenant!" I chimed in.

But why the follow-up adjustment, to bring it right on top of himself—and ask for it in unrelenting quantities? Not even a Marine second lieutenant was that stupid!

The shells impacted all around us with tremendous noise and concussion. Over the radio, we could hear the grunts around us frantically yelling for the guns to cease fire. Hearn, Richards, and I had buttoned up the tank to wait it out, all of us pondering the same two questions. Where was Embesi? And could a tank survive a hit from a five-five projectile?

More shells crashed into the perimeter. Over the radio, several voices screamed, "Cease fire! Cease fire!" which added to the confusion back at the artillery battery. But the same familiar voice came over the air again.

"Repeat. I say again, repeat." He was asking the guns to keep firing. The guns didn't know who to believe, and after pumping out about ten rounds, they ceased fire.

We waited about a minute. Then we stuck our heads out to see the results of so many large shells impacting in our perimeter. After the horrific noise and those concussions we had felt through the tank, it was hard to imagine that anyone could still be alive. A haze of smoke hung a foot above the ground. Out of the darkness came muffled cries from between clenched teeth, "Corpsman!"

We soon discovered that one of the tanks from 1st Tank Battalion had come close to answering our question. One of the five-fives had landed right in front of the vehicle. It blew off everything including the searchlight, the TC's machine gun, both aerials, and most of the personal gear stored in the gypsy rack. The crewmen were slightly deaf—but alive—and their tank was still operational.

Then, almost magically, Embesi appeared from out of the smoke-filled night.

"Where the fuck have you been?" Hearn asked him. "We thought you bought it!"

"I waited it out in a hole with one of the grunts."

"That was some big stuff," Hearn added, referring to the size of the artillery attack we just experienced.

Embesi shook his head. "Believe me," he said, pointing over his back, "it's a lot bigger when you're out there."

It was a miracle that no one was killed and only a couple of grunts were wounded.

That request for the fire mission, we later learned, hadn't originated from our battalion at all. It was our first experience with a mysterious voice we would hear from again. Whoever he was, he was fluent in English and knew our radio procedures, call signs, and map coordinates—even the lingo for requesting a fire mission.

We heard from the voice the next day as it attempted to redirect our own air strikes on us. Our solution to the problem was one of the cleverest deceptions of the war I ever witnessed. Like many great solutions, its very simplicity made it so beautiful.

It started the following morning, after we stepped into it again with Mr. Charles. Once more we called for air support. Our luck held. We got another pair of little Skyhawks that circled to wait instructions from the FAC.

Before the pilots would deliver an air strike, we had to let them know exactly where the friendly lines were located. This we accomplished by popping a few smoke grenades along our lines to mark our boundaries for the pilots. The FAC's job was to tell the grunt CO when to throw out a smoke grenade of a particular color, and then to inform the pilots when the smoke would appear and what color to expect. The infantry CO, using a different radio frequency, sent the order out to his unit commanders.

That hot morning, the grunts waited for the word to throw yellow smoke grenades in front of their position.

The FAC was standing next to our tank. "Flight Leader, yellow coming out on my command," he said.

"Now!" he told the CO, who immediately repeated the order to all his unit commanders.

Ten seconds went by. Clouds of yellow smoke began to blossom up at three intervals along our lines. But a fourth plume of yellow smoke was issuing out of the tree line across from us—the very tree line we wanted the air strike on.

No matter how the FAC tried to direct the pilots to the "bad" yellow smoke, they wouldn't drop any ordnance for fear of hitting fellow

Marines. That fourth plume effectively nullified our air support for the rest of the day—making it painfully obvious that somebody was eavesdropping on our radio frequencies.

That night, a lone helicopter swooped in from out of nowhere, picked up the FAC, and left without ever touching the ground. That sent a very clear message that we wouldn't be getting any close air support for the remainder of the operation.

We were pissed. The FAC had given up and left us on our own. Goodbye! We all wished we could have told him. Enjoy your hot shower and hot meal, you chickenshit! At least he should have tried to work the problem through, although we couldn't figure out exactly how.

Dawn broke to the groans of grunts all around our tank. They scraped their stuff together and ate a can of whatever C rats they had left. We were getting ready for another sweltering day with no hope of any air support. Suddenly we heard the distinctive noise signature of an H-34's blades slapping the air. It came diving into the perimeter, throwing dust and grass all over the place. We all hunkered down to wait for the mortars that were sure to follow.

But the chopper didn't even touch the ground. It brought no water, no supplies, no ammo, and no mail, just a lone individual, who jumped off the bird before it quickly pulled away. It was the FAC!

We were speechless. What the hell was he doing back here? This guy had it made, and he came back? He must be crazy!

Our morale picked up at the prospect of having air support once again. Word quickly went around the perimeter: No one was to throw any smoke grenades unless the CO ordered it. More importantly, the color designations were going to be changed—yellow was now red, and vice versa. Suddenly the plan became obvious to everyone. We only hoped that our mysterious eavesdropper would take the bait.

It didn't take long before we were back into it with Mr. Charles. The call immediately went out for air support. Two F-4 Phantoms loaded down with Nape and Snakes circled our position while they established contact with the FAC. We were near enough to hear him tell the pilots that our position was about to be marked with yellow smoke. The message went out over the radios for the grunt units to be ready to throw a "yellow" smoke grenade.

A few minutes later, the FAC spoke into his handset. "Yellow smoke on my command." He turned to the grunt CO and yelled "Now!" The grunt CO ordered his units to throw yellow smoke grenades.

Ten seconds later, red smoke billowed up from our lines. But yellow smoke came out of the tree line in front of us!

"Get some!" was all the FAC needed to add over his hand mike. Unwittingly, the NVA had pinpointed their position better than any neon sign could have done.

We never again had trouble with anybody eavesdropping on our transmissions, and we never heard from the mystery voice again. Napalm and 500-pound bombs had obliterated the area, ending someone's career in radio. The FAC, whom we had all cursed for leaving us the night before, had worked out the ruse with his fellow pilots back in Da Nang.

A rumor began that an American had been turned by the NVA. Later, the story would include alleged sightings of a tall Caucasian among the NVA, packing an American PRC-25 radio. It made for a great rumor, but we all believed it was just that—scuttlebutt.

During an air strike, the grunts counted every bomb that left the underside of each plane against the number of explosions they heard. As luck would have it, we ended up one detonation short, meaning that one bomb hadn't gone off. It further meant that someone had to go in and find the dud before Charlie did, because he was sure to make use of it. For an hour, the grunts made a fruitless search for the 500-pound Easter egg. It was no surprise that they couldn't find it—the ground was really marshy, and the bomb had probably buried itself dozens of feet below the surface.

WE CONTINUED THE SWEEP into wetter and wetter ground. Embesi, who was growing very concerned, gave the driver a lot of pointers over the intercom. This was no place for an inexperienced driver to do something stupid and throw a track. It was easy in such marshy terrain to have a track walk off the sprocket much like a bicycle chain. Even so, it didn't take long before one amtrac became hopelessly mired. A tank was sent over to help out, but it sank into the same predicament itself as it struggled pulling against the trac's dead weight.

Now we had two vehicles stuck, and the closest dry ground we could safely pull them from lay a hundred feet to their rear—way beyond the reach of our tow cables. Some of us wondered if we would have to abandon them both and blow them where they stood. But leaving equipment behind was seldom a Marine option.

Someone, maybe Lieutenant Scott, remembered that there was a Navy LSD in Da Nang, where we could borrow some cable ("rope," to those who spoke Navy). Time was critical, because the longer an object sat in mud, the more it succumbed to suction, which was often so strong that a tank or amtrac might never get free. Also, it was getting late.

A frantic call went out to 1st Tank Battalion's CP, asking them to arrange for a helicopter to pick up the cable from the ship and get it out to us.

An hour later, we heard a Sea Knight chopper coming in with the desperately needed cable. Well before it arrived, Embesi had four tanks line up in a column, each one cabled to the next, sitting on the nearest dry ground behind the two mired vehicles. As soon as the chopper dropped off the cable, they ran it to the last tank in the column and hooked the other end to the mired tank. Then all four tanks pulled up slowly, taking the slack out of the tow cables.

Anyone with half a brain stood well clear of the cables. They were known to snap and cut a tanker in half. On Embesi's signal, all five tanks—the mired one included—slowly and steadily applied power. Like four diesel locomotives in tandem, the lead tanks belched black exhaust, straining against the tonnage assigned to them. Slowly, inch by inch, the mud gave up its prize. We repeated the same process for the amtrac. At first it didn't look like the swamp was going to release it, but eventually, after several minutes of 3,000-horsepower persuasion, the muck surrendered its victim.

Now the two vehicles were freed, but the afternoon was getting late. We had to find some spot to set up a perimeter for the night. One thing was for sure: The tanks and tracs were not capable of going any farther east on the island due to the marshy ground. The CO has made the decision that he wasn't going anywhere on this island without his tanks in support.

WE SPENT ANOTHER SLEEPLESS NIGHT with everyone up and in position, awaiting an attack that never came. Each and every night, we had been so certain we would be hit that Charlie's inactivity began to perplex us. It just wasn't like him.

Morning came on May 12; it was Mother's Day. We set out to return to drier ground on the other side of the berm. We retraced our steps and headed back toward the underpass. Because it was a vehicle's only way in or out of the area, we knew Charlie wouldn't miss such an obvious opportunity twice. This time, it would be mined for sure. Once again we called upon the minesweeping teams.

The two teams swept their instruments back and forth, like old-time farmers scything at invisible fields of wheat. Each operator, through his set of headphones, listened for the telltale beep that indicated buried metal. The two teams extended their search all around the area in and out of the underpass.

The grunts never liked sitting in one spot for too long. They got restless after waiting for about twenty minutes. But as far as the tank crews were concerned, the minesweepers could take all the time they wanted. For all we cared, they could sweep all the way back to Hill 55. Imagine our incredulous surprise when the sweepers declared the area free of mines.

"No fuckin' way!" said Embesi in disbelief. He struggled to extricate himself from his seat and called for me to take the TC's position. Once in the TC's spot, I watched him ease himself to the ground and painfully hobble toward the minesweepers.

Charlie had missed a few opportunities during this operation but never would he pass up one like this. Every tanker knew there was a mine there somewhere, hence Embesi's reluctance to move ahead.

From my new perch, I saw a few of the TCs and minesweepers in a heated debate. Embesi was making animated hand gestures, pointing to the underpass and the area right in front of it. Although I was fifty meters away and couldn't hear a thing, I could tell he was refusing to move his tanks through until they checked it again. Finally the minesweepers lost the argument. Reluctantly they turned to resweep the underpass. Another half hour went by, but they came across . . . nothing.

While Embesi was arguing with the minesweepers, Sergeant Kimbrew was on the ground next to him. After the second sweep, when it became obvious that the TCs didn't have much of an argument left, Kimbrew turned back to his tank and circled one finger in the air. His driver cranked up the V-12 diesel engine. All the other tank drivers took Kimbrew's gesture as a signal to start up their engines as well. It suited us just fine to be moving out of here.

Up until then, we'd been the lead tank during the entire operation. Now, for the first time in a week, we were second in a long line of vehicles. Kimbrew's tank, coming from the northern side of the perimeter, joined up with the column of tanks and amtracs. Kimbrew was part of our regular platoon, so it didn't make sense to break it up. Ordinarily, he would have waited for our entire column to pass before falling in behind us, but Embesi halted the column and signaled for Kimbrew to cut ahead of us.

Embesi was still in a lot of pain; he limped slowly back to our tank. It looked like the show was finally getting underway. I climbed out of the turret and down onto the fender to help him climb up on the tank. Then I climbed back up on the turret, slid down through the TC's hatch, and settled into my solitary chair next to the main gun. After a lot of difficulty, Embesi finally got back on his makeshift chair. We put on our comm helmets, and I could hear him talking to Kimbrew. Embesi warned Kimbrew to be ready for a possible ambush on the other side of the underpass.

Sergeant Kimbrew was justifiably cautious as his tank approached the underpass. Like a blind man looking for a curb that he knows lies somewhere in front of him, he crept forward cautiously, almost hesitantly. Even though the engineers had proclaimed the underpass clean, we all knew that Charlie wasn't about to let us pass unmolested. If it wasn't a mine, it had to be an ambush. Just in case it was, a company of grunts had already passed through the tunnel and set up a perimeter on the other side. Slowly Kimbrew's tank inched into the gap. Suddenly, the entire area was rocked by an earthshaking blast.

I felt the concussion through our tank. Kimbrew's tank was lost in a huge cloud of dust, dirt, and smoke that engulfed the entire underpass and everything around it.

"What the hell was that?" I asked.

"Son of a bitch!" Embesi wasn't using the intercom, but I could hear him plainly. "I told those cock-sucking engineers there was a mine there, goddamn it!"

It took a minute or two before we could finally see the tank. It was down on its right front; the blast had thrown two sets of 200-pound roadwheels in different directions.

"Goddamn it!" Embesi repeated, again loud enough for us all to hear. "I told the motherfuckers!"

I wasn't able to get a glimpse of the tank because I was scanning the closest tree line, about one hundred meters out, off to our left. It wasn't uncommon for a mine to signal the start of an ambush, and we had to be ready just in case. But the longer we waited, the more obvious it became that this was an isolated event.

Gary Gibson was aboard Kimbrew's tank. We were indebted to him for saving our tank from the two NVA a few days earlier, with that well-placed beehive round. After such an explosion I prayed the crew was okay.

Over the radio, Embesi kept calling for Kimbrew or any crewman on the wounded tank to answer. All four were still inside, but none of them acknowledged. Finally, after what seemed like hours, we saw the first sign of life. Kimbrew re-emerged from his TC position. Then over the radio came Gary's voice, responding to Embesi's questions about the crew. It turned out everyone was all right, just slightly dazed and shaken up. Kimbrew was temporarily deaf; his head was outside when the mine went off.

Their tank wasn't so lucky. The explosion had carved out a large hole you could have easily sat in. It must have been made by a large antitank mine, but how could two mine detector teams have missed such a large object? Embesi, who was really pissed, verbally vented his frustration on the minesweepers—and their mothers, too.

Half of the tank crews dismounted. Two men stayed on each tank to cover the surrounding area. All the tanks alternated their gun tubes' direction, so as to cover both sides of our column. Once again, Embesi told me to stay with our tank and assume the TC's position. I would make sure I didn't have another sinking-tank fiasco, but I considered myself lucky. Repairing a wounded tank was a backbreaking job that called for sledgehammers, giant crowbars, and gallons of sweat. A lot of spare track would have to be taken off other tanks and bolted together.

Someone called up to me, and I turned to see that it was Johnny Cash. We had been stationed together in California and shared the same barracks. He had been thrown into a makeshift crew when its regular driver was hit in the mortar attack that had caught me outside ferrying ammunition. Now he asked to borrow our tow cables.

I climbed out of the TC's cupola and started to unhook the cables from the back of our turret. We talked about the spectacular luck of Kimbrew's crew, particularly the driver's. Whenever a tank hit a mine, the driver was the most vulnerable because he sat so low in the tank's hull, only a few feet away from the set of roadwheels that triggered the blast. That was why we never left our main gun aimed straight ahead, directly over the driver's head. Too many drivers, ejected from their seat by the force of an explosion, had broken their necks against the main gun. I wanted to know if Kimbrew had ensured his driver's safety and Johnny confirmed that he had.

Finally I got the cables unfastened from the back of the turret.

"How bad is it?" I asked him.

"They're missing the first two sets of roadwheels on the right side. Embesi thinks we'll be able to short-track it and tow it."

Taking one of heavy cables' ends in each hand, he dragged them behind him toward Kimbrew's tank.

The grunts were quick to forget how valuable we had been to them so far on this operation. Their adage was, "It's not what you did for me yesterday, but what are you doing for me now?" This latest setback meant they weren't going anywhere for a while. They would have to stay with us until we repaired the wounded beast, giving Mr. Charles time to regroup. The longer we sat in place, the longer Charlie could exploit the situation to his advantage.

Just as Johnny said, Embesi's quick fix would have us moving again in fifteen minutes. He had rigged up Kimbrew's tank so that it could be towed, but he didn't want to take the time to short-track it. Embesi had decided that Kimbrew's tank could be towed on its roadwheels with no track at all. When needed, the driver could apply a little extra power to help it move forward on its one track. We wouldn't be here too long after all.

Hearn walked back to Better Living Thru Canister, had our driver crank it up, and told him, "Follow my signals." Then he walked backward, giving the driver hand signals to maneuver our tank in front of Kimbrew's tank. Then Hearn signaled our driver to back up—very slowly—until Embesi, who was behind our tank, clasped both hands together, indicating that Better Living was close enough to hook up the tow cables.

Cash and Gibson hooked up the cables from the lame tank to us and signaled for Hearn to pull ahead. Putting tension on the tow cables was always a delicate task, so those on the ground took several paces back. Hearn guided the driver slowly forward until the cables were taut. Kimbrew's driver slowly applied power at the same time we began to pull. Fortunately, this wasn't the rainy season, or towing a tank in this manner would have been impossible. If we hit some softer ground, Kimbrew's driver could add a little power to his good side to help compensate.

After we had pulled the tank ahead a short distance, Gary Gibson went over to inspect the crater where the mine had been. He found splinters of wood, the remains of a large box mine whose nonmetallic materials had made it invisible to the mine detectors. We had all known the underpass was mined, but we had made the cardinal mistake of underestimating Mr. Charles.

Everyone returned to his vehicle. Now it was our turn to go through the underpass, pulling what should have been our tank, had it not been for the mix-up of Kimbrew's taking the lead. As we cleared the underpass, a quick look around showed one tree line on our left, about two hundred meters away. We no sooner made that observation than our tanks came under fire from a second tree line about three hundred meters in front of us. While I took that tree line under fire with the machine gun, we pulled ahead about seventy-five meters to give the tanks behind us room to maneuver as they exited the underpass.

Our delay, brief as it was, gave Charlie time to marshal his forces—just as the grunts had feared. As our last two tanks exited the underpass, a sudden firefight erupted and quickly developed into a slugfest along the tree line. Our job was to tow Kimbrew's tank; we were at the lead of the battalion. Two other tanks under Staff Sergeant Siva and Staff Sergeant Pozner were with us. Kimbrew's tank was still able to fight; his guns all worked. His turret faced the tree line to our left as his .30 suddenly opened up.

In an instant, control was taken out of my hands as our turret snapped around to the left. "Gunner," came Embesi's voice, over of my earphones. "Thirty. Gooks in the tree line." His command told me to target the machine gun on NVAs in the nearer of the two tree lines.

"Identified!" I yelled loudly enough that I didn't have to waste time keying my microphone.

The turret came to an abrupt halt and power was handed back to me instantly, so I could lay the gun. Seconds later I had the red aiming circle of my periscope set just ahead of a large group of NVA that was running along the tree line, trying to join the firefight that had begun at the rear of our column. The red circle was the aiming point for the .30. As they ran into my red circle, I squeezed the triggers. I worked the machine gun into the group, watching as red tracers tore into them, killing about twenty. Some just fell, others were knocked off their feet by the impact of the rounds, as still others tumbled head over heels. This was one of the few times that I saw the enemy out in the open, and I really enjoyed it. This was too easy, I thought to myself.

"Got the motherfuckers!" yelled Embesi over the intercom. "Good shootin'!"

Our column had stopped as soon as the shooting began. The last two tanks maneuvered to their left to support the infantry by taking on the attackers in the thick tree line. Farthest to the rear was Lieutenant Scott's tank; the other tank was made up of ex-amtrackers we picked up in Pendleton. Except for Johnny Cash, the driver—the entire crew was ex-amtrackers.

Both tanks were giving it to the NVA as good as they got it. The grunts were hunkered down, hidden in the eighteen-inch grass. We remained in position, saddled with Kimbrew's tank; we could only provide cover against the sporadic firing coming from our front.

Cash's tank started to advance on the tree line, which was totally uncalled for. More dangerous still was his tank's lack of infantry support; withering fire had all the grunts pinned down. My headset rang as other TCs screamed for Cash's TC to back away from the tree line.

But the former amtracker put his inexperience on display for all to witness. Maybe he thought he was being aggressive. Instead, he was being plain irresponsible, needlessly risking the tank and its crew. Why he brought his tank right up to the tree line remains a mystery; he would have been just as effective from a hundred meters back. Covering the tree line's wide expanse was more difficult while he was right on top of it. Now, if a target popped up, instead of moving his main gun only a few inches to the left or right, he had to swivel it several feet one way or the other. Even worse, he had removed the safety that distance provided from enemy RPG fire. Those few extra seconds could spell the difference between a living tank and a smoking hulk.

As the lone tank approached closer to the tree line, the firefight grew more vicious. Embesi sensed that something was about to go wrong; he got on the radio and ordered Kimbrew to unhook us. Gary Gibson jumped down from Kimbrew's tank to remove the tow cables. Embesi ordered our driver to kick it in the ass and get the tank into the fight. We did a one-eighty and raced toward the battalion rear to thwart an impending disaster. The cavalry was coming to the rescue.

As we sped to the scene, Embesi was on the radio, telling Siva and Posner to get on line with us at the end of the column, assault the tree line, and try to provide the errant tank with some additional cover. The three tanks rapidly advanced toward Lieutenant Scott's tank and Cash's, right near the tree line.

I had the main gun pointed just to the left of Cash's vehicle. We still had one hundred meters to go. I heard Scott on the radio, ordering Cash's TC to back down and put some distance between the tree line and his precariously positioned vehicle. There was no response.

Just as we got up to the lieutenant's tank, we watched in horror as the errant tank raised its gun tube until it was aiming at the sky. Every tanker on the field knew what had happened. The .30-caliber machine gun had jammed, so the inexperienced TC was raising the main gun to give the loader room to work on it.

It was a fatal mistake. Instead of backing down, the inexperienced TC tried to use his .50-caliber machine gun, which was all but useless, because the elevated main gun tube was in the way. Voices yelled over the radio to order the TC to pull back, but in vain.

We had just started to close on the tree line when the lone tank was enveloped by two blinding flashes in rapid succession. Two RPGs struck the front of the tank. We were all surprised to see the tank commander leap out of the turret and run behind the tank.

Seconds later, the loader and gunner realized that they had no TC, so they bailed out of the tank and followed their moronic, gutless TC. It filled us with anger to see a Marine tank crew abandon its vehicle in the middle of a firefight and leave their driver behind!

They had taken no weapons with them, a sure sign of their panic. We saw exhaust from the abandoned tank's engine, indicating that it was still running. The tank's outside appeared to be okay, although a wisp of light blue smoke was coming from out of the turret.

Staff Sergeant Siva tried to raise the driver by calling his name repeatedly: "Cash, are you all right? Can you back the tank out of there?"

There was no response. We all wondered if the driver was still in the tank. Was he still alive?

Siva's, Pozner's, and our tank moved up to the tree line, guns ablaze. Our vehicle halted to the left of Cash's tank while Siva pulled up behind the stricken tank.

"Take over," Embesi told me. He started to leave his position when several bullets ricocheted of the turret, forcing him back down. At the same moment, Siva suddenly exited his tank to sprint toward the imperiled tank. His gunner, Tim Matye, immediately took over the TC position.

As Siva made his twenty-five-meter dash, fire from the tree line doubled in intensity. We tried to give Siva as much covering fire as we could. While Embesi was working his .50, I saturated the tree line with everything I had.

Directly in front of Siva, Cash's tank provided some shelter. He ran up behind it and climbed up on the back, using its turret for cover as bullets ricocheted all around him. He waited a second, then made the most dangerous part of his run, fully exposing himself as he dove into the TC's cupola. Short, stocky Siva wasn't built to pass easily through a tank's hatchway. That afternoon, however, he vanished through the hatch like a greased eel.

Ten seconds went by. Then the turret swung around 180 degrees, to the rear of the tank. Every tanker knew that Siva was traversing the turret to the one spot that permitted him access to the driver's compartment. Another twenty seconds went by, then the tank's exhaust blew a few puffs of black diesel smoke as it began to back away from the tree line.

Over our radio came Siva's voice: "The driver is dead. The tank took two RPGs through the slope plate. There's nothing else wrong that I can see." His last statement pissed off every tanker on the field.

He backed the tank up about one hundred meters, and we backed up along with it, putting as much fire into the tree line as we could. The lieutenant's tank, about seventy-five meters to our left, was backing up, too, when suddenly it just disappeared. There was no cloud of smoke, no hint; it just vanished. A few seconds went by and there was no sign of the tank!

Then the LT's voice came over the radio: "I've backed into a hole and I can't get out."

Embesi finally noticed the very tip of an aerial sticking above the ground. That was some hole. "Only a lieutenant would fall into the only hole around," Embesi said over the intercom.

As it turned out, that hole could have held three more tanks. The LT had backed into a bomb crater. Sergeant Siva, who was now back on his own tank, pulled up to the hole, jumped out again, and attached his tow cables and pulled Lieutenant Scott's vehicle out.

As Siva was hauling the LT back on level ground, a Marine infantry captain got up on our tank. "I'm going to flank the tree line," he told Embesi. "I want some tanks for support."

Embesi told him there weren't enough grunts available to make such an assault. Besides, we had a wounded tank to attend to.

A few seconds later, the captain was replaced by a lieutenant colonel, the battalion CO. As he looked up at Embesi, his face showed all the emotions of a man with many men's lives at risk. "Sergeant?" he pleaded, "can you help me get my men out of there? They're stranded up near the tree line."

"Yes, sir. Get some men behind us and my three tanks will advance toward the tree line. We'll lay down fire until we get to where they can retrieve your men. Once they're behind our tanks, we'll back away and give them cover."

"I'll have you your men in two minutes!" the colonel said.

Embesi got on the radio to tell the other tanks what we were going to do. Three tanks would advance on line with ours in the middle and provide cover to allow the grunts to retrieve their people. As the colonel promised, small groups of men gathered behind the three tanks, so we started to advance. The grunts walked half-crouched, as if walking into a pelting rain and trying to avoid as many drops as possible.

The tanks that were still in the column behind us opened up with everything they had.

We got up to where we thought the remaining grunts were, but we couldn't see them. Suddenly, as if we had come upon a town of prairie dogs, heads began to pop up out of the grass and back down. We were surprised at how many grunts appeared out of nowhere, glad as hell to see us. We were the last lifeboats for the survivors of a sunken ship. They knew we would never leave them behind; it was only a matter of time until they would be rescued.

We didn't have to tell them what to do; they dragged their dead and wounded behind the tanks. During our advance on the tree line, we had run out of canister and beehive. All we had left was high explosive rounds for the main gun. HE wasn't very effective against nonspecific targets like a tree line, so Embesi had Hearn set the fuses on delay. He then told me to do something I had never heard of.

"The enemy's dug in, so you fire into the ground, about ten feet short of the tree line. Try and ricochet the HE rounds into the tree line, so they explode in the air over the gooks."

Tim Mayte saw a tank shoot at the ground and wondered what in hell its crew had been drinking.

The enemy fire increased substantially as the grunts gathered behind us. Several RPGs streaked wildly out of the tree line. We were up against a well-entrenched NVA force. Several of them were clearly visible, and more were moving along the tree line, trying to meet our rescue attempt. The grunts didn't take long to gather all of their stranded people behind the three tanks.

We began a slow withdrawal, careful not to run over the infantry. That meant each TC had to spend more time watching the Marines in back of his tank than the NVA to his front. My job remained unchanged: Cover our withdrawal by keeping the tree line hosed down with machine gun fire. Hearn worked at a breakneck pace supplying the 90mm gun and .30-caliber machine gun. He had no idea what was going on outside, he only knew that we were burning up enormous quantities of ammo.

We finally stopped our withdrawal about two hundred meters back from the tree line to allow the grunts to tend to their wounded. The colonel yelled up to thank Embesi for rescuing his men.

After things quieted down and the battalion regrouped, it was late afternoon. We moved half a klick north of the ambush site to set up a defensive perimeter for the evening in the same spot near the railroad berm and the river as two nights earlier.

Embesi left the tank to attend the CO's evening sitrep meeting, still limping on badly bruised legs. That night, the colonel spoke to Embesi about decorations for the tank crews who had rescued his men, but Embesi turned him down.

"We only did our job," he told the colonel—and he was right. By then, I had known Embesi for almost two years, and his philosophy was that we all had a job to do, and doing your job didn't warrant a medal. He thought decorations were given out too freely, particularly among officers. I agreed with him: That afternoon, the men on the ground deserved medals far more than we did.

All the tank commanders got together to review the situation and decide what they were going to do with the wounded vehicle. When Embesi came back he brought with him the details about Cash's tank. As we suspected, its .30-caliber machine gun had jammed. With guns no longer firing at him, Mr. Charles was able to get off two well-aimed RPGs. Both of them entered directly through the tank's bow, where its armor was thickest—twelve inches of solid steel. The successive rapid impacts and explosions inside the tank panicked the TC, who abandoned ship without alerting the rest of his crew.

The two other crewmen left behind in the turret took their TC's lead and followed him out. The driver had been killed instantly by the first blast, but because his position separated him physically from the rest of the crew nobody bothered to check on him.

Who killed John Cash? Not the NVA, but an incompetent, ill-trained TC who drove too close to the tree line and foolishly elevated the main gun instead of backing away to fix the problem. That day's hero was Staff Sergeant Siva, who was later decorated with a Silver Star for saving the tank.

Embesi also shared with us the latest scoop: Division G-2 (Intelligence) suspected that we were surrounded.

"Shit, Sergeant Embesi," I grinned sarcastically, "Those clairvoyants figured that out all by themselves? Whoever said Intelligence wasn't intelligent?"

Embesi went on to tell us that due to the delays earlier in the day caused by the mine and the later ambush, the NVA had time to consolidate and move up more men. It would be another sleepless, terrifying night we would never forget.

WE WAITED UNTIL AFTER SUNDOWN before we took up a position on the battalion's line. There wasn't any need to make it any easier for Mr. Charles to plan an attack. That procedure, which we had initiated early in the operation, kept the NVA from seeing exactly where the tanks were located. As it got pitch dark we cranked up the tanks and guided them to positions around the perimeter.

Our tank was located on the western side of the position, with the railroad berm behind us and the river off to our right about a hundred meters away. These two geographical boundaries gave our battalion a strong tactical advantage because it allowed us to concentrate our tanks along the two sides of the perimeter most vulnerable to attack. But our very strong position left us no room to maneuver. If the NVA overran us, we had no place to fall back to. It was a last-stand position. If we couldn't hold, it meant a "Go tell the Spartans" ending. We had to stop them at the perimeter or die trying, as the Greeks had done at Thermopylae.

The last helicopters that passed overhead had made sightings and passed the information on to our infantry CO. They could all see we were surrounded. We were long overdue for an attack, and now Charlie had us right where he wanted us. This was certainly the night we were going to be hit. Embesi explained that, in the face of such an imminent attack, the CO had decided not to send out any listening posts. He wanted every man on the perimeter.

It was highly unusual not to have any LPs, patrols, or ambush teams outside the perimeter at night. LPs, composed of one or two men, provided an early-warning system for the battalion. Their unenviable job was to sneak out about two hundred feet beyond the perimeter and warn the parent unit, via radio, of anything they saw or heard. Their chance of survival was based solely upon their ability to stay awake and, above all, to keep quiet. They had to hope that an attacking force didn't stumble upon them during the night. They had to position themselves so that they were not in a direct line of fire from the battalion at their rear. Tonight, however, the battalion CO decided not to risk sending anyone out. We were going to get hit hard, and the CO didn't want to risk any more men.

Embesi and I had the first watch. The grunts loaned us a starlight scope, the first such device I had ever seen. The scope, which was a handheld device, looked like a very large riflescope with a single eyepiece. By amplifying ambient light, it provided the user a ghostly green image of whatever it was pointed at, even on the darkest nights. They were very rare, only a few people had them, but the grunts were happy to lend us theirs because our height above the ground increased its effectiveness.

Around 10:30 p.m. I was using the scope when I clearly saw movement in front of us at about the two-o'clock position. There were a half dozen well-equipped figures crawling through the grass. I tapped Embesi on the shoulder without taking the scope off what were surely enemy soldiers and whispered, "I've got half a dozen guys snoopin' and poopin' through the grass at two o'clock, maybe a hundred meters out."

Embesi took the scope and confirmed my observation. He immediately notified Gary Gibson, whose tank was fifty feet away, and they worked out a plan. Anything out in front of us was definitely not friendly, and because we had the starlight scope it was decided that our tank would do the initial firing. We would use the .30-caliber machine gun to fire short bursts as Embesi guided me to the target by watching our tracers. When we were on target, Gary was to open up with the .50 on his tank and follow our tracers to the target.

I had to fire only three five-round bursts before Embesi had me on target. Once on, I thoroughly saturated the area while Gary opened up with his .50 and followed our tracers to the same spot. It worked perfectly; we totally blanketed the area. Nothing could have survived such a devastating fire. The whole episode lasted less than a minute.

Just as we ceased fire, two grunts ran up to our tanks screaming, "Ceasefire! Ceasefire! There's friendlies out there!"

"Bullshit!" we replied. "We just took out a patrol of six or seven dinks in the grass." We were cocky, for we had just caught an enemy patrol in the open and had drilled every one of the little bastards. It had probably been a probe gathering information for the attack that was surely to come. It was a standard NVA tactic.

"Those are our guys!" The men yelled pleading with us not to fire any more. "You're shooting our own men!"

"It was a gook patrol," Embesi insisted, hoping to God that the grunts were wrong. "Besides," he added, "no one was going out tonight. Didn't you get the word?"

At that moment doubt began to fill the air; there were too many voices screaming at us from all directions.

Dear God, I thought to myself, please tell me they're wrong. It was about the only time I turned to God during my entire tour.

"No! Cease fire! Some of our guys are out there!"

Embesi and I couldn't believe what we were hearing. We had done everything by the book. We tried to convince ourselves that we faced a group of uninformed grunts, which wasn't unusual; they were always behind in the news department.

There was just no way we could have killed our own people. There was a standing order that no one was going outside the perimeter tonight—no LPs, no patrols, and no ambush teams.

Only a few minutes later it was confirmed that it was indeed a friendly patrol outside the wire. Word quickly went around the perimeter that the tanks had killed six Marines, and a small patrol was sent out to retrieve them. It hit us hard. Our denial turned to intense anger—but we were not alone. For the rest of that night, while surrounded by the North Vietnamese, we now had a new enemy in the form of grunts all around us as well.

A voice came out of the pitch-black night air after the patrol was brought back in. "We'll get you, tanks!"

"Watch your back during the next firefight, tanks," came another.

It was impossible to defend our action; the grunts were in no mood to listen. We tried to keep quiet. After all, the enemy was all around us, but didn't seem to deter the furious grunts. We told the grunts near us what had happened and to pass the word. We could only hope that our story would make it around the perimeter but the catcalls continued, convincing us that our side of the story never made it around the lines. It was their final straw. They had had no sleep for several days and little or no water. They were exasperated, looking for someone to take it out on. They were angry and wanted revenge.

We had our own anger to contend with. The fact that we were part of such a horrible yet avoidable mistake weighed heavily on us. The thought of killing six fellow Marines was a horrific burden. We were sick about what we had done, but we had to listen to the faceless voices that threatened us. It terrified us to think that the grunts were only waiting for the next firefight to kill us. Embesi raised the TC's hatch to the half-cocked position to protect his back.

The threats continued for another hour, becoming more and more frequent and strident. We were despised as much by those inside the perimeter as by those outside. We literally feared for our lives, convinced we would end up shot by our own troops during the coming attack. Anyone standing watch on a tank would be a sitting duck, his death written off as a combat error, with no questions asked.

Gary Gibson was standing watch at the same time we were. He too had raised his hatch to cover his back. Two hours had passes since the incident when his infamous Irish temper finally snapped.

We had towed Gary's tank into a position only fifty feet away from ours. I could barely make out the shape of the tank in the moonlight. A commotion of voices erupted from the far side of Gary's tank; there was shouting back and forth. The crescendo increased until we could clearly make out Gary's voice.

"Come on, you motherfuckers! Let's start it right fuckin' now, you gutless fucks! I'll blow your asses away just like the others! Come on, you chickenshit motherfuckers!"

Gary had swung the .50-caliber machine gun around and depressed its long barrel toward the line of Marine foxholes from which the threats had originated.

"Oh, fuck!" was all Embesi said. He extricated himself from the cupola and got down off the tank. No one knew Gary's Irish temper better than Embesi, who realized that he had only seconds to act before Gary's hair trigger would fall. Despite his bad feet, Embesi managed to climb down off our tank and hobble as fast as he could over to Gary's tank. He knew he had to intercede before Gary let loose with the .50.

He got to the far side of Gary's tank and placed himself squarely between the machine gun and the grunts; the .50 -cal's barrel was pointed at the middle of his chest. Embesi stood there with both hands on his hips. "Gibson, you get that fuckin' gun off me right now, or I'll come up there and kill you with my bare hands," he said.

"These fucks wanna kill us!" Gary yelled as he looked down at Embesi.

Embesi summoned all of his command presence and said in a voice I had never heard before: "I'll say it one last time: Get that fuckin' gun off my chest!"

Gary slowly and reluctantly turned the .50 back toward the front of the tank, cursing the grunts as he traversed the TC's cupola. Embesi then turned around and addressed the voices, faceless and unseen in their black foxholes. He had both hands on his hips. "If any of you mother-fuckers want a piece of us, you can come up here right now. I'm the one who gave the order to fire!" he shouted into the night. "Come on, you gutless motherfuckers, I'll kick every one of your fuckin' asses right now. It was your battalion CO that gave us permission to fire!"

No one took him up on his challenge, not a word was said back to him. If anyone could carry out the threat of taking on several grunts, it was Staff Sergeant Embesi. It was the most awesome display of "command presence" I witnessed in the Marine Corps.

The anger we shared over the terrible shooting accident, for tankers and grunts alike, was looking for a way to vent. We were irate over the tragic mistake, and we all wanted to blame someone.

CHARLIE HAD TO BE WONDERING what the hell was going on with this Marine outfit what with all the screaming and yelling going on in the dark. He must have thought that the battalion had lost control, which was a very good sign for him.

Embesi no sooner got back to the tank than a loud drone overhead caught our attention. We all recognized it as Puff the Magic Dragon.

But tonight there was something different about it. The engine noise was much louder than normal; we assumed he was flying lower than usual.

"Puff" was an old C-47 from World War II, twin-engine, propeller-driven sister of the venerable DC-3, he specialized in ruining Charlie's nights. It was equipped with three 7.62mm Gatling guns that were pointed out of the left side of the plane, each of which could spit out 6,000 rounds a minute. It was said that a two-second burst could put one bullet in each square foot of a football field.

We had seen Puff many times before, always at night, and always a long ways off, its three laserlike fingers of red light massaging the ground, as if the Hand of God had suddenly appeared out of the sky in search of mortals to kill. Each of the red lines appeared solid, as a continuous neon bolt of red lightning. They were actually the trails of every fifth bullet that left Puff's Gatling guns. The fifth round of all automatic weapons had a tracer element in the rear of the bullet to aid the shooter in directing his fire. It was hard to believe we saw only twenty percent of the bullets leaving the guns.

What happened next was something that none of us had ever seen before or since. The pilot, who used night-vision equipment, reported that there were so many people all over the area that he was unable to differentiate friend from foe. It was just after midnight when we received the strangest order any Marine unit ever got in the field. It passed from hole to hole in a controlled whisper, "Get a cigarette lighter ready or a flashlight out. Cover it and get ready to light it."

"What?" we gasped, totally flabbergasted at the insanity of the order. The grunts, justifiably scared of exposing their positions to the gathering NVA, muttered among themselves as only enlisted men can, "Who's the dumb shit that thought this one up?"

They were instructed to wrap a poncho around their light source so it was shielded from the enemy but could still be seen from the air. Tanks were instructed to use flashlights from down inside the turret, pointed up to the sky through one of the open hatches.

We were convinced that all hell would break loose as soon as we lit up the perimeter. It took only twenty seconds—but they were the longest twenty seconds of our lives. Puff was now able to get an exact fix on our position. The pilot confirmed what he had suspected, that we were surrounded by several large masses of enemy troops.

Without warning, six laserlike fingers began kneading the earth around us—there were two of them! That explained the loud drone. We listened to the delicious sound of their guns, which was reminiscent of someone tearing paper next to your ear. They circled in tandem, both firing their mini guns all around our perimeter. It was the first time anyone had ever seen two of them flying together, and no one had ever seen Puff used in a tactical ground support role as it was that night.

We had at least one plane circling overhead all through the night. It was reassuring to know that we weren't alone out here, that someone was aware of our plight. It was the closest any of us had ever been to Puff and its truly majestic display of firepower.

This was the night we were going to be hit. Puff confirmed that the NVA had been massing for an assault. The arrival of the gunships couldn't have been better timed. Thanks to them we got through the night without getting hit. Charlie was not able to marshal his troops under such lethal fire.

In the morning the truth about the night's friendly fire incident came out. The grunts found out that it was caused by an overzealous FNG lieutenant who sent out the patrol without telling anyone.

I wondered what the six families back home would be told? "Your son died bravely in the defense of his country?" Would they ever know that fellow Marines had killed their sons? I hoped not. The parents of those men did not need to know the truth. It would have served no purpose and would only add to their anguish. As tragic as it had been, their families didn't need to know the specifics—dead is dead. Those of us who were involved have had the rest of our lives to live with it.

THE NEXT MORNING we began heading back to Phu Loc 6 with what was left of 1/7 and 3/7.

Our heavy reliance upon the .30-caliber machine gun during the operation had burned out both of our spare barrels and also the spare electric solenoid. It was the solenoid that actually fired the machine gun through the electrical impulses from the gunner's trigger switch on his hand controls. Without it, the gun was almost useless. It could only be fired manually by the loader, who had to stand by it and pull the trigger at the gunner's command; it was very ineffective and prevented the loader from servicing the main gun.

Embesi had a fix for the problem. Was there anything this man couldn't do? He took a six-foot-long piece of comm wire and tied one end around the gun's trigger, routed it up through the chain-hoist eye-bolt in the roof of the turret over the main gun and back down to the gunner's position. He tied a short stick to my end of the wire as a handle; I simply had to pull down on the wire to fire the machine gun. We gave it a test, and it worked.

It was late afternoon, and the heat inside the tank was way above the outside temperature of 120 degrees. Usually by this time of day, with no fresh air coming down into the turret, the heat would start to get to me. I was half-conscious, almost delirious. My sweaty forehead was up against the gunner's periscope, slowly traversing the turret back and forth across the umpteenth tree line. My role was that of a sniper with a fifty-two-ton rifle. As the tank slowly kept pace with the infantry, its slow side-to-side movement jostled me as we crossed any rough ground at no more than three miles per hour.

From almost the beginning of the operation, we had learned to depend on a technique called "recon by fire." This was firing the .30 into tree lines before we got close to them, in the hope of actually tripping an ambush early, making the NVA think we had discovered them. It was an effective method that could prevent one from becoming trapped in the kill zone of an ambush.

While bobbing along inside the moving tank, I had to be conscious enough to keep the gun aimed at a given tree line. Not only did I have to traverse the turret left and right, I had to elevate or depress the gun as the ground changed beneath us.

The tank must have started going down an incline. I found myself elevating the main gun to keep it on the tree line. The huge breechblock next to my left shoulder began to move down as the gun tube outside went up. Half-delirious from the afternoon heat and half-numb from several days without sleep, I was unaware of what was quietly taking place next to me.

The wooden handle of Embesi's makeshift contraption had become entangled with the cocking lever on the breechblock. I was preoccupied elevating the main gun in order to keep it pointed at the distant tree line. I was looking through my periscope for potential targets, unaware that the breechblock was dragging Embesi's stick down with it. Without warning, the .30 exploded to life beside me, almost giving me heart failure. Through my periscope I saw a grunt in the middle of the red aiming circle fall as the machine gun bullets impacted all around him!

Over the intercom, Embesi screamed, "Cease fire!" at least twice.

"Hey! It ain't me, goddamn it!" I yelled. I thought it was him doing the firing from the TC override control handle, which—had my brain not been fried and had I thought about it—was impossible, because the solenoid was burned out. I looked over at the runaway machine gun as it chattered away. The adrenaline had entered my bloodstream and the fog had cleared from my brain. I suddenly realized that Embesi's hung-up invention was firing the machine gun. The wire was as taut as a guitar string.

I immediately tore at the wire and broke it, which stopped the clatter. The entire scenario lasted about five seconds, which in machine gun time was about forty-six bullets. It seemed like it had taken a week to stop the runaway gun.

I quickly went back to the aiming circle in my periscope, fearful that we had killed the grunt I had seen going down. Immediately I keyed my intercom switch, "Please tell me we didn't kill somebody!"

Embesi and Hearn, who stood with their heads and shoulders out of the turret, would have seen the consequences of the gun's moment of insanity. Again I keyed my helmet to ask them if we had hit anybody. Their silence only confirmed my worst fears. The moment I asked the question, I heard the sounds of a huge firefight erupt outside. I heard Embesi yelling to someone off the tank, "They're in the tree line!"

Then Embesi's voice came over the intercom, "Fire two rounds of HE into the tree line!"

"Where in the tree line?" I asked frantically, trying to get an idea what and where the enemy was.

"It don't matter! Just shoot, goddamn it! Shoot now!"

It was the dumbest order I had ever heard. It wasn't like Embesi to just waste ammunition, but I did as I was told.

"On the way!" I yelled for all to hear, and the gun fired and I followed up with the same command again when I heard the breech close behind the second round. The firefight quickly died down, so I got on the intercom again, "Please tell me we didn't kill some friendlies?" I pleaded.

I still didn't get a response from either one of them. I pulled my comm helmet away from one ear and leaned back with my head at the TC's feet, looking straight up at Embesi. I couldn't believe what I was seeing. I was staring straight up at someone in a hysterical fit of laughter! I could hear Sergeant Hearn laughing as well.

"Did you see that guy jump?" asked Embesi, barely getting the words out before he and Hearn broke into more uncontrolled laughter. "The whole battalion was shooting," he added, gasping for breath.

"Would someone tell me what is so fuckin' funny about killing somebody?" I yelled over the intercom. "And what the fuck was that stupid fire mission all about?"

My demand was met with another round of laughter even louder than the first. I was on the outside of some inside joke, and I didn't like it one bit. My thoughts were on the grunt we—no, I—had just killed.

That night, as we sat in our crew positions and ate some C's, I learned the rest of the story. When our machine gun began to fire, it was as big a surprise for the lone grunt as it was for me, probably bigger. He suddenly found himself in the middle of a dust cloud of bullets that hit all around, some even between his legs. His immediate reaction was to hit the deck, convinced that he was under fire from an enemy machine gun.

It was at that moment that I had managed to cut the wire to stop the deranged machine gun; I was certain I had cut down the grunt as well. The rest of the battalion, seeing one of their men under fire, assumed our tank was returning fire at an unseen enemy machine gun. They opened fire blindly into the tree line. It was the typical response of a veteran grunt unit that suddenly came under fire—return fire, and in prodigious quantities.

Embesi, who was aware that the grunts were looking back at him to get a sense of where the enemy was, yelled, "They're in the tree line!" It was then that I wasted the two HE rounds, which the grunts could follow with their own eyes.

No one ever suspected that it was our wired contraption that started the whole thing. Our screw-up remained our secret thanks to Embesi's quick thinking.

The lone grunt whose execution I was sure I had witnessed was the luckiest son-of-a-bitch on earth, having lived through a stream of bullets from what he thought was a North Vietnamese machine gun. He and all his buddies were grateful for the tank that took out the "enemy" machine gun! Suddenly the grunts thought we were great!

WE WERE CLOSE TO PHU LOC 6 when we met up with our relief force, 3/27. Our appearance dispelled any hope they were going to have a cakewalk. The two units didn't say much as they passed one another. The blank, expressionless faces of the men of the 7th Marines told the story. They were faces of Marines who had been on the edge a little too long. There was no exchange or banter that usually went on between two units that pass one another. The relief troops didn't like what they saw.

The grunts had been worn to the point of exhaustion; they needed to be refitted, regrouped, replenished, and rested. We had been in the field for twelve days without a break and were totally drained. Too many sleepless nights and the constant harassment by sniper and mortar fire had taken its toll. True to Marine tradition, we came out with all of our dead, wounded, and equipment.

We were almost within sight of Phu Loc when suddenly, wham! My world was shattered by a violent explosion. The tank had taken a solid hit! A cloud of dust immediately replaced the air in the turret. My first thought was that it was an RPG but I didn't see the telltale flash inside the tank. Over the radio, Embesi immediately wanted to know how everyone was. The driver didn't answer right away. A few seconds later he said that he was fine, but he wanted to know, "What the hell was that, Sergeant Embesi?"

Before Embesi could answer the driver, I reported that everything appeared okay in the fighting compartment, as the turret was called. I asked him the same question, "What the fuck was that?"

"We hit a mine."

So that's what it's like, I thought. I had always thought that the blast would be more severe.

Embesi said, "Peavey, get up here and man the fifty." That told me that he was getting off the tank and I was to take his spot in the TC's position. I jumped at the chance to stick my head out into the cooler air.

As I crawled up and into the TC's position, I could see Embesi was on his hands and knees, looking over the edge of the tank's fender as he inspected the suspension system. There was a corpsman next to the tank, working on a wounded grunt who had been hit by shrapnel from the mine.

Embesi was smiling as he turned to Hearn and me. "We hit an antipersonnel mine. I think we're okay." He was still on the tank next to the driver's position when he told the driver to slowly pull ahead.

"Okay, stop!" he yelled. He was inspecting the track without getting off the tank. He was not about to risk stepping on another one of Charlie's surprises.

"We're okay!" he said, "All we did was flatten one set of roadwheels slightly. We didn't even break track!"

The damage was light—unbelievably good news because it was too damned hot to have to replace track.

It represented the pinnacle of our luck for the entire operation. When we thought about all the things we had gotten away with, we started laughing among ourselves. After all, there had been a number of things that could have been disastrous:

The RPG that sailed in between the driver and me
The RPG that should have killed Embesi
The NVA on top of our tank
The two A-4 "angels" that appeared out of nowhere
My getting caught off the tank during a mortar attack
The never before seen appearance of two Puffs
Winning the coin toss as the weapons tank
Not cutting the grunt in half
Hitting a mine without breaking the track

We were giddy and laughing over the intercom as we resumed the sweep with the grunts. The wounded grunt had been put up on the back of the tank.

I was certain of one thing, however: If that was an antipersonnel mine, I did not want to hit an antitank mine.

We had moved about one hundred meters; the fire base was within sight as we gloated over our phenomenal luck. We were like kids who had just found out they had a snow day and didn't have to go to school. The end was in sight and we were about to end this long exhausting operation.

Embesi said, "I am glad as hell we didn't have to repair that track. That was really lucky!"

And as he uttered that last word, it happened. The tank immediately pulled hard to the left. Embesi screamed over the radio louder than I had ever heard him before, "Stop! Driver! Stop, goddamn it!"

The track had decided that it had been abused long enough and had finally just let go. It must have heard our gloating and decided that we had, in fact, been too lucky. Fortunately for us, the driver stopped the tank before the track ran off the tank.

After a careful inspection, Embesi discovered that the track had separated at the spot where the mine had detonated beneath it. The mine had cracked some of the end connectors, which weren't visible when he had inspected it. It decided it had had enough after it made a few circuits around the drive sprocket.

It took us forty-five minutes to replace the section of track, but there was nothing we could do about the flattened roadwheel. The grunts had to set up a perimeter around us; it was especially frustrating for them with their goal in sight. They were so close to getting out of the bush, and now the tanks held them up—again. Some of them blamed us for wounding one of theirs when we hit the mine. The alternative, I suppose, was to let them find the antipersonnel mines with their own feet. Sometimes there was just no winning with grunts. They suddenly forgot who supplied them with water, who covered and rescued their asses more than once. They acted as if we hadn't done a damned thing for them.

We soon resumed the slow procession toward the little fire base. We no sooner got into the fire base and dismounted than someone broke out several cans of warm beer—from where I don't know. A few of us gathered around and someone got out a camera to record our Kodak moment.

We were all talking as if we were on amphetamines or speed, unable to speak at a normal rate, each of us doing more telling than listening and all of us giggling with the sudden relief and an outpouring of our pent-up emotions. Then the shakes started; we tried to chase the moving beer cans with our mouths, our hands betraying our adrenaline rush. We were still alive; we had made it through a horrible twelve days.

We spent the night at the fire base. The following morning the three tanks of our platoon formed up for a fast return trip to 1st Tank Battalion's CP. It would be roads all the way and for the first time in two weeks we would feel a breeze, albeit the artificial one we created. I was still forced to stay down in the gunner's position, because we were still in Indian country. I so desperately wanted to feel the wind. Now I had nothing to do; I could only sit there and imagine what it looked like outside.

We had been on the road for twenty minutes, still going flat out when I heard Hearn ask Embesi over the intercom, "Do you smell that?"

"Yeah. Smells like someone's burning tires, don't it?"

We never skipped a beat as we headed back to civilization, anxious to get off the tank and get a decent night's sleep. A voice I didn't recognize came over my comm helmet, "Bravo Two Four, you got a fire." It was one of the tanks behind us telling us we were on fire. Embesi and

Hearn quickly looked over their shoulders toward the engine exhaust where one would expect a fire to show itself. There was no sign of anything unusual coming out of our exhaust. There was, however, black smoke trailing from the left side of the tank.

"Driver, stop the tank."

When we came to a stop, I began to smell the burning-rubber odor. Embesi and Hearn had exited the turret. I took advantage of the open TC position to stick my head out. The left side of our tank was billowing black smoke.

"Holy shit!" I thought to myself. I couldn't imagine what was burning until I got a whiff.

Embesi yelled up to me to hand down one of our five-gallon cans of water that was strapped to the turret. "What's burning?" I asked as I was undoing the can.

"The damned roadwheel's on fire," he said. The egg-shaped roadwheel wasn't turning, and the friction of it rubbing against the track caused it to ignite.

He took the almost empty water can from me, unscrewed the top, and threw water at the blazing roadwheel. There wasn't enough water to do the job; it continued to burn.

"Everybody off the tank!" he ordered. "We're gonna have a pissing contest!"

How comical it must have looked, four grown men, standing in a semicircle, pissing on their tank. The urine steamed back off the burning roadwheel, adding mightily to the already awful stench. Fortunately, the contents of our collected bladders were sufficient to extinguish the fire. We climbed back up on the tank and got ready to move out.

"Damnedest thing I ever saw!" Embesi said just before he told the driver to kick it in the ass.

And so that is how we ended Allen Brook—pissin' on Better Living Thru Canister!

ALLEN BROOK CONTINUED FOR ANOTHER MONTH, but without us. According to Marine Corps lists, casualties for Allen Brook in May totaled 138 killed and 686 wounded. There were 283 nonbattle casualties, mostly heat-stroke victims. In many engagements, the number of heat casualties equaled or exceeded the number of Marines killed and wounded.

There was a total of 1,017 confirmed North Vietnamese killed. We were not in the habit of inflating numbers to accommodate the unseen enemy wounded and dead dragged off the battlefield, so actual enemy KIAs would probably approach closer to two or three times the confirmed count.

We got back to 1st Tank Battalion and found orders waiting for us as soon as we fixed the roadwheel and the machine gun solenoid. We would get two days' rest, then head back to our CP at the 2/27 fire base.

Chapter 10

Not So Tough

With our role in Allen Brook over and Better Living repaired, the next day we made our way back to our platoon CP at 2/27's fire base. Awaiting us were orders that would send our platoon quite hastily to Hoi An, a city twelve miles south of Da Nang. We had been assigned to support an American ally in a war the American public thought was all their own. There were several allies in Vietnam including Australia, New Zealand, Thailand, and South Korea. The South Koreans had several major units in-country, and now we would work with the Korean Marine Corps, or KMC.

We packed up all our gear and left the fire base, bound for Marble Mountain, headquarters for Bravo Company, 5th Tanks. The following morning brought us to Hoi An, the only time I saw tanks driving through the streets of a major Vietnamese city.

Our orders told us to get there as soon as possible to relieve a platoon from 1st Tank Battalion. We didn't know they had already left Hoi An—rather suspiciously. When one unit relieved another, that wasn't the way a change of command usually took place. We couldn't exchange information to find out the lay of the land and, more important, what

185

it was like working with the Korean Marines. We never suspected the reason they had departed so quickly was that 1st Tank Battalion HQ didn't want them talking with us. Consequently, there was no one to warn us of what we were driving into.

Overnight, with no help, Embesi and our new lieutenant had to learn to deal with the Korean command structure—a task made all the more difficult by the differences in language, customs, and food, not to mention the Koreans' operating procedures.

When we pulled into our platoon CP we thought we had died and gone to heaven. It was like the set of South Pacific, complete with a white beach and hardback hooches that were constantly bathed with cool breezes—as close to a Far East vacation as we could get. At first, we were certain that this was one of Embesi's practical jokes, so nobody dismounted the tanks. We just sat there, waiting to be directed to the shit hole we were really supposed to occupy. Then we saw the LT and Embesi hauling their personal gear into one of the hooches.

Could this be the real thing?

We accepted our fate. As we unpacked we began to hear stories from a nearby U.S. Marine amtrac unit, also attached to the Koreans. This was our first inkling that the previous tank unit had had some kind of friction with the Koreans. Also, we heard tell of a tank that was lost while supporting the Korean infantry. But the craziest rumor—that we would be turning our tanks over to the Koreans—came from the Koreans themselves.

Axiom Number Six: The stranger a rumor is, the more likely it's true.

That idea sounded so totally weird that it just might be on the level. Naturally assuming the worst, we figured that we'd be assigned to the grunts . . . but in which Marine Corps, American or Korean?

SO HERE WE WERE, a rogue platoon, out of the mainstream and living on our own. Embesi had his own truck, driver, cook, and corpsman. Our tanks were immediately assigned to various KMC units. Embesi and the lieutenant would monitor the tanks by radio—a very similar arrangement to the one we had had with 2/27, when our tanks were spread around to support different units and bridges.

I was reassigned as the gunner on Kimbrew's tank. We were ten miles away from the rest of the platoon, stuck in a small Korean Marine combat base in the middle of Dodge City, an area, as bad as they came, full of mines and booby traps. The Koreans referred to the outpost as the Mud Flats. That name didn't do it justice, because it was now July, the height of the dry season. Surrounding the compound was a sea of dry, red-cracked earth that could have been on Mars. Not only was the terrain bizarre, but we were also surrounded by aliens who spoke no English.

The Mud Flats was a nameless spot on the map at which a road and a railroad line intersected. Neither of them was recognizable to the naked eye. The rail line was a slight berm whose rails and ties had been stripped years earlier. The road, unless someone pointed it out to you, looked more like an abandoned, overgrown path. A look at the map showed that it was clearly an extension of the same railroad line we had fought for during Allen Brook. In fact, we were only three klicks (3,000 meters) north of the river and its eight spans of steel bridges leading to Goi Noi Island. It was hard to imagine that the long mound, one foot high and ten feet wide that ran through our compound, was the same rail line. The road, impossible to see, showed up on our maps as Highway 4. "Highway" was a gross misnomer; it hadn't seen traffic since the French left, more than a decade before.

Our tank sat parallel to the railroad berm that ran through the Korean position. The previous Marine tank crew had dug a bunker into the side of the berm and covered it with sandbags. It became our daytime sleeping area, and the only place we could get out of the sweltering July sun, which boosted the mercury to a constant 120 degrees every day.

The mud all around us, dry as concrete, amplified the heat beyond measure. The thick air made our least exertion a Herculean effort. I swore that once I got back to The World, I would—to paraphrase Scarlett O'Hara—never, ever go hungry again . . . for air-conditioning.

I WAS REALLY PISSED THAT Embesi had assigned me out to this god-forsaken spot. To make matters worse, the more I got to know Kimbrew, my new tank commander, the more I was convinced he wasn't playing with a full deck. He was a nice guy, but not the sharpest knife in the drawer. I increasingly distrusted his ability as a TC. During one of our conversations he said he would never use the .50-caliber machine gun on Charlie because it was a violation of the Geneva Conventions. The .50 was considered inhumane against soft targets and thus to be used only against vehicles and aircraft. Although Kimbrew was correct, a lot of Marines died on Allen Brook assaulting .51-caliber Chicom machine guns. I felt my chances of survival were severely limited with this tank commander and I wanted off this tank in the worst way.

Many years later I asked Embesi, "Why did you assign me to Kimbrew's tank?" He laughed. "I had to have at least one man on each tank I could count on if the TC got hit. Somebody I knew that could at least tie his own bootlaces. That's why I had Gibson on his tank during Allen Brook."

The Mud Flats compound's most prominent features were the square green bunkers the Koreans had built. None of us had ever seen sandbagged fortifications to rival these. They spent so much time filling sandbags and meticulously shaping and placing each bag that their bunkers appeared to be constructed of green bricks.

Several days after our arrival, we noticed that not one Korean had yet set foot outside the wire. Were they too occupied filling sandbags to send out patrols? Their perimeter looked like the Maginot Line, yet it never seemed to be strong enough. The Koreans kept at it continually, always digging, filling, and tying. Each and every bag was shaped, set in place, and tamped square. If an enlisted man can recognize anything, it's busy work, and that combat base had to be the greatest monument to busy work ever created.

One single trench, lined with sandbags, traversed the entire perimeter. The ring was broken only at the compound's two entrances, two hundred feet apart and directly opposite the other. A tank was positioned by each entrance; we would know if anyone came or went. But I had doubts about the soundness of the base's design. If attacking troops could breach the defensive line, couldn't the enemy run around the entire perimeter through the uninterrupted trench line?

We were as remote from our platoon CP as we could be, and we were at the fringes of our radio's range. Embesi's job was to interface with the KMC commanding officer's staff and keep us supplied with ammo and food. Mail was the high point of any week spent in the Flats, but we got it only sporadically. Embesi had a hell of a time getting a U.S. Marine helicopter to make a run to the Mud Flats; for them, a Korean outpost was a low priority.

To avoid going hungry we often had to eat Korean food, which was unbelievably and inhumanely hot. It brought tears to the eyes of the bravest of us. While stationed in Southern California, where the nearby Mexican border strongly influenced the local cooking, I had grown accustomed to spicy food, but nothing could have prepared me for the volcanic kimchee. About the only Korean food we could manage was what they called pop, or rice, which they ate with every meal.

Eating was almost a ceremony. Groups of about six Koreans would cluster around a small fire, waiting for their rice to cook in an empty .50-caliber ammo can. They drooled over it while it was cooking, each chef giving his own verbal input, as if they were watching a filet mignon on the grill.

We mixed rice with our C rats to stretch out the meal. There were twelve meals in each case of C rats, and each of us had his likes and dislikes. Two of them were absolutely horrible and defied improvement, no matter what you added to them. But all over Vietnam, be it Army or Marine Corps, the hands-down winner of the Worst Meal Award was ham and lima beans.

I can confidently say that of the five million–plus men who served in The Nam, not one could bring himself to eat that disgusting meal. It was the same color and consistency as the contents of a baby's diaper—and smelled like one, too! We called it ham and motherfuckers, usually just motherfuckers for short. Nothing you mixed with motherfuckers could make it palatable; rice only increased the quantity of the inedible mess.

Each box of C rats came with a few accoutrements. There was always a little pack of toilet paper in each box. One was never enough for a single session, so it was necessary to pool our resources. We saved the packets in a communal pile, awaiting the next crewman's needs. Some meals had a can of either apricots or sliced peaches, which, in the extreme heat, were worth their weight in gold. Often we would open a can of fruit just to drink the sweet juice. But it only made us thirstier.

Some of the meals came with a small tin of cheese and crackers. The dry crackers tasted like hardtack. Most of our C rats had manufacturing dates on them from the early 1950s, making them at least fifteen years old. Ever eat a fifteen-year-old cracker?

One of the most sought-after items that accompanied the C's was a small flip-top box holding five cigarettes. Winston was the most common brand. You didn't have to smoke to want those cigarettes. They were quite valuable as a trading commodity.

There was a packet of instant coffee and packets of sugar and dried creamer. But the most prized drinkable was the instant cocoa, which didn't come with every meal.

Certain C ration meals contained a tin of peanut butter or cheddar cheese. The peanut butter was saved in another communal pile next to the toilet paper—appropriately enough, because C rat peanut butter had the mysterious, unique ability of stopping the runs. It certainly wasn't whipped up with that in mind, but we found it to be more effective than any over-the-counter diarrhea medication.

For many of us, a tour in Vietnam was one endless cycle of diarrhea and constipation—or peanut butter and soap. Everyone would get hit with a case of the runs several times during his tour, which is where the peanut butter came in handy. But often it worked too well. The only sure way to get "unplugged" was to ingest a small quantity of soap. Many peanut butter overeaters like me preferred Wisk. Because it was a concentrated liquid, you needed only a small swallow to do the trick. Often a man's entire tour was one nonstop cycle of soap that gave him the runs that only peanut butter could stop.

One last little item in every box of C's was so thoughtful, only a woman could have thought of including it: a tiny box containing two Chicklets. Someone thought it would be nice if America's fighting men didn't have bad breath while sharing a foxhole with a buddy. The Chicklets' sweet taste was prized by all.

TWO MONOTONOUS WEEKS CREPT BY in which not a single Korean patrol went out, day or night. That was something unheard of in an American unit, because patrols and ambushes kept Charlie off guard. A U.S. Marine outfit of this size would have sent two patrols out during the day, plus two or three ambush teams at night. Charlie owned the night, and we could never take it away from him, but at least we could instill some fear into him.

Lieutenant Kim, a Korean officer who lived near our tank, told me that the Koreans thought it was too risky to send patrols out into Dodge City during the day, and sending men out at night wasn't even an option in their minds. Those were the first signs that maybe these guys weren't all they were cracked up to be. After trying to reason with them, to no avail, we passed our concerns on to Embesi, who took them up with the Korean CO back in Hoi An. His prodding must have worked, because one afternoon we got the word that tonight the Koreans would be sending out an ambush team—their first ever! We were glad to see them finally taking some initiative, to lessen the chances of the fire base being attacked.

Typically, a U.S. Marine ambush team would go out after sundown or drop off from a large daytime patrol and set up for the night. A typical team consisted of five to ten men—seldom more than that, because the more people you had with you, the more chances for making noise.

That afternoon, the Korean CO briefed us on the intended location of the Korean ambush team that was going out. From the tone of the briefing, it was obvious they were worried less about Charlie, more about the tanks firing on them after sundown. They were scheduled to go out at 10 p.m. through the north gate, right in front of our tank.

As usual, our crew was up on the tank just before sunset. We would stay until 10 p.m., when night watch started. At 9:45 p.m., a group of Koreans slowly formed up in front of us. More and more men appeared. Finally, when more than forty soldiers were standing in front of us there, I turned to Kimbrew and asked, "What are all these guys doing here?"

"I think it's the ambush team," he said.

"Team?" I asked. "This isn't a team. It's a herd. There's no way this many guys, with all that gear, can keep quiet!"

It was an invitation to disaster. An ambush team's survival depended upon stealth. You couldn't make the faintest sound, nor wear any bug repellent, due to its smell. No bug juice meant insect bites all night long, which you didn't dare slap for fear of giving away your position.

The Korean ambush platoon was more like a route-step parade than a stealthy fighting unit. But they were afraid to send out anything less than a full rifle platoon. We tried to explain the lunacy of what they were planning, but they said we were the crazy ones for even suggesting a night ambush. That was our first inkling into how these guys operated—totally missing the point.

It was no surprise when, in the middle of the night, two NVA soldiers caught them totally by surprise. From our tank we could see the explosions and hear the eruption of gunfire. Charlie ran through the middle of the Korean ambush site, throwing grenades to either side—and got away unharmed! But the Koreans must have expended five thousand rounds of ammunition, firing relentlessly for several minutes. We immediately noticed that all the tracers in the night sky were exclusively red in color. The NVA used green tracers.

The ambush team suffered two wounded, all the proof they needed that this was a very "hot" area, far too dangerous to justify sending out any more patrols.

That was just the tip of the iceberg. A few weeks later, we were working with them on a sweep: Operation Mameluke Thrust, a joint U.S. Marine and Korean Marine op. The Koreans insisted they had to be back inside their perimeter by nightfall, because spending a night in the field was way too dangerous.

We began having some serious operating difficulties with the Koreans on the first day—as soon as we got outside the wire, in fact. They refused to go out ahead of the tanks, insisting it was our job to lead the way. We stopped and argued with the Korean captain, who wanted to keep his men behind our tanks—way behind. They didn't understand that we depended on the infantry to uncover enemy RPG teams. We had heard rumors about a previous Marine tank lost to enemy fire. Purportedly, it had taken six RPG hits from all directions—an impossibility if the grunts had been around the tank.

Kimbrew refused to move, and it developed into a stalemate. To Kimbrew's credit, he got on the radio and explained our predicament to Staff Sergeant Embesi, who was monitoring the radios at the Korean CP, in Hoi An.

Embesi then argued with the Korean executive officer and tried to explain what the infantry's role was when working with tanks. After it became a heated argument, Embesi demanded to see the Korean commander, who was a general. Getting no response from the XO, he stormed out of the CP and into the general's private quarters, waking him up. Due to the language barrier, Embesi didn't get very far until he noticed a nearby blackboard. Grabbing a piece of chalk, the Marine staff sergeant diagrammed for the general just how infantry and tanks worked together. The "conversation" turned heated when Embesi threatened to pull his tanks out altogether.

A U.S. Army officer, acting as an adviser to the Koreans, had overheard the entire exchange. Later, he accused Embesi of creating a potential international incident between two allies. Embesi said he didn't give a damn; those were his men out there and no one was going to fuck with them. That was Embesi for you.

During all that time we remained in a deadlock, sitting outside the perimeter at the Mud Flats. Finally, instructions were given to the KMC infantry leader over the radio. The Korean field commander suddenly ordered his men to move past the tanks. Embesi had gotten through to the general.

That same morning, we came across a small village and got to see that all the stories we had heard about the Koreans were true. They were brutal toward all the Vietnamese, women and children alike, riflebutting any civilian who didn't move fast enough. We couldn't believe it. As if a switch had been turned on, the laid-back Koreans became tyrannical and ruthless. We were no fans of the Vietnamese, but certainly they didn't deserve this kind of treatment. We could only wonder what the Koreans would be like when the shit hit the fan. Their ferocity was legendary throughout I Corps. So far we only saw them in action against defenseless civilians.

After we left the village, we continued what became an uneventful sweep. By mid-afternoon, the Koreans decided it was getting late, so we turned around to make our way back to the Mud Flats. We had just pulled into our old position next to the berm when Embesi called; he wanted to know how much ammunition we required. He also wanted to know the condition of our crew, which we thought was odd. Embesi was trying to organize an emergency resupply run before sundown. We couldn't imagine what the rush was all about until he asked how much ammo we had gone through.

Kimbrew was holding the radio's mike in his hand. He and I just looked at each other and shrugged.

"Do you know what he's talkin' 'bout?" Kimbrew asked me.

"No," I replied. "I think he's losin' it."

"Is everyone okay?" Embesi wanted to know.

Kimbrew and I glanced at each other. "You think they're drinkin' back there?" he asked me.

"Maybe they spent too much time on the beach and fried a few brain cells."

Kimbrew keyed the mike and said, "Everyone's fine. How are you? Over."

With that, we both broke into laughter. It sounded more like a friendly phone conversation than standard military radio traffic.

"Why does he give a shit about us all of a sudden?" Kimbrew asked me.

"Maybe their pinochle game back on the beach broke up early," I said. "And while they're waiting on the steaks to cook, Embesi had a few spare minutes to see how we're doing."

We hated the rest of the platoon, particularly Embesi, for living the life of luxury on a movie set while we were stuck on the dark side of the moon.

Embesi came back on the radio to explain that he had been at KMC headquarters the whole time. He was there when the shit hit the fan and said that we must have gone through a lot of ammunition. He was concerned that we might not have enough left for the coming night.

Kimbrew and I looked at each, now more confused than ever. Finally Kimbrew spoke into the mike, "What the hell are you talking about? Over."

Embesi explained. The Korean CO on our sweep had just reported 250 NVA dead, while only sustaining light casualties.

"I don't know where you're getting your information, but we didn't see anything, let alone shoot anything! Over."

This was our first insight into why the Koreans' record in I Corps was what it was: They simply lied about their kills. A little investigative work by Embesi uncovered what these "allies" were up to. They would report fictitious engagements and proclaim huge numbers of enemy KIAs. And then, true to the agreement the United States had with them, we would replace their ammunition.

Embesi decided to do some follow-up detective work. Using the truck he had at his disposal, he waited for the truck convoy to deliver the replacement ammunition to the Koreans a few days later. He watched the ammo being unloaded, and stayed with it until he saw it reloaded on Korean trucks, which he then followed to the docks of Da Nang and to a waiting Korean ship.

The Koreans were in this war for reasons of their own.

ON OUR VERY NEXT SWEEP WITH THEM, we made contact with Mr. Charles. The NVA sprang an ambush, and the Koreans turned and ran behind the tanks, leaving us totally exposed.

The other tank working with us, which was from 1st Tank Battalion, took an RPG hit on its searchlight. Luckily, there were no casualties. The tanks had to back away from the fight alone and unescorted because the Koreans had run.

After the sweep, the two Marine TCs got together to vent their disgust at the Korean captain. They told him that from now on, one tank would keep its gun tube facing to the rear and would fire at any fleeing Koreans. The captain accused the tanks of almost running down his men while we were backing up!

We never got the chance to go back into the field with these worthless noncombatants. But we did learn something about how rumors can lionize a unit that really hadn't done anything. We found out first-hand that working with the Koreans wasn't any different than working with Marvin the Arvin—our nickname for South Vietnamese troops, the Army Republic of Vietnam, ARVN. The ARVN were terrible fighters and couldn't be depended on any more than the Koreans. The lone exceptions were the Vietnamese Marines, who were pretty good because they had been trained by their U.S. counterparts.

IT WAS MID-JULY and it seemed to get hotter with each passing day. During the six weeks we sat at the Mud Flats we hadn't felt the slightest hint of a breeze. The heat got so miserable we actually welcomed the nights. That was a first!

It was one of these cooler nights that had the Koreans really freaking out. It was at the start of the first watch around 10 p.m. when voices came screaming out of the night. They were obviously coming from North Vietnamese loudspeakers outside the wire. Stranger still was that we couldn't understand them because they were speaking in Korean. Suddenly the little guys were scurrying around the compound, convinced they were about to be overrun. We were convinced that they were close to panicking, and that began to worry us. It was a tense night for the two tank crews; we didn't know if the Koreans would run out on us or not.

Embesi tried to make life a little easier by rotating one crewman out of the Mud Flats every week, via the weekly resupply helicopter. It was a mini R&R vacation. During that time, the lucky guy got to visit the rest of the platoon and loll on the beach. They made the best of a great situation, even decorating their hooches with Vietnamese fishing gear they found around the area. It was a pleasant break from the tension of being the minority out in the middle of nowhere surrounded by non-English-speaking troops. It also meant a few nights of uninterrupted sleep.

But all wasn't right in Shangri-La. Our crews had reported several bad incidents while trading with the Koreans. They were merciless in their bargaining and would gang up on the tankers and amtrackers to take what they wanted. It got to the point where Embesi had to curtail all trading with these allies—adding more fuel to the fire, pissing off the Koreans even more.

Evidently problems with the previous tank platoon had gotten to the point that one tanker found a Korean booby trap under his cot. The Marine tank officer threatened to leave the Korean base and return to Da Nang. On hearing that, the Koreans demanded the Marine tanks, which they claimed had been promised to them in exchange for their participating in the war. Hence the hasty exit of the previous Marine tank platoon. But why had no one warned us before our arrival?

There was an abandoned fishing village a quarter mile from the platoon compound. For weeks, scores of tankers had made the short walk to the nearby village to scavenge old fishing nets, floats, and anchors to decorate their hooches. One day our truck driver—whose last name was Ford—was scrounging for some knickknacks. He found a particularly large wooden anchor and was dragging it back to his hooch when the ground underneath him blew up.

At the sound of the blast, Embesi grabbed his pistol and medical pack, flew out of his hooch, and ran down the oft-traveled trail. Ford was on the ground, one leg completely gone. Embesi shot him up with morphine and had him carried to a nearby LZ.

"Why me, Sergeant Embesi? Why me?" Ford repeated over and over.

Embesi could only tell him to hang on. He applied a tourniquet and yelled for the corpsman. They quickly drove him to the LZ and loaded Ford on a Marine medevac helicopter, never to be seen again.

Later, Embesi went back to the site to look for clues. He uncovered a small fragment of green metal from a U.S. machine gun ammunition can. Embesi found the lot number printed on the side of ammo cans that identified the manufacturer and date.

Because he was a well-connected staff sergeant, it didn't take him long to track down the lot number and trace it back through the supply system. In a matter of days, he had his answer; the lot number had been on a large quantity of machine gun ammo sent to the Korean Marines. With his suspicions confirmed, Embesi immediately terminated all fraternization with the Koreans and put the fishing village off limits.

THERE ARE CERTAIN MOMENTS in everyone's life when we can look back and say, "This is where I changed" or "After that, my life was affected forever." We don't usually recognize these turning points when they occur.

One of my most important moments was about to begin, strangely enough, at my lowest point. It happened halfway through my Southeast Asia Senior Class Trip, as we sometimes referred to our tours of duty in Vietnam. It was a fit expression for this war, where the conscripts' mean age was nineteen, the youngest average of any American war.

A Marine unit was sweeping through the Dodge City area, and with it were several tanks from our platoon. That morning, we received word over the radio to be ready to join the sweep as it passed by the Mud Flats. We would be leaving our inept, worthless little Korean "allies" behind.

This operation found us working with a newly relocated unit—the 26th Marine Regiment, which had just stepped out of Marine folklore after enduring the siege at Khe Sanh. Now they were reassigned to the 1st Marine Division outside Da Nang, some 170 miles south of the DMZ, and found themselves in an unfamiliar and different kind of war, with our tank platoon for support.

The 26th Marines came into our TAOR with all the cockiness of a unit that knew it had triumphed over a terrible ordeal. They arrived totally unaware of our kind of war, never having heard of Dodge City or the Arizona Territory—two areas known for their wild shoot-'em-ups. They thought that coming down here was a well-deserved, in-country R&R.

Our first sweep with the Khe Sanh veterans went into Dodge City, where the Korean Marines refused to tread. It was the mother of all booby-trapped, punji-pitted, and mined areas in all of I Corps, if not all Vietnam, and the scene of countless vicious firefights.

It was late July when we began the sweep south of Hill 55. We had our aerials tied down, sacrificing the range of our radios but reassuring the tank commander that his head might stay connected a little longer. We were only two klicks away from Hill 55 when the first explosion went off. Immediately we heard the call, "Corpsman! Corpsman up!"

Our sweep came to a stop almost as soon as it had started. Those of us who had worked in this area before knew what to expect. Sure enough, with the approach of the helicopter, all hell broke loose. Mortars started dropping among the grunts, while Soviet .51-caliber machine guns opened up on the bird. More men were wounded.

The chopper got away with its cargo of casualties, and we resumed our advance. Five minutes later, another explosion went off, and the cycle repeated itself. This unit's mental effectiveness became seriously affected. The 26th Marines had little experience in identifying and disarming booby traps. They were almost frozen in place, psychologically paralyzed by this new and different type of warfare.

While waiting for the medevacs, we got to talk with the grunts around the tank. "This is bullshit!" said one.

"Is it always like this?" another asked.

"Welcome to Dodge City," Hearn told them. "Ain't the same as sittin' in a bunker, is it?"

Neither were the 26th Marines accustomed to the roving enemy mortar teams that nipped at a unit's heels wherever it went, waiting for the opportunity to catch a helicopter on a resupply or medevac mission.

We hadn't moved two klicks in two days, yet we took several KIAs and WIAs from mines and booby traps without so much as sighting Charlie. For the grunts, who didn't know if they would still be connected to their legs with the next step they took, movement became disconcerting and painfully slow. It was a mind game, and Charlie was winning.

The sweep turned into a two-day stop-and-go exercise until it was decided to back out of the area. The heroes of Khe Sanh had experienced the uncertainty of casualties from deadly booby traps, and they needed training in dealing with this different type of threat. At least that's why we thought they were taken out of the field.

Around this time, rumors started circulating that elements of the 5th Marine Division would be returning to the States. Any rumor that good . . . wasn't possible, but in a few days we found our entire tank company back at 1st Tank Battalion's CP. Axiom Number Six had come into play: The stranger a rumor is, the more likely it is true.

WE LEARNED THAT THE 26TH AND 27TH MARINES would be the first units to return to the States as part of a gradual U.S. withdrawal. Along with them would go supporting units that had mounted out of California in response to the Tet Offensive back in February. Hey! That was us! It was too good to be true. I might be going back six months early.

But I was naïve about the workings of the military. We were on a high from which some of us would come crashing down.

Our tanks no longer looked like the showroom models we had started out with. Now ours had the missing fenders, headlights smashed and missing, RPG holes, and mud caked all over the suspension system.

We soon learned that the only men returning to the States would be the veterans caught up in the February mount-out. Short-timers from all over northern I Corps were gathered up and reassigned to units that were slated to go home. The rest of us first-timers would be reassigned to other Marine units of the 1st and 3rd Marine divisions. Half our company celebrated, while us first-timers were absolutely devastated at the prospects facing us.

When you were assigned to another unit, there was no guarantee you would keep the job you had trained for. If the Marines needed more grunts—well, you know. I had seen enough to know that humpin' the boonies wasn't something I was cut out for, so the certainty of getting reassigned to a new outfit filled me with apprehension. Having grown accustomed to being surrounded by several inches of steel, I was terrified at the prospect of becoming a grunt. We first-timers didn't know where we would be going, what we would be doing, or all the new people we would be thrust in with. It was most dismal point of my entire Marine Corps experience, and our morale was as low as you can imagine.

As a final insult—it felt like a punishment—we first-timers were kept around to clean and disinfect the tanks that would be returning back to The World! It felt as if we were having it rubbed in our faces. We all wanted to tell the veterans, "They're your Goddamn tanks! You clean them!"

The next morning, after we completed the dirty work, they called a company formation, the last time for Bravo Company, 5th Tanks, as we knew it. After the formation, each platoon sergeant notified his first-timers where they were being assigned. It was done by roll call, and we were notified publicly, one by one.

Embesi read off the assignments alphabetically from a clipboard. As he called out each man's name, he waited for an acknowledgment, then announced the unit to which he had been assigned. As he went down the list, my colleagues' destinations became increasingly worrisome. One after another, they were assigned to infantry units; only a few were assigned to tank units.

By the time Embesi got down to the middle of the alphabet, I was certain of my fate. I imagined myself in a hot thick jungle, leeches clinging to my legs, loaded down with 782 gear, barely able to walk, being pushed along by my fellow grunts.

"Peavey! . . ." The sound of my name startled me. ". . . 3rd Tank Battalion."

I couldn't believe my good luck at being reassigned to a tank unit!

We said our good-byes and good lucks to one another. Never again were we going to see men we had lived with intimately for the past six months. It was over—or, depending on how you looked at it, just beginning. I remained a tanker, but I had no idea what my new job was to be or where it would take me. I knew only that I was about to go north—farther north than I could have ever imagined. I packed up my stuff, slung my M14 over my shoulder, and took a truck to the Da Nang airbase.

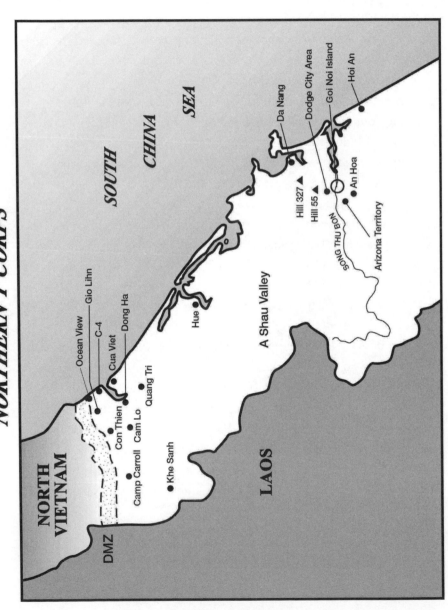

Chapter 11

Movin' North

I received orders instructing me to catch a ride to the Da Nang airfield for the next plane to Quang Tri, home of the 3rd Marine Division. Where would I end up? What kind of crew would I spend the next six months with? I was only a corporal, but my fourteen months in grade and six months in-country ought to count for something. Both of these factors would become far more important than I realized right then. Well, at least I wasn't an FNG reporting in for the first time.

No sooner had I reached Quang Tri and 3rd Tank Battalion's head-quarters than they issued me a pistol and told me to catch the next plane north to Dong Ha. I learned that my timing was perfect; the next plane for the short hop to Dong Ha was leaving in an hour. Ten other men would be on my flight. Some were coming back from R&R, a few were FNGs, replacements, and others were holdovers from the departing 26th and 27th Marines.

Two hours later, a Marine C-130 cargo plane pulled up on the tarmac and we were guided to a ramp to the rear of the plane. We, its sole cargo, sat on two long benches that ran along the airplane's bulkheads. The plane's cargo master pressed a large button that closed the cargo ramp.

"When we land in Dong Ha," he yelled for us all to hear, "we usually come under artillery fire. I want you men running down that ramp when I tell you. This plane won't stop, and I suggest you don't either. Someone on the ground will guide you over to the nearest bunker."

Holy shit! This was getting pretty serious!

Within only fifteen minutes the plane dove steeply for the ground and quickly flattened out onto a bumpy dirt strip. Billowing clouds of dust rolled past the windows. The plane came to a hard stop, turned around, and quickly taxied back down the strip while lowering its cargo ramp.

The cargo master had put a headset on. "We'll be stopping after all," he said, turning to us. "When we stop, run down the ramp away from the plane. Someone on the ground will direct you."

We gathered up our stuff, glad that we didn't have to exit a rolling aircraft. As soon as the plane came to an abrupt stop, we ran down the ramp clutching our personal gear. A dozen men ran past us, getting on. They were paired off, each holding one corner of a large plastic bag. I didn't give it any thought as I passed them. I was more concerned about where I was supposed to go.

We were directed to a slit trench alongside the landing strip. We piled in, certain that enemy artillery was about to find us.

The plane revved its engines and started to move away. Its deafening noise finally abated. One of my travel companions, an FNG, asked no one in particular, "Was that what I thought they were?"

"Is what, what you thought it was?" I asked him.

"Those green bags," he said, referring to what the men getting on the plane were carrying. I hadn't wondered about it until that moment, but I realized he was right. I had never seen one before.

"Hey, man," I said, getting up and not looking at the FNG, "you're smarter than them. Just be glad it ain't you."

When it came to travel arrangements in The Nam, you were on your own, especially as you tried to track down an outfit. I hitched a ride with a couple of other guys going to Charlie Company, 3rd Tanks. Once I got there, I found I had been assigned to 1st Platoon. I asked where they were. "North of here," came the answer, "at a place called C-4."

No name, just C-4. I expected to be going someplace I would recognize, like the Rockpile, Camp Carroll, Razorback, Vandergrift, Cam Lo, maybe even Khe Sanh or Con Thien—two bases that had earned themselves a solid place in Marine folklore.

The next day, a supply truck left for a place at the mouth of the Cua Viet River, on the coast of Vietnam, where I was to meet a Mike boat to take me across the river. From there, C-4 was straight up the shoreline. It didn't take me long to find a truck driver headed for C-4. He said it was only three or four miles north, straight up the beach, but he wanted to wait for a few more trucks.

"Ya don't make that run alone," he said. "Not around here, ya don't." He pulled out a military map to show me where I was and where we were going. It wasn't hard to miss the quarter-inch gray line a couple of miles north of C-4.

"Is that the DMZ?" I asked.

"Yup!" he smiled. "Can't go much farther north than that!"

He was wrong on that point, as I would later learn. Right then, however, I was busy wondering what I had gotten myself in for and began to feel sorry for myself. I didn't know anybody. Hardly anyone knew where I was going, and it sure was close to North Vietnam.

Another truck came across on the Mike boat and it was obvious the two drivers knew each other. They agreed to "make a run for it!" I was never so happy to have my M14 with me as I climbed in the back of the truck and pointed it over the edge, toward the sand dunes. The trucks drove like hell up the beach until we reached a fortified area about one hundred meters inland. We then made a left turn into the fire base known as C-4.

It was right on the South Vietnamese coast, only four thousand meters south of the DMZ. C-4 was made up of dozens of large, very solid bunkers. Obviously built by engineers or Seabees, only their top halves stood above the ground. Their roofs were composed of 12 x 12–inch wooden beams able to support the dozens of layers of sandbags stacked on top. The bunkers' sides were equally well protected. I never saw a fire base that looked so professionally built; C-4 looked as if it was meant to be here for a while.

The driver stopped his truck inside the compound, and I asked him where the tanks were located. I just followed his pointing finger, knowing that eventually, someplace, I'd find a tank. Then, behind a row of bunkers, I spotted what looked like tank aerials. Sure enough, three tanks were parked on the other side. I was relieved to have finally found my destination. I didn't figure that going any farther north could be an option. Weren't we almost on the Z?

I approached the bunker opposite the tanks, mentally preparing to meet my new platoon leader and greet the dozens of strangers I would be living with for the next seven months. I hoped I'd get a good tank commander.

Outside the bunker's entrance, six men were sitting around, working on a .50-caliber machine gun. Two were trying to get the bolt out of the machine gun's receiver assembly. One of them—I couldn't believe my eyes!—was my friend John Wear.

I spoke to him before he saw me. "Well, if it isn't my pet boy Sherman!"

He looked up with a big smile across his face, jumped up and came over. "Hey, Mr. Peabody!"

John and I had met back in tank school. He'd always looked young for his age, and his Marine Corps–issue glasses gave him a resemblance to Mr. Peabody's pet boy, Sherman, on TV's *Rocky and Bullwinkle* cartoon show. With a last name like Peavey, I naturally became Mr. Peabody.

We shook hands, glad to see each other.

"What the hell you doing up here?" John asked. "I thought you were down south leaving the war to us Third Tankers!" He couldn't have imagined how good it felt to finally see someone I knew, let alone a good friend. Also, his recognition helped me establish instant credibility with the other five.

Looking over at the table and the .50 they were working on, right away I saw that someone had put the bolt in backward, a situation almost impossible to correct. They were all puzzled as to what to do next.

I walked over and said, "I can fix that if you get me two screwdrivers."

"No, man. We been workin' on this all mornin'. Its gotta go back to battalion to be fixed," said one of the strangers.

"Get me the screwdrivers, and I'll save you the embarrassment of having to turn in the weapon." They didn't know I was a graduate of the Embesi .50-Caliber School.

Someone came back with the screwdrivers, and thirty seconds later I had the bolt out—to the amazement of all hands.

Anyone freshly checking into a unit, no matter what his credentials, was immediately assumed to be an FNG. Even if you were a lifer in the Corps, it didn't matter. If you had no combat experience you were just somebody apt to get some veteran killed. Between my fixing the gun and John's confirming who I was and where I had just come from, like a wiseguy in the mob, I was spoken for.

Then came one of the greatest coincidences of the entire Vietnam War. "You're not going to believe this," said John, "but I just got a package from your mother today. Four baby bottles full of Scotch!"

After my mother's first attempt to send John a bottle ended with a visit from a postal inspector I had asked her to use plastic baby bottles next time—along with a fictitious return address. That night I voluntarily stood watch with John on C-4's perimeter. We enjoyed ourselves immensely, swapped war stories, caught up on the war and our mutual friends, and polished off the baby bottles of Glenlevit.

It was lots of, "Did you hear about so-and-so . . ." and who the latest KIAs were. I brought him up to date on what it was like down south, in the Arizona Territory and Dodge City area outside Da Nang, all about Allen Brook, and our mutual friend, Johnny Cash. Wear couldn't believe how we got stuck with all the amtrackers when we left the States. He was disgusted at the stupidity of Johnny's death and the inexperienced tank commander and crew.

Wear had been with 3rd Tanks since he first arrived in-country. He filled me in on the battle for Hue and the short life expectancy of TCs in the house-to-house fighting. The death of his good friend, Bob Minetto, really affected him. Back in The World, he and Bob had been very close.

THE NEXT MORNING, I met my new platoon leader—another "never going into the field lieutenant"—and discovered what my extensive time in grade and six months in The Nam was really worth: I was made a tank commander! Not only that, but a section leader as well, with another tank under me. One day I had been trying to figure out which C rat meal to eat, the next I had the responsibility of organizing the resupply of food for two tank crews.

In the eyes of a gunner, ammunition was there to be shot up. Now I had to ration it out between two tanks and account for it. Seven men's lives rested in the hands of a twenty-one-year-old corporal whose decisions, if wrong or slow, could result in serious, even tragic, consequences. Suddenly I was forced to think about others and deal with their problems. It was a situation that quickly forced me to become a man.

When I asked which two of those tanks outside would be mine, the surprising answer was "None."

"Well, then where are my two tanks?"

"At Oceanview, about two miles north of here."

I didn't think it was possible to go any farther north! Oceanview, right on the DMZ, was the northernmost outpost in all of Vietnam. Any farther north would require a visa!

In 1967 Marine engineers had plowed a path a thousand meters wide and thirty klicks long about two miles south of the DMZ. This strip of land, known as The Trace, was part of the Strong Point Obstacle System (SPOS). Along and beyond The Trace was a string of fire bases that crossed the neck of South Vietnam beginning with C-4 on the coast, followed by Gio Linh, Con Thien, the Rockpile, and Khe Sanh on the Laotian border. Marines referred to the whole system as the McNamara Line. The job of plowing such a huge swath of land never went any farther west than Con Thien following the loss of many bulldozers and their crews.

The Marines were bitterly opposed to the concept. Marine philosophy was to take the war to the enemy, not sit behind barbed wire. But we had to live with it, even though it tied us down to static defensive positions like C-4.

The tanks at C-4 and Oceanview rotated once a week, and my section's two tanks were due to return the next day. I would have one week to become acquainted with the crews, look the tanks over, and get a feeling for what had been thrust upon me.

The next morning, "my" two tanks from Oceanview rumbled into the C-4 compound and proceeded to the bunker area housing the tank crews. The LT greeted them and introduced me as their new TC and section leader.

Both crews immediately had me under scrutiny. All they knew for sure was that there was a new corporal in town. Confronted by this unknown leader, they were naturally leery. I knew what they were thinking: Does this new guy have any combat experience? I explained my background, assuring them their new TC was no FNG. In fact, I had logged more time in-country then they had, which gave me instant credibility. John's good words helped to ease their concerns.

I immediately wanted to look over both tanks, particularly mine. When the crew pointed to my vehicle, I couldn't believe my luck—it was brand new, a recent replacement for an older tank that had been in-country since 1965.

We stood watch as a crew for the first time that night and I immediately ran afoul of their procedures. As soon as we pulled into our position on C-4's berm, I told my loader. Bob Steele, to load a canister round in the main gun.

I couldn't believe the looks on their faces. "They don't let you do that in Third Tanks" said the loader. "It's against battalion policy to have a loaded main gun."

That was a stupid order, written by some pencil-pushing, noncombatant officer back in the rear who had never stood a night on watch or faced a human-wave attack. If we got hit I wanted a canister round going out first. "The round stays," I told him, "until the battalion CO starts standing watch with us."

Looking over the ammunition mix stored on board, I saw another thing that disturbed me. Of all the places we stored ammo on the vehicle, the ready rack was the first place the loader reached for when shit hit the proverbial fan. Because this rack held only nine rounds, what we chose to carry there was an important decision, to be made only by the TC.

Down south, Embesi's ready rack had a heavy emphasis on canister, five rounds' worth. The other four rounds were two each of HE and beehive. Imagine my shock when I looked down through the loader's hatch to find three rounds of HEAT in the ready rack's prime location, along with four flechette rounds and only two canister rounds.

"Steele!" I shouted. If anyone knew why the ready rack held such a dumb mix of ammo, it would be my loader. Bob Steele, a young, light-skinned black man from Pittsburgh, climbed the tank and joined me near his hatch. "What the fuck is all this HEAT doing in the ready rack?" I asked him. "And why isn't there more canister?" Little did I know that I was about to get my first lesson into the differences that 170 miles made.

Steele seemed surprised that I didn't like the mix I was pointing at. "That's how all the tanks are set up."

"You really think we're going to need HEAT in front of the next tree line we take on?"

"Hell, no! It's for the Russian tanks!"

"The NVAs got tanks up here?" I asked. "You got to be shittin' me!"

"We ain't seen 'em yet, but their tracks have been spotted a few times."

Bob Steele turned out to be the fastest, strongest loader I ever knew. Built like nobody's business, he could easily muscle the large rounds around with agility. With him as my loader we would win a bet against two other tank crews on a feat that was almost impossible—getting three main gun rounds in the air at once!

AFTER MY EXPERIENCE WITH how Better Living Thru Canister's name turned out to be prophetic, superstition told me that this new vehicle needed a good name, too. What brought good luck once might work again. I refused to name the tank Michelle after my sweetheart back home, as so many TCs did. I wanted the crewmen to feel they were part of a group effort in this decision. As my first deliberate act of trying to build a team, I shared with the crew Better Living's name and its ironic outcome, then asked them to come up with some ideas for this one.

My gunner was Bob Truitt, a nice guy who always wore a smile. John, the driver, was from Las Vegas. Cool and laid-back, he kept mostly to himself. If "dude" ever fit an individual, it was John. He was in love with an Okinawan woman, and for good luck, he had painted her name in very small letters on the front of the tank, close to where he sat. He always looked like he was on drugs, but it was just his nature, not his habit. John said that until he rotated back to The World, his only request would be, "Hey man, how about cuttin' me a little slack?"

The DMZ had been a little too intense for his liking, and he thought he deserved a break. So did the rest of the crew. They agreed they could all use a little more slack from the war on the Z—and that kicked off the christening process. After spending thirteen months in Southern California before reaching The Nam, I thought the popular surfer's motto, "pray for surf," had some merit as a starting point—particularly if we changed the noun.

I got some masking tape and began to outline "Pray for Slack" on our gun tube. Pray for Slack was as fitting a name as my last tank's, every bit as prophetic, and certainly more original than Judy. We never worked with grunts who didn't comment on that name. It was one they could bond with—and, as I'd learned from Embesi, bonding with the grunts was added life insurance.

NOW IT WAS OUR TURN to go up to Oceanview. I listened on the tank radio for word that the tanks up there were leaving. Before long, I got the messages and circled a finger over my head, "Crank 'em up!" Looking over at my other tank, I saw they were doing the same. I left behind John Wear; it would be the last time we'd see each other for quite a while.

We pulled out of C-4 and raced up the beach, skirting the ocean's waves to avoid any possible mines planted in the dry sand. Pretty soon we could make out two tanks coming toward us. I told the driver to steer a little deeper into the surf to give them room to pass. We were quite close as we passed one another at thirty-five miles an hour.

The TC and his gunner waved to us from their tank, and we returned the same. My driver knew where to turn left into the tiny little fire base of

Oceanview, or I would have gone right by it. There wasn't much to look at. If not for its thirty-foot wooden tower, I'd have missed it entirely.

The small outpost was only a hundred meters in diameter surrounded by a single strand of razor wire. Can't be too many troops here, I figured. Maybe a platoon, at the most. Then I spotted two Army M41 Dusters sitting on the western perimeter. Up until then, I had seen only pictures of these potent vehicles, with twin 40mm antiaircraft guns—also called pom-pom guns—mounted on a small-tracked chassis. I didn't know the Army was operating this far north in I Corps.

What was the purpose of this little cluster of sand dunes? There was no artillery at Oceanview, so technically it wasn't a fire base, just an outpost. I couldn't get over how few grunts were manning the perimeter. What had we gotten ourselves into?

Pray for Slack drove to the top of the second highest sand dune—the tower was sitting on the tallest one. John stopped right on top of the dune, and already I began to see some problems. The dune ran north and south, parallel to the beach, which was one hundred meters behind us. Our tank's position was to cover the western approaches to the outpost. In the soft sand, it wasn't possible to dig a slot for the tank to pull into, and the dune was too steep to allow the tank's bow to face due west. Therefore, the tank could only sit parallel to the perimeter, which wasn't its best defensive orientation. Generally, we tried to keep a tank's thicker bow facing the enemy.

I could see one thing we would have to do immediately—build a wall out of sandbags, the entire length of the tank and as high as our fenders. I was surprised this hadn't been done before. The crew wasn't happy with their new TC's decision, but they knew I was right.

Eventually I grew to like the tank sitting sideways, relative to the perimeter and parallel to the wire. It had advantages over the usual front-in-first position I was used to. For one thing, it increased our mobility two-fold. Now, in an emergency, I had two directions I could move in, whereas a tank parked in a slot could only back out. And the sideways orientation gave the grunts an unexpected benefit by extending the main gun farther out over the perimeter—reducing the effect of the muzzle blast, which could knock a man over.

Oceanview was only one hundred meters inland from the South China Sea. Stand on top of the tank's armor plate—the flat area over the tank's engine—and you could look up the coast into North Vietnam. The farther north you looked, the more the shoreline swung out into the ocean. Using the main gun's telescope, I could see up the beach for ten miles. Occasionally we saw North Vietnamese soldiers swimming or fishing in the surf, but never more than two or three of them at a time. This became the basis for a game that helped ease the boredom of sitting around doing nothing.

The effective range of an M48's main gun was 4,400 meters, or just under three miles. If you could see it and it wasn't more than 4,400 meters away, there was an eighty percent chance of hitting it on the first shot. Anything farther away was beyond the range of the tank's ballistic computer. That called for a crapshoot involving parallax, wind speed, wind direction, the cant of the gun, wear on the barrel, and a liberal employment of Scientific Wild-Ass Guesswork. SWAG was what made a game of it, because everybody had a different opinion as to how much elevation or deflection to add to the gun. In short, it took a lot of luck to land a round even remotely close to a target—like these soldier-fishermen, who were at least six miles away.

Back in The World, one of the many things Embesi had taught me was the dilemma of parallax in tank gunnery. It wasn't mentioned in any training manual, just something he had learned in his years of experience: Why would a projectile sometimes hit to the left or right of a target?

The cause of the problem, Embesi realized, was that a gunner's sights were four feet to the right of the main gun. When we bore-sighted the gun and optics, we aligned the two at a known target 1,200 meters away. Therefore, the farther away from 1,200 meters any target was, the more the main gun began shooting to its right.

To see for yourself what I mean, close one eye and point your finger at some object. Then close that eye and open the other one, and you'll see your finger's no longer pointing at the same spot. When looking at a target as far away as the fishermen, this problem only multiplied.

Our seaside shooting gallery game cost Uncle Sam $200 a pop (in 1960s dollars, when a new Corvette sold for $5,000). We weren't content to waste a thirteen-cent rifle bullet. Expense wasn't an issue; our ammunition was free. Besides, the shots we were attempting were five to eight miles out—ten times the distance made by any sniper with a rifle. For our purposes, 90mm projectiles were ideal because the large tracer element in their tails made their flight easy to monitor. We needed to see where each projectile went in order to adjust for the next shot.

The first time I got to play Shoot the Fishermen was during our first week at Oceanview. My crew introduced me to it; they said that due to the ridiculous distances involved, nobody was very good at it. The day they let me try a hand at it, I got my chance to impress my crew just how good I really was—and I found out just how lucky I was.

Truitt, the gunner, was sitting up on the turret, looking north through the TC's binoculars. "Hey! Bob!" he yelled down, "We got us a fisherman!"

I climbed up on the tank. The rest of the bored crew scurried up for a look. Truitt had already jumped down into his gunner's seat and was traversing the turret to the north, trying to acquire the target through the tank's powerful telescope.

Picking up the binoculars, I discovered Charlie standing at the water's edge, fishing in the surf; I guessed he was about six miles away. Using SWAG, I made my best estimate and laid the main gun. This was always a fun moment, because everyone offered his own opinion and expertise on where to point the gun. However, I had a distinct advantage over my crewmen because I remembered the parallax dilemma and compensated for the additional range.

Using Embesi Windage (a good guess, factoring in the wind), I moved the gun a few degrees to the left. That immediately prompted a string of four-letter words from Truitt, who moved the gun back again so that his crosshairs were back on the fisherman. Once more, I moved the gun off the target and told him to leave it alone.

"You ain't gonna hit shit with that," he warned me.

"From what you've told me, you haven't been able to hit shit anyway. Right?"

"You're way off to the left!" he protested.

"Well, we'll see, won't we?" My shot might land long or short, I thought, but at least be it would be on line with the target.

There was no convincing Truitt. "You're crazy!" he added helplessly.

I asked the loader for an HE round. I rechecked all my guesswork, particularly the lateral offset of the sights and the elevation.

"On the way!" I yelled, signaling to all that I was going to squeeze one off.

Boom! We watched the projectile and its tracer speed away from us. Early in its flight, it appeared to be way too high. But then it started to arc on its trajectory, right on line with the fisherman, as it almost vanished from sight.

"Damn!" Steele said. "We just might hit this guy!"

Just when the tracer looked as if it was going to hit the NVA fisherman in the head, it passed by what must have been only a foot in front of him!

"Holy shit!" said Steele.

"Damn, you're good!" said the doubting Truitt.

I had already experienced the sound a rifle bullet makes as it passes close to your head. Like someone snapping a twig, or the cap in a toy gun, it's actually the sound of the bullet—an object only a third of an inch in diameter—breaking the sound barrier. The tank projectile we were watching was three and a half inches in diameter, so I could only guess at what Charlie must have heard as it passed inches in front of him. From the way he jumped and dropped his fishing pole, it must have made one hell of a crack.

The HE round impacted what looked like fifty feet farther down the beach from him. Already the fisherman was bolting for the sand dunes, leaving behind his fishing pole, a small pile of clothes, and his weapon. It had to be one of the all-time closest misses a tank ever made. Evidently, the crew had attempted these shots before, but judging by their loud and boisterous reaction now they had never gotten even remotely close to hitting anything.

Suddenly I wasn't just an FNG tank commander. My credibility and esteem grew enormously, right when I needed them most. The crew talked about my prowess with the other crews. They never realized I had made only one phenomenally lucky guess that surprised even me—but I sure wasn't about to tell them.

THE BORING DAYS RAN TOGETHER. We never knew what day of the week it was. While sitting on top of the tank on yet another hot afternoon, I turned my head north to peer into the DMZ when movement caught my eye.

By sheer luck, I happened to be looking in the right direction and saw something most everyone else missed until it was over. It occurred so quickly that, at first, none of us was sure exactly what happened. It was an oddball moment when the war became very real for somebody else, and I was just an innocent bystander.

Half a mile inland, an F-4 Phantom was flying due south out of the DMZ at a terrific speed, about as low to the ground as a jet can without taxiing. Just as the plane got even with our outpost, my attention was drawn to a brown blur trailing behind it. At first, I guessed that the plane was dragging something—until I saw that the "something" was closing on the aircraft, and rapidly. As the blur got closer to our position, still on the Phantom's tail, it began to look more like a flying telephone pole. As we learned later, it was a Soviet heat-seeking surface-to-air missile—fired from North Vietnam, no doubt—that had locked onto the Phantom's exhaust.

Hugging the ground, the jet roared by us about half a mile away. The missile looked to be only two hundred meters behind when suddenly the plane went into a steep, near-vertical climb, issuing a huge plume of exhaust, followed by a thundering ka-boom! An instant later, the very point where the Phantom had turned upward, the SAM exploded in mid-air.

Later, a FAC told us that the jet's radar intercept officer (RIO), sitting behind the pilot, would have been aware of the SAM on their tail. But the Phantom was too low and too slow to try any evasive maneuvers. Its only hope was to draw the missile in and then, at the critical moment, light both afterburners. The idea was to leave a significant hot spot behind in the air to fool the heat-seeker on the SAM, making it think it had entered the plane's exhaust pipe. Monitoring the missile's progress electronically, the Phantom's RIO told the pilot when to make his desperate pull-up maneuver. The ka-boom was the jet's afterburners kicking in.

I knew exactly how the jet's crew must have felt, to still be alive after pulling off such a gutsy maneuver. By sheer coincidence, I'd been looking in the right direction, because the entire incident lasted only three or four seconds. Steele and Truitt missed the whole show except for the finale of the SAM exploding in midair.

"What in hell was that?" they yelled up to me.

"There go two of the luckiest bastards in The Nam today," I said. "Headed home to warm showers, hot food, and a cold brew—after they change their underwear." Truitt and Steele didn't understand a word until I explained it all.

OCEANVIEW WAS VERY PRIMITIVE, with no cooking facilities—not uncommon for any base along the Z. C rats became breakfast, lunch, and dinner. The bathing facilities were even more primitive. Even though we were only a stone's throw from the ocean, walking the hundred meters to take a dip in the South China Sea was out of the question. The beach was too far outside the perimeter to be considered safe; mines and unexploded ordnance were all over the area.

Marine ingenuity came up with the easiest of solutions. Inside the base was a medium-sized bomb crater. Our proximity to the ocean meant for a very high water table, so any hole in the ground naturally filled with water. This one was no exception, so it stayed full all the time—always with the same water. You can imagine (but wouldn't want to) how foul that communal washbasin was, because forty men used it day after day, week after week.

The only thing that changed about that small pond was its color. Mornings found it covered with thick scum that called for a prebath ritual. Before entering the Oceanview Public Baths you brought with you four necessities: towel, soap, Ho Chi Minh sandals, and the ubiquitous fragmentation hand grenade. The frag, for short, went into the water first. Its explosion did nothing to sanitize the pond, but did take care of the floating crud that covered the surface. Down below, I'm sure, lurked organisms that would have thrilled the Centers for Disease Control. But, hell, we were young and indestructible. What was a little greenish-black water going to do to us?

A grenade in the bathtub was always the highlight of a boring day at Oceanview. In fact, everyone brought a frag to the hole, just for the fun of throwing one in. We were just a bunch of unsupervised kids with some really cool fireworks—that is, until the day we got a batch of defective hand grenades.

I had just opened a new case of grenades for the morning's pool party and finished handing them around to my eager playmates. We moseyed down to the pond and laid down our stuff in neat little piles. At the edge of the swimming hole, I pulled the pin on my grenade. "Fire in the hole!" I yelled for everyone to hear, and threw it in the drink.

For you to appreciate this story, I must remind you just how a hand grenade works. It has a handle called a spoon, contoured to the shape of the grenade body. When you want to throw it, you grip one hand around the grenade and the spoon as a single unit. Then, with your other hand, you pull the pin. Beneath the spoon is a strong spring that drives a striker that starts the weapon's fuse. The spoon keeps the grenade "safe" until it leaves your hand and flies off. Once it does, the fuse ignites, giving the thrower a three-to-five-second delay before the grenade detonates.

I lobbed my grenade into the pool. Even before it hit the water, I knew something was wrong. "Did anybody see the spoon fly off?" I asked.

But no one had paid any attention. They all had been backing away from the water. After we waited about ten seconds, I said, "I don't think the damned spoon came off!"

What to do next? No one in his right mind wanted to wade into that inky water and grope for a grenade with his feet. That blind touch might just dislodge a hung-up spoon.

We waited another minute.

"I don't think the spoon released," I repeated. "Throw in another grenade. Maybe that'll dislodge it."

Driver John stepped up to the plate and pulled the pin on his grenade. All eyes followed it as it left his hand. But before it broke the surface of the water, all three of us shouted in unison, "The spoon didn't come off!"

We again waited, not sure what to do—then unanimously decided to throw another one. Certainly there couldn't be three duds in a row!

"Fire in the hole," Steele yelled. He pulled the pin and threw his grenade.

The spoon flew off, and the grenade splashed into the middle of the pond. "That'll take care of 'em," he said cockily, looking at us as if we had all done something wrong and he had gotten it right.

There was no explosion. Three feet below the water's dark surface lay three live grenades.

Who had the guts to go in and retrieve them? Well, no thanks, guys!

At moments like this, there were always one or two big-mouth braggarts around who tried to egg on the others to do something.

The name-calling started, followed by taunts of "chicken!" More men from inside Oceanview began to gather around, and soon the betting started.

The amounts of money kept increasing, tempting only the dumb and the poor. The rest of us smart, rich chickens kept betting more money. I couldn't imagine anyone wanting to take such a risk.

Finally, the sum rose to the point at which a grunt stepped forward. For $125, a score of onlookers got to watch a fellow Marine risk blowing himself to Kingdom Come. This was a crowd that went to a car race only to see the wrecks. Anything for a bet.

Then the fool said that he would be right back before he took care of the problem and collect his money. So, we waited. Five minutes went by without our pool boy returning.

"Where is he?" several men began asking. Everyone became itchy waiting for this guy to return, wondering what he had up his sleeve.

A few more minutes went by and our pool cleaner returned with a towel and two huge sausagelike sections of line charge. To get rid of mines, a specialized amtrac could fire a missile that dragged a hundred meters of line charge out in front of the vehicle. Each link was equal in size and weight to a five-pound bag of sugar, and consisted of C4, a plastic explosive. The amtrac would set off the charge, which would clear a safe path through the minefield.

We all stepped back to watch this would-be bet winner push a blasting cap into the soft C4. He attached a two-foot length of time fuse to the cap, then wrapped it all up in his towel so that two people could pick it up between them and swing it into the pool. He asked for a light.

Nobody had one, so I volunteered and ran back to our tank. What I really wanted was my camera. On my return, he and another volunteer held the contraption between them, and I got the honor of lighting the pool-cleaning bomb.

The fuse was long enough for a twenty-second burn, giving us more than enough time to get away. They swung their homemade device back and forth and, at the count of three, let it fly. It splashed into the middle of the pool. The crowd dropped back a hundred feet from the edge and waited.

And waited. And waited some more.

After a minute went by, we started laughing at the totally impossible odds of all these munitions not going off. People began arguing over the $125. The clever inventor pleaded for more time.

"It could be a slow fuse," he offered, after another minute passed.

Another three minutes, and the moneylenders wanted him to pay up. And there was no way anyone was going into that pool, ever again.

"Nice going, asshole," someone said. "Now nobody can take a bath!"

As we turned to go back to our tanks, we were nearly thrown to the ground by an enormous explosion. Recovering quickly, we looked up and saw a geyser reaching its apex. A solid column of water hung suspended in mid-air. It then collapsed in a torrent back into the spa. I had the presence of mind to snap a picture before the last few gallons had returned to the pool.

"Shower's open!" said the pool cleaner. "Pay up!"

MANY A CLAYMORE ANTIPERSONNEL MINE was pried open in Vietnam to get the C4 explosive inside. A marble-sized ball of C4 could be harmlessly ignited to heat C rats in its intense heat, and we used the plastic compound's explosive qualities for a variety of odd jobs when we didn't have the right equipment or needed an expedient fix to a problem.

For example, there was the day a couple of tanks came up from C-4 to go on a sweep with a couple of amtracs full of grunts. We would join them the next day to sweep toward Gio Linh, west into the dangerous Leatherneck Square area. Leatherneck Square was the area between Con Thien, Go Lihn, Dong Ha, and Cam Lo, which on a map marked the corners of a square. It was as notorious as Dodge City had been down south. The next morning, as the grunts and tanks began forming up just outside the perimeter of Oceanview, one of the visiting tanks hit a mine.

It was a bad start for a long sweep, and the grunt CO was pissed to be held up almost before we left the perimeter. Another TC and myself took charge of tackling the repair process. They had to remove some damaged track first, so I went out to scrounge all the tanks for spare track blocks.

I climbed up on Pray for Slack to remove a large piece that had been bolted to the sides of the turret months earlier. Somebody, I soon discovered, had put the bolt in backward, making it impossible for me to get a wrench between the head of the bolt and the turret wall. Worse, it had rusted in place, so there was no way to loosen it. This was a job for C4!

I got out a small amount of the white putty and molded it halfway around the bolt's rusted head. Without my packing something around the charge, it would just dissipate and not do the job. The charge had to be partially covered, so it would channel the explosion and cut off the head of the bolt. I found a couple of half-filled sandbags and packed them around the charge, stuffing them in the space between the track block and the turret wall.

I lit the fuse and ran to the other side of the tank with my crew. The charge went off and the track block fell loose from the side of the turret. Damn, I'm good! I thought to myself.

Using that section, we were able to piece together enough spare track to get the tank back in shape so that it could be towed back to Dong Ha. Even though we fixed it in record time, I was acutely aware that we had held up the entire sweep. I was the last one back on Pray for Slack, and we quickly got underway.

Just as I was putting my comm helmet on, gunner Bob Truitt's voice came over the intercom through my earphones. "Hey, TC?"

"What?" I asked.

"Er, ah, you might want to come down here and look at this."

After all the time we had just wasted with the injured tank, I couldn't believe he expected me to leave my position. "Not now, damnit!" I told him. "We're holding up the sweep. We gotta get going."

"Okay," he sighed. "I sure hope you don't plan on shootin' anything except canister."

As I watched the other tanks around us preparing to move out, I was about to ignore his remark. "What are you talking about?"

"It's no big deal," he said with a drop of sarcasm, "If you don't mind the ballistic computer hangin' off the wall."

"Driver, stop the tank!" I dropped down to take a quick gander at whatever Truitt was trying to tell me. There, hanging half off the turret's interior wall by one of its drive couplers was the computer. Nobody could have done this much damage accidentally.

"What the hell did you do?" I asked, thinking he must have really whacked it hard with something.

"Don't know," Truitt said. "It was like that when I got inside."

"Look, it didn't just fall off the fuckin' . . ." Then I realized, Oh, shit! That piece of track I had blown off the outside of the turret was directly opposite the computer. The shock wave from the explosion must have gone through the wall and knocked the computer off its mount. I must have either packed the C4 charge a little too well, or used too much. My ass would be in deep trouble over this. When they found out I had used C4, they would throw the book at me.

Whenever confronted with a problem, I always asked myself what Embesi would do. Face it, if he was clever enough to convince an entire Marine battalion of a nonexistent machine gun in that tree line on Allen Brook, surely he could figure out a way around this.

Then it came to me! I told Truitt that he didn't yet know what I knew—that during this sweep, we were going to be hit by an RPG.

He understood what I was driving at. "Man! If it hadn't been for that track block hangin' outside the turret, it might have gotten all of us!"

"Exactly!" I replied. "You should thank God for that track block. You're lucky to be alive!"

Chapter 12

The Night the War Was Lost

Our sweep didn't turn up a thing—something unheard of in Leatherneck Square. We went back to Oceanview. We remained there for two months, without being relieved.

It wasn't so bad. Certainly it beat going out in the bush, and up at Oceanview, there were no officers or staff NCOs to bother us. Nobody wanted to come this far north just to check on two tanks.

The highlight of a stay at Oceanview was the fuel run down to Cua Viet to meet up with a tanker truck. It also meant a visit to the Navy perimeter on the south side of the river's mouth. This was a wind-in-your-face, full-out, run-down-the-beach, half in and half out of the surf. Once there, we had a few hours to kill before we had to head back. Sometimes there would be an LST—Landing Ship, Tank—unloading supplies, which also brought the possibility of getting a hot meal.

The squids loved to trade for anything North Vietnamese in origin—AK-47 rifles, SKS rifles, pith helmets, and pistols. But the item most sought-after by real NVA aficionados was an officer's brass belt buckle with an enameled red star in the center. That was your ticket to a first-class hot meal.

Once we topped off our fuel cells and stomachs, we made the twenty-minute run back north—with our turrets facing inland, always anticipating an ambush. Fortunately, we never had a problem on the stretch of no man's land between Cua Viet and C-4, nor on the run between C-4 and Oceanview.

Running a tank through saltwater had a corrosive effect on its moving parts. After each romp in the surf we had to go over the entire suspension system with a hand-pumped grease gun, injecting fresh grease into the myriad small grease fittings that adorned the suspension system. You had to keep pumping in fresh grease until you saw clean fresh grease ooze out of the seals, thereby purging any saltwater that might have seeped inside.

The day I took command of the tank I had noticed that one set of our roadwheels had a broken grease fitting. The crew told me it had broken off months earlier. Without a new fitting, we couldn't possibly grease the wheel bearings for that particular set of roadwheels. I had notified maintenance via radio, but nothing could be done in the field; the broken fitting would have to be "tapped" out before installing a new one. They said to wait until our next PM, when we would have to go to Dong Ha to have the pack pulled. For now, there was nothing we could do, so we simply ignored the problem.

For several months, this fitting—which normally channeled grease into the roadwheels' high-friction environment—went without lubrication. At the same time, saltwater bathed the bearings and wheel spindle during every run we made up and down the beach.. The result, although perhaps predictable, was still quite dramatic when it finally came to pass.

We were finally due for our scheduled PM, at which time we would get the grease fitting fixed and the gunner's ballistic computer repaired—the one the RPG had knocked off. It meant three days off the Z and we all looked forward to that.

We crossed the Cua Viet using the Mike boat and were on the main highway toward Dong Ha. We were traveling alone—unusual, because tanks always traveled in pairs—but this was a major highway and considered relatively safe, even though it ran atop a berm elevated about five feet above the ground. The road was considered paved by Vietnam standards, which meant it was regularly sprayed with diesel fuel. All that fuel didn't go to waste, because the combination of dirt and oil made for a surface almost as hard as asphalt, difficult for Charlie to mine. Any hole he dug would stand out like a sore thumb.

Flying wide open along a smooth, straight road was always a real rush. Fifty-two tons running full out created a strong wind in our faces, particularly on a road as lightly traveled as this one. Our size combined with our noise gave us command over indigenous traffic—and a tremendous ego trip. After all, here was a killing machine on a highway full of jeeps, scooters, and microbuses. The noise of our tracks, accompanied by the throaty whine of our V-12 diesel engine's turbo-chargers, provided all the warning necessary. The locals looked over their shoulders at the noise coming up from behind. As if Moses himself was driving our tank, the lanes would magically part.

Never slowing for anyone or anything, we sped on as if on some life-and-death mission. We loved staring down on their upturned, half-terrified faces, seeing them cling desperately to the edge of the road, giving us road hogs all the room they could without plunging five feet down the steep embankment. At moments like these, a tanker wouldn't trade places with anyone. All the attention we drew only added to our self-esteem. We were arrogant and contemptuous, we were King Shits of the highest order—and we played the part for all it was worth.

Sure, the locals despised us. That was fine by us, because we didn't like them, either. We were proud of who we were and what we did. Here we were, fighting their war, and they didn't act the least bit grateful. Well, we really didn't give a damn; they'd just better not get in our way.

We were riding in the middle of that two-lane road, going flat out. I scanned the countryside and, as far as I could see, the road was completely free of traffic—so much so that I began to get concerned. Lack of local traffic might indicate that something was up.

Suddenly my peripheral vision picked up a hint of movement. Off to my right a blur had come out of nowhere and was rapidly gaining alongside of us, trying to pass us. For a split second, it startled the hell out of me until I looked down and did a double take. Right below me, passing us by, was a set of wheels that looked exactly like the roadwheels off a tank.

"Where the hell did they come from?" I asked Steele, who was equally stupefied. We turned quickly to see if another tank had appeared out of nowhere behind us. But no, there wasn't any. I was baffled.

The wheels had just passed my side of the tank, still moving faster than we were.

"Who's fuckin' roadwheels are those?" asked John the driver.

They couldn't be our wheels; I was sure of that. There hadn't been the slightest shudder or whimper, nor the slightest change in the ride of the vehicle. No smoke, no audible sound or vibration of any kind. The mysterious set of roadwheels rolled down the road ahead of us.

"Driver. Stop the tank," I suddenly ordered. Then I told Truitt to take my position in the TC's seat while I jumped down off the tank. If nothing else, we could always use an extra set of roadwheels. I yelled to John to get out of the driver's seat and help me pick them up.

I was certain that these orphaned wheels weren't ours. But where else could they have come from? The phantom set had come to rest down off the side of the berm. Waiting for John, I looked back toward the tank. And there, like a grinning kid's missing front tooth, was a large gap where our third set of roadwheels should have been. Our grease fitting, broken for some time and ignored long enough, had finally decided to pay us back for our neglect.

It took three of us to pick up the double set of wheels and haul it up on the back of the tank. We would add it to the list of things that needed repairing during our PM. The timing was uncanny.

ON HALLOWEEN—OCTOBER 31, 1968—President Lyndon Johnson ordered a bombing halt in the naïve hope that North Vietnam would reconsider and possibly curtail its invasion of the South.

It was pitch-black the night of November 1, and I had the night's first watch. As always, our tank was on the western side of Oceanview, sitting on the second highest sand dune inside the perimeter. It was another ordinary watch, on an ordinary night, except that we had been informed of the presidential order restricting offensive action against North Vietnam. The only way it would affect us, we thought, was that we no longer could fire into North Vietnam. It meant we had to curtail our Shoot the Fisherman competition. We had no reason to expect anything would change, aside from Charlie's enjoying unrestricted access to the DMZ. How could we have guessed he was about to rub it in our face?

I was looking into the night for any movement, scanning the sand dunes directly to our west, with Pray for Slack's gun tube pointed in the same direction. Close to midnight, near the end of my watch, something out of the corner of my eye caught my attention. I turned my head to the right, looking almost northeast, toward North Vietnam's darkened coastline.

What I saw, several miles north of the DMZ, was so bizarre and fantastic that at first I couldn't believe my eyes. Since the war started, no one had witnessed anything like this. Coming straight down the coastline toward me was a long line of lights. Once I realized they must be headlights, I muttered "Holy shit!" out loud.

Then came a complete mental disconnect. For, if they really were headlights, all of us were dead men—maybe not tonight, but very soon.

The rest of the crew, unable to sleep, was suddenly standing next to the turret alongside me, wondering what had me so excited.

"You see something, TC?" Steele asked.

Borrowing my binoculars, it took him a while to reach the same conclusion. We were looking at an endless freeway of trucks driving due south, right down the beach.

"Those little bastards!" I said through clenched teeth. "They had the nerve to turn on their lights!"

The NVA knew we couldn't shoot at them, so there they were, driving boldly down the coast. None of us could believe—wanted to believe—they were so bold as to turn on the headlights of a goddamn convoy of trucks. Until now, Charlie wouldn't so much as smoke a cigarette at night. The sheer gall he was exhibiting really fried us.

And so we sat, wide awake, unable to take our eyes off the lights, staring at the potential death sentence driving straight toward us, our hands tied by presidential edict. Our lives hadn't even been considered. With a stroke of his pen, LBJ had prevented us from defending ourselves until that convoy crossed the DMZ. For those of us standing there helplessly, that southern migration became the single most demoralizing sight of the war, and this was only the first of many nights to come. We felt sick to our stomachs with desperation; we knew that our own country had sold us out.

Up until now we all felt the war was winnable if we were allowed to fight it. Tet and Mini-Tet had been huge victories for the U.S. forces. We felt we were seeing the first glimmers of the proverbial light at the end of the tunnel.

As we stood there, our eyes fixed north, we realized that our country had turned its back on us. We were not even a consideration in the minds of the politicians, particularly the president and his idiot secretary of defense. In their eyes, we were expendable. It's hard to describe how it felt to suddenly realize that we were simply pawns in a politician's war, not even permitted to defend ourselves.

That night, we became totally disillusioned with what was being asked of us. As Steele, Truitt, John, and I watched the distant truck lights heading ever nearer, one thing became very clear—in that moment, America lost the war.

We all sat up late, talking and trying to come to grips with finding ourselves in a unilateral truce while the enemy stockpiled munitions with no fear of retribution. Every one of us, from the lowliest buck private on up the ranks, knew how to end the war: unleash American air power to bomb real targets. Reduce Hanoi and Haiphong to rubble.

The next morning, we saw a huge North Vietnamese flag flying on the north side of the DMZ. They were cocksure that we wouldn't fire at them, because they knew that we good guys played by the rules.

After that night, my job became more difficult, because suddenly my crews had different motives entirely for carrying out their mission. In their minds, the question had shifted from willingness to win the war to simply staying alive until their tours of duty ended. For Marines in the field, the unspoken aim became to risk little and do the minimum to get by. Personal goals suddenly superseded those of Corps and country. Even TCs were less willing to expose themselves, which hindered their close cooperation with the grunts.

What was the use? Our country had sold us out.

NINE DAYS LATER WE KNEW the Corps hadn't sold us out. There was only one day in a year when a Marine in the field could expect a hot meal—November 10. No matter where a Marine was in the world, even on the loneliest and most remote Vietnamese mountaintop, he was assured that a hot turkey dinner would find him. November 10 is the Marine Corps' birthday and the single most important day on the Marine Corps calendar.

A chilly November 10 morning found me at Oceanview, miles north of the nearest mess hall. But true to tradition, two amtracs made the run up the beach to bring the tiny outpost contingent our turkey dinners. It would have been unthinkable for our fellow Marines to do less. Semper Fi!

Chapter 13

Life's Certain Flavor

It was a cold, damp, foggy morning on the DMZ, a far cry from the blistering heat and rice paddies that America witnessed on TV. To those watching the TV war back in The World, Vietnam was either rice paddies or tropical jungles, and the enemy wore black pajamas and hid in tunnels. And, of course, there was the weekly body count—Charlie's and ours. But this was northern I Corps, where both the weather and the fighting were different than everywhere else in The Nam.

Late 1968 was the bloodiest period of the Vietnam War, and we were still on the Z, the scene of countless, nameless bloody engagements. The Demilitarized Zone was a strip of land no more than a mile wide, devoid of trees and scarred with bomb craters—some deep enough to swallow the tank I commanded.

That chilly morning found us on a road leading directly north to one of the Z's most infamous Marine positions. Con Thien was two small knolls surrounded by a couple of rows of razor wire and interlaced with mines and trip flares. The perimeter was made up of interconnected bunkers. Stacked on their roofs were layer upon layer of sandbags, and each one was supported by any and every kind of material that could be scrounged up.

The long road up to Con Thien was straight and red in color. Eerily, for two hundred meters on either side, lay complete desolation. Large bulldozers called Rome plows had flattened swathes parallel to the road. My first reaction was relief—the sanitized area would make it harder for Mr. Charles to mount an ambush. But it was the second impression that was the lasting one: apprehension. If this road could speak, I was certain it could tell only of heartache. We were en route to one of the most notorious Marine positions on the Z.

Up here on the border between North and South Vietnam, northern I Corps was waging a conventional land war, similar to combat seen in World War II.

The year before, Con Thien had been routinely hit by 1,200 artillery shells a day from the other side of the DMZ, and it still took a sporadic pounding. It was as bad a place as you could go in The Nam. In fact, living there was so inimical to its inhabitants' mental health that Marine units were usually rotated out every two weeks. Hence the purpose for our drive up the road that misty morning.

Both tanks in my section were prepared to escort a column of trucks up to Con Thien. Tanks never operated alone. This was to ensure that if one gets mired in soft ground, a large enough tow vehicle was available. But, more importantly, a second tank could scratch your back in case the enemy overran you and brush off enemy infantry from one another, à la Allen Brook.

A tank platoon consisted of five tanks, divided into two sections, a "heavy" section of three tanks, and a "light" section comprised of the remaining two. Normally, the platoon leader was a lieutenant and he controlled the heavy section. A staff sergeant was the platoon sergeant and he commanded the light section. But that was according to the book, and like so many other rules in The Nam, these applied only in an ideal world, which sure wasn't here.

Traveling up the road to Con Thien that morning was a heavy section of tanks with me, a corporal, as tank commander and section leader. On this day I was the heavy section leader when a third tank joined our convoy.

In Vietnamese, *Con Thien* means "place where angels dwell," an appropriate name for one of the unhealthiest couple of acres in the entire country. My tanks were to provide security for a convoy of trucks loaded with a company of grunts from the 1st Battalion, 9th Marines, 1/9.

When I first learned I was to escort troops from 1/9, I exclaimed, "Jesus H. Christ!" I had heard way too much about these guys; every Marine in Vietnam knew about 1/9.

Tanks were never permanently assigned to any one grunt unit. We were constantly moved around to provide support for any infantry unit that needed us. Each grunt unit had its own individual peculiarities and personalities, but 1/9 suffered the worst reputation of all. Some would have considered it a death sentence upon receiving orders to work with 1/9. It meant you were going to see a lot of shit.

One-Nine was one of the oldest American units in Vietnam, a top-notch fighting unit with emphasis on fighting. It established a legacy known to every Marine in Vietnam. Theirs was a battalion infamous for its numerous desperate actions and last-ditch stands, a unit that continually found itself outnumbered, outgunned, and always in the thick of things. The near-legendary battalion had earned itself a nick-name, something not easy in the Corps: One-Nine was known as the Walking Dead.

THE ROAD CLIMBED SLOWLY IN FRONT OF US. We could barely make out the smudge on the horizon, at the end of the long road to Con Thien, which was about three or four klicks due north. Its nasty reputation had us feeling as if we were traveling up the road to Hell, if such were possible. The tree lines that had been bulldozed back seemed to converge in the distance, making the road appear like a funnel.

This was my first trip to the combat base, and I was quite apprehensive and curious. I placed two of my tanks in the lead of a column of half a dozen deuce-and-a-half trucks, which were trailed by the third tank. Our greatest fear was hitting a random mine and becoming stalled in the open.

Pray for Slack was second in the column, which might sound like an advantage; it's logical to think that we were in the safer position. That would be so in the case of an ordinary mine. But in the event of an ambush, the second vehicle in any column—be it truck or tank—was in the most dangerous position. The North Vietnamese standard operating procedure was to let the first vehicle go by, then immobilize the second. They often initiated ambushes by detonating a mine manually, at a time of their choosing—and Charlie always chose the second vehicle in a convoy. The detonation was the signal for the enemy to open fire, often with an onslaught of RPGs aimed at the last vehicle in the column.

Knocking out the last vehicle trapped the column between two immovable wrecks. This isolated the lead vehicle—which they could deal with later. For all but the worst NVA marksmen, trucks in the middle of the sandwich were easy pickings. Those concerns justified the efforts to roll back the vegetation on either side of the road.

You might make it without incident to the isolated, besieged combat base, but then you had the next two weeks to worry about traveling back down that road. Con Thien had a nickname earned at the height of the siege a year earlier—The Meat Grinder.

My lead tanks had their gun tubes facing in opposite directions, toward the tree lines on the left and right sides of the road. The last tank's gun was pointed to the rear. All the trucks were lined with sandbags and the grunts were hunkered down, with their M16s pointing out over the sides. Each of us was making the same silent prayer: God, please get us through this. To keep your sanity you always had to convince yourself the other guy was going to get it, or else you would become ineffective, even incapacitated. You secretly hoped that it would be another truck or tank that got it, not yours.

We were on what was called a Rough Rider—an all-out, balls-to-the-wall, nonstop race up the driveway to our new home. This was the only part of the journey I looked forward to because we only rarely got the chance to rev up our engines to full speed and go off hell-bent.

The synthetic wind made our faces feel even colder. I scanned the tree lines while I continually glanced at the lead tank as well as the convoy behind me—to make sure no one was straggling. I also had to monitor the radios. Occasionally I touched base with the tank at the very rear of our column, to ask how he was doing and if we needed to slow down. I also monitored the infantry CO, who was hunkered down in one of the trucks behind me.

I also had to continually update my location on the map in my left hand. In a place like this, a map could spell the difference between life and death. If we ran into an ambush with no map I would have a hard time summoning artillery support. In this case, the artillery was several miles away, at a Marine fire base called the Rock Pile. The TC was one very busy man.

We made it to Con Thien without incident. As the lead tank approached, a few of the inhabitants pulled aside a razor-wire barrier to allow us to enter the base.

As we passed through the wire, I saw a hand-painted sign that said, WELCOME TO CON THIEN, PLACE WHERE ANGELS DWELL.

Directly beneath that was a phrase that struck me then and stays with me to this day: For those who must fight for it, life has a certain flavor the protected will never know.

That sign lifted me out of the doldrums. It was so right! It did indeed feel great to be alive. I decided at that moment it was to become part of my life.

THE ENTIRE CONVOY PULLED INTO the infamous combat base. I removed my comm helmet and took a minute to look around, to take it all in, and to locate the command post. Very little, if anything, protruded above ground. With its grim appearance, this didn't look like any base I had ever seen.

According to the map, the base was made up of two "hills"—an over-generous term for those small connected knolls. Even from the top of them looking north, the advantage to the defender was barely percep-tible. But turn around and look southward, and it became immediately obvious why we were here: You could see all the way back to Dong Ha. Allowing the enemy such an advantageous position would have made life in Dong Ha untenable. A single enemy artillery observer could precisely call in artillery fire over the entire area.

I found it a little disconcerting that Con Thien sat in the open on an exposed plain, covered with scrub growth and scarred by shell craters. Comparing it to a moonscape would be a cliché. But given that there were lots and lots of overlapping shell craters, I can think of no better description. Then I saw that some of the shell craters had craters! This place was even worse than I had expected; it was our "turn in the barrel," as a tour in Con Thien was known.

There wasn't a lot to see, just the tops of sandbagged bunkers peeking about two feet above the ground. Only a few men were visible; the rest opted not to leave their burrows. Residents' heads popped up randomly here and there, then dropped back down. Those I did see all wore genuine smiles. Then it dawned on me: These guys were happy to see us because they would be turning Con Thien over to the guys we had just escorted up into the base. Tomorrow morning, they would return to a safer base.

I divided up our tanks and proceeded to relieve the three tanks that were located up there; they would escort the convoy on its return trip. Con Thien was going to be our home for the next two weeks. Each tank was in what was called hull defilade—positioned in a bulldozed revetment or slot that left only its turret exposed above ground level. I placed my tank on the perimeter's northwest corner. On either side of the tank, the grunts had bunkers with roofs amalgamated from whatever was lying around—ammo crates, runway matting, old stretcher poles, and stray pieces of corrugated roofing material, all covered with at least five layers of sandbags.

If the tanks exchanging positions disturbed the grunts, we never knew it. Nobody even bothered to come out and look. Soon we realized that nothing seemed to faze these guys. There was none of the usual grab-assing and kidding that went on between two Marine units as they mingled together. All these men looked worn. Some had hollow, deep-set eyes that were almost lifeless.

It was my first sight of something I had only heard about, the thousand-yard stare, which was symptomatic in troops who were wound long past tight. It took a lengthy process to produce it; it didn't just happen during a two-week stint at Con Thien. Probably it was the result of being on the Z for too long, with no break from the strains and stresses of constant incoming, patrolling, and firefights. Also contributing to these symptoms could have been who they were—the Walking Dead.

As section leader, my job required that I break Axiom Number Two. I couldn't possibly stay permanently fixed to the vehicle, any more than had Staff Sergeant Embesi during Allen Brook. I had to get off the tank for direct face-to-face contact with the infantry CO—who was always a Marine officer—as well as to attend briefings. Those briefings, I found, meant endless questions about tanks' capabilities and limitations from a usually uninformed, uninitiated grunt officer.

Some officers had absolutely no experience with armor and thus brought with them lots of preconceived notions, most of them fallacious. Most common was the idea that to save their troops from the heat and labor of carrying heavy loads, they could let them ride on the tanks during an operation. Likewise, some officers couldn't distance themselves far enough from tanks. The Marine Corps was going through officers so fast they often received limited training, forcing them to learn in the field what they had missed in the States. I had to become a salesman and technical adviser, but I rather enjoyed the role. I liked the respect they had for my knowledge, even if I was only a corporal.

I had to sell them on the mutual advantages of combined tank-infantry support. Also, I had to explain that tanks weren't as impervious as they might think, and warn them not to let their men bunch up behind our tanks—a common but understandable reaction during a firefight. The danger was that if we couldn't maneuver, Charlie could easily overrun us. I had to convince them that we needed to work together as an integrated team, as well as dispel their fear that tanks drew too much fire.

Tanks did, of course, draw fire. But seldom did grunts realize the plus side of misdirected enemy fire: It was no longer directed at them. My obvious, everyday responsibilities also included provisioning food and ammo for two tanks and their crews, plus maintaining each vehicle. But during the few seconds of a firefight, not fulfilling the crucial responsibility of making the right decisions could prove fatal.

THAT FIRST NIGHT AT CON THIEN, our convoy's arrival had swollen the defending force to almost twice its normal size, so our chances of being assaulted were very slim. I was glad we didn't have to go back down that road right away. I needed two weeks to gear up for that return trip.

I was assigned to a night fire mission. I was provided with map coordinates at which the CO wanted us to pump five rounds of harassment and interdiction (H&I) fire at an area the NVA used for troop movement. H&I was our way of keeping Mr. Charles on his toes by not surrendering the night on a platter.

I set the azimuth and elevation settings that represented the intended target on the main gun. The target was a trail intersection that lay to the northwest of our location, within South Vietnam. We were all well aware of the presidential ceasefire; it had been in effect for several weeks. It was really directed at halting aerial bombing of the North by our Air Force and Navy, but it also forbade us to engage enemy units across the DMZ.

The frustration of watching our enemy build up his matériel while being denied the right to protect ourselves prompted some personal action on my part. I had become a short-timer, with only a few months left in this crazy country. Back in The World, the threat of being sent to Vietnam was commonly used to keep servicemen in line. But that intimidation didn't work over here anymore. Anyone caught in trouble simply had to ask, "So what are they gonna do? Send me to Vietnam?"

At this late stage of my tour, I felt I could definitely afford to get a little cocky. That night, I decided to take out my frustrations by defying the lunacy of the entire war.

The fire mission called for a five-round "killing cross" of H&I fire at 2 a.m. Determined not to waste the rounds south of the DMZ, I swiveled the gun 40 degrees more to the right and then elevated it to maximum. Five rounds were about to travel several miles north, into North Vietnam.

Whenever we were about to fire at night, I made it a habit of warning the grunts nearby to cover their eyes. Now, should anyone be watching, they wouldn't be the wiser because the accompanying muzzle flash would ruin their night vision. They would know the gun had fired, but I was betting that no one would notice the gun's new orientation.

When 2 a.m. rolled around, Steele and I discharged all five rounds in less than fifteen seconds. We were feeling pretty satisfied at doing our little part to piss off Charlie. The fact was, I really didn't care about this goddamned war anymore. We had been made expendable by the Johnson administration.

I had grandiose dreams that we might have hit some hidden ammo dump that would light up the North Vietnamese horizon. If caught, I even had ready my standard I Corps retort—"I'm already in Vietnam, what are you going to do, put me on the DMZ?"

A voice called out from the dark: "The guy in charge of the tank report to the CO," meaning Con Thien's ranking officer. Oh shit! I thought. Somebody must have seen what I had done. Nervously I jumped down off the tank, map in hand.

When I approached the speaker, my fears were realized. There stood a Marine captain, both fists on his hips. I was somewhat surprised—I hadn't thought officers stayed up this late.

"Were you the one responsible for that?" he asked.

"Do you mean the fire mission, sir?" I replied. "Five rounds H&I fire in a killing cross, at these coordinates?" I lied as I pointed at the map.

"Don't get smart with me, corporal. That fire mission went due north."

I maintained my innocence. I gave him my best impression of a choirboy. "What do you mean, sir?"

"You know damn well what I mean! You defied the bombing halt."

"Sir, here are the coordinates we set up for and fired on. Could the muzzle flash have distorted your perspective, sir? It's not uncommon to be fooled at night, sir. We see it happen all the time."

"If this were any other place," he said, "I'd run you up on charges and have your ass court-martialed and thrown in the brig! Get out of my face before I decide to."

I saluted, gave him the only answer a Marine can say to a direct order: "Aye-aye, sir!"

As I turned away, I heard him say, under his breath, "I hope you hit something." Obviously, he was just as frustrated as the rest of us with our president. I was off the hook.

It was the only time I ever lied in the Marine Corps.

Chapter 14

The Steel Ghost

The war along the DMZ was unlike anywhere else in Vietnam and rarely covered by the media. Of the few who risked getting the Marines' story on the Z, only two photojournalists come to mind: David Douglas Duncan and Larry Burrows, who lived with the Marines at Cua Viet, Khe Sanh, and Con Thien.

Duncan is best remembered for his photo essays of Pablo Picasso at home and in his studio in France, but he and Burrows admirably captured the living and dying going on in northern I Corps. Years later, after I became a photographer, I wished that I had met them. Their photographs of Marines in combat were some of the best of the war.

The American public was so inundated with footage of Vietnam's lowlands, rivers, and rice paddies that the sight of mountains surrounded by cold, damp fog would have seemed foreign to them. Many parts of the DMZ were rolling hills of low scrub and tree lines, with terrain not too dissimilar to that of upstate New York.

It was good tank country. There were few rice paddies to bog down in, and no villages and civilians to worry about. The DMZ didn't hold to the same rules of engagement that we ran into down south. It was open season all year around, at least until the bombing halt.

241

Up north, what made Mr. Charles so effective was his direct artillery support. Down south, he simply harassed us with mortars or the occasional 122mm rocket. Up north, however, the NVA just didn't nip at your heels, they grabbed your leg like a pit bull with rabies. They could call in 130mm and 152mm Soviet artillery pieces, hidden in caves just across the DMZ, away from the prying eyes of U.S. aircraft. Once locked in a fight with Mr. Charles, you could expect to receive incoming, for they had artillery spotters with their grunt units, the same as we did, who called on artillery for support, just as ours did. After the first incoming round of NVA artillery, you could watch each subsequent explosion move closer, as their spotter corrected their aim. This was conventional warfare, on a scale not seen anywhere else in The Nam.

A year earlier, Mr. Charles had shown just how well equipped he was by attacking Con Thien with flamethrowers and almost overrunning the base. Also, there was the incident while we were refueling at Cua Viet, when two NVA bodies washed up on shore, wearing wet suits, fins, masks, SCUBA equipment, diver's weights, and satchel charges. They had fallen victim to the occasional random hand grenade, thrown in the water at night to deter enemy swimmers.

Later on, we saw a battalion-sized unit out in the open only three klicks away. We couldn't tell if they were "theirs" or "ours," so we called in the sighting to make sure it wasn't a friendly Marines unit, then waited an eternity for division HQ to give us permission to fire. This was a part of the war that America rarely saw over the dinner table.

Dawn and dusk were slow to develop; they were the longest parts of the day, and also, the most common times for the NVA to attack. When on an operation in the field, I always had the entire crew up at the first hint of dawn. Tonight, though, we were inside the confines of Con Thien, whose population had been doubled with our arrival. Mr. Charles wouldn't be dumb enough to attack tonight; he would wait until tomorrow, when the garrison was back to its regular strength.

Once morning broke, the LPs began coming in from beyond the perimeter. I admired the guys who spent their night alone outside the wire, with nothing but a radio and a rifle between them and the garrison. They drifted in through the wire, and slowly the rest of the combat base started to come alive. At least half the Marines anticipated they would be leaving in a few hours.

This was the morning when the usual biweekly rotation routine was deliberately broken. The grunts who thought they were about to be relieved soon found out that something else was in the wind. The CO asked for a bunch of men—all platoon leaders, supporting arms commanders, the forward air controller, the air and naval gunfire people, and me—the tank section leader—to report to the CP immediately.

Instead of the return to the rear they had earned, those who had already served their two weeks in the barrel were being sent on a search-and-destroy mission into the DMZ. My worst fear—an operation with 1/9—was suddenly thrust upon us. Worse still, we would be going into an area that was notoriously hot.

We thought LBJ was pretty damned naïve to think his bombing halt would bring the North Vietnamese to the peace table. Now, with complete immunity from air attacks, the NVA enjoyed free access to the river that separated the two Vietnams. Charlie never stopped walking, digging, humping, and planning his ultimate outcome of total victory. If our government had the same resolution to win, the war would have been over by late 1968.

No one in his right mind wanted to go into the DMZ. There was no telling what we would run up against. At Ocenview we could see the NVA trucking their equipment and material south every night. Eventually it would find its way across the DMZ, and we would be its victims. We couldn't let North Vietnam build up its forces on our side of the river, or else Con Thien and all the other little bases strung along the Z might be overrun. So this morning we had orders to move north and find out what our little friends were up to.

Understandably, lots of bitching and moaning was heard from the bunkers surrounding the perimeter, from Marines who thought they were about to ride out of there. The word was given: "Mount up!" With that command, a mass of grumbling Marines in full battle gear began emerging from their burrows in the ground. Con Thien suddenly looked like a giant anthill under attack.

A semblance of two infantry companies formed up, with a single platoon in the lead. The grunt platoons assembled into a wedge formation, with us behind them in a similar configuration. It was the strongest formation to be in, but it still allowed for flexibility if the shit hit the fan. We exited the base and proceeded straight north.

We all hoped this deliberate break from our normal two-week rotation pattern might surprise the NVA and catch them off balance. In The Nam, one thing you never wanted to do was slip into a routine, because routine was what Charlie looked for most of all. For all we knew, that rotation change might have saved the usual returning southbound convoy from getting ambushed, but I'd much rather have gone back down that road and taken my chances.

The tanks stayed about a hundred feet behind the grunts, with a platoon of infantry covering the rear. We'd crossed into the Z, a no man's land of craters, fresh and old, some small and others big enough to lose a tank in. We were approaching the Ben Hai River, which nominally separated the two Vietnams, when the grunts stumbled on several camouflaged gun pits, complete with ammunition for their Soviet-made 130mm artillery pieces. As we knew they would, the NVA had taken advantage of our bombing halt to move their artillery across the river. We found everything but the guns themselves. That meant it was only a matter of time before Mr. Charles crossed the river, too. Thanks, Mr. President.

We set up a perimeter while the engineers destroyed the gun pits and their ammo. We continued the sweep in the early afternoon anticipating that the NVA would make a stand to protect their supplies. We were passing through a tree line when one TC reported seeing tracks that didn't belong to any U.S. tracked vehicle. Northern I Corps had reports that the NVA were operating tanks, but so far no one had seen any. Nevertheless, the threat was taken so very seriously that, just in case, our tank's ammunition ready rack was loaded with three HEAT rounds. Down south, we had only carried a few that were squirreled away in hard-to-reach ammo racks for use against rare hardened enemy bunkers.

Just as we began to enter a tree line—always a precarious time—something past the trees caught my attention in the field beyond. It looked like another tank. I shot a quick look at my own two tanks, just to make sure one of them hadn't gotten ahead of us, but none had.

The last thing a tanker wanted to run across was an enemy tank, so my adrenaline was pumping. For an instant, I thought that this would be the first tank-to-tank shootout of the war.

"Gunner. HEAT. Tank!" I yelled over the intercom.

John immediately stopped the tank. I grabbed the override control and quickly swung the turret so that the gunner could acquire the target.

"Identified!" Truitt shouted.

My heart rose in my throat as I dropped down to use the rangefinder that would feed the distance into our computer. Steele had already loaded a HEAT round into the main gun, and the breech slammed shut with a resounding ka-chung!

This whole complex ballet took place in about seven seconds, in a space no larger than the smallest of bathrooms with a five-foot ceiling. We were a second away from Truitt warning the rest of the crew that he was about to fire when I realized the target was an M48—one of ours! My God, we were about to pump a 4,400-foot-per-second HEAT round into another Marine tank!

How was that possible? I quickly checked my other tanks. Were they all where they ought to be?

"Up!" the loader yelled.

"Cease fire! Cease fire!" I screamed over the intercom an instant before Truitt would have squeezed the triggers. Getting on the radios, I warned the other tanks not to fire on the friendly. The two other tank commanders were gazing back at me, as confused as I was.

In front of me stood a Marine tank, its gun tube pointed almost right at us. It was the second time I had seen such a tank, the first being on the docks of Da Nang, back when I first arrived in-country. This tank, too, was empty—the victim of an earlier fight, its crew incinerated when an RPG set off its main gun ammo. Tank ammunition doesn't explode, as you might expect; it burns like a giant blowtorch. Twenty-foot jets of flame, like the exhaust from a jet fighter, shoot out of the tank commander's and loader's hatches, and from around the base of the turret. No one could survive such an unlucky hit; the crew would have been vaporized.

We Marines always prided ourselves on coming out with all our equipment. I had never heard of a tank being abandoned and left behind without being destroyed. Totally unprepared for this ominous sign, we rode closer to the vehicle. The grunts seemed to pay no attention to the dead beast, as if they had seen it many times before. It had never occurred to them to warn us.

But for us, the war and all our frailties suddenly struck home. Realizing our own unavoidable vulnerability had a chilling effect. We desperately wanted to know its history. Who had the crew been? How did they get hit from the side? Were they overrun?

There was one final question in our minds: Were we all going to end up the same way? Suddenly, the other TCs hunkered down in their cupolas, their eyes just above the steel rims. But no one said anything. We just stared at the tank. We left it behind to continue its solitary vigil, a Flying Dutchman on the plains of the DMZ.

Chapter 15

Apricots

The rest of our search-and-destroy mission passed without incident. But as late afternoon came on, it became obvious that we weren't going back to Con Thien. We would spend the night in Indian country, alone.

That night, the infantry COs directed me to set the tanks in position like covered wagons, in a circular or "laager" formation, dispersed equally around the infantry's perimeter. Listening posts went out after sunset. There was no wire between us and the night, no revetments for the tanks to lower their silhouettes. We were as exposed as tanks could be. The only thing standing between us and Mr. Charles were a few Claymore mines and some trip flares.

Back when I first arrived at 3rd Tank Battalion from Da Nang, there were many things I had to learn and adjust to. First was the obvious difference in the kind of war being waged along the DMZ—up north, the terrain was totally different, far more hospitable to tanks. Due to the sparse population of northern I Corps, there were no villages to support local Viet Cong units. Here, mixing it up with the enemy meant encountering only hardcore NVA regulars, who had their own artillery support.

But what really surprised me were the strange superstitions shared by the Marines up north.

Superstitions varied from unit to unit. Sometimes they changed with the dictates of the moment. Nonetheless, they were taken very seriously, as I was about to find out.

Once we had circled the wagons, the tank crews got busy going over the guns, checking fluid levels in the engines and transmissions, and grabbing boxes of cold C rats for dinner. I wanted to avoid surprises the next morning, so I walked around our tank, carefully inspecting every component of both tracks. Another crewman checked on the water levels in the batteries and topped them off. Then I visited the other TCs and looked at their positions. The Steel Ghost took up most of our conversation; it had gotten to the others, too.

When I returned from the meeting, I noticed that my gunner was carrying a track block he had borrowed from one of the other tanks. He threw it up onto our tank, then immediately turned back to get another one.

I was alarmed. Had somebody seen something I had missed? I was afraid one of the crew had spotted a damaged piece of track and was about to replace it. This wasn't the time or place to break track with night coming on. The process was like changing a link in a very large chain. With so little light remaining, it was the last thing I wanted to do. Breaking track was a laborious job that would have us working in the dark, making lots of noise with sledgehammers and wrenches. That wouldn't endear us to the grunts.

I yelled up to Bob Steele and John, "What's wrong with the track?" They shrugged their shoulders, but I heard Bob Truitt's voice behind me.

"Just gettin' some spare track, TC." He was carrying another track block, which he threw up beside the first one.

"Why the extra track blocks?" I demanded.

"Nothing's wrong, TC," said Truitt, "I just wanted to borrow some blocks."

I told him to go back and help the crew with the maintenance work before it got dark.

"Can I make one more trip? I'll be right back to help out." I let him go.

Every fighting man had his own philosophy about death, which was referred to by any number of euphemisms. A deceased Marine variously "got greased," "got wasted," "bought it," "got hit with a bullet with his name on it," "went to the big tank park in the sky," or "his time was up." Death was always analyzed or rationalized to fit the philosophy of the living—who generally fell into two categories: fatalists and determinists.

Determinists believed that some giant cosmic clock ticked off every predetermined minute of one's life. To them, it explained why some men in a firefight could be totally reckless, exposing themselves to enemy fire, and never get hit. Somebody else could be totally safe in a foxhole, only to have a mortar round fall in his lap. There might be no logic to it, but determinists accepted it as simply preordained: When your time was up, your time was up. Even though determinists liked to think that death was predetermined, I never saw anyone stand up in the middle of a firefight to prove his theory to the rest of us.

The fatalist held that such occurrences were sheer happenstance, a fall of the dice or a spin of the wheel. The key difference between him and the determinist was that the fatalist thought he could load the dice or cheat the wheel—improve his odds by avoiding unnecessary risks and taking reasonable precautions.

Me, I was solidly in the fatalist's camp and would do anything to minimize risk. I stayed low in the TC's cupola, wouldn't smoke on watch, wouldn't sky-mount a machine gun on top of my cupola.

This later modification was popular with 1st Tank Battalion, down south. But with the large-caliber artillery at Charlie's disposal up on the Z, it was totally out of the question. I hung spare sections of track on my side of the turret, as did most tank crews, thinking they would make it harder for an RPG to penetrate. Even though I had seen an RPG go quite handily through twelve inches of steel, the extra layer of track lent a false sense of protection and made my fellow fatalists and me feel better. Rumor had it that a track block had saved an unknown tanker—once, years ago—but that was all the evidence a fatalist needed.

John, our driver, was a fatalist too. To put more distance between himself and an RPG, we had had brackets welded to the tank's front that allowed sandbags to be stacked tightly on the front slope plate. Bob Steele, my loader and fellow fatalist, hung extra track block all across his side of the turret.

Our gunner was the lone determinist of the crew. His philosophy was that if it was your turn to go, there was nothing you could do about it. But tonight Truitt was on a personal mission, going from tank to tank borrowing spare track blocks. How come? I wondered.

When he returned to the tank to add to his track block collection, all the work had been completed. The rest of us were opening a box of C rats. What we witnessed next was a miraculous conversion, a change in faith that was as significant as Jesus leaving Judaism. Our gunner skipped dinner to bolt track blocks to his side of the turret.

No man enrolls in a new school of thought on a whim. Something had gotten to Truitt, something powerful enough to cause him to rethink his entire philosophy. We had always argued over which philosophy was the right one, each of us providing examples to prove whichever theory we adhered to. The gunner might as well have just enlisted with Mr. Charles, his conversion was that significant. The enormous amount of kidding he would take from us determinists had to weigh in his decision. When asked why he was hanging the track block, he gave no reason except "I just felt like doing it."

"You just felt like it, Mister-when-your-time-is-up-it's-up?"

"Well," he answered, "it can't hurt nothing to try, right?"

As John and I ate our C's, we sat on the warm armor plate that covered the engine on the back of the tank, deliberately keeping the turret between us and would-be snipers. Loader Steele ate while standing in the TC's position keeping an eye out in front of us. We three talked among ourselves, wondering just what had gotten into our gunner that outweighed even hunger. As we replayed the day's events, the answer became obvious: The Steel Ghost must have really spooked him.

When I first met my crew after being assigned as their tank commander, I quickly became aware that they lived by an unfamiliar system of local superstitions. The first time I broke open a case of C rations, I saw that someone had already rifled through all twelve boxes that make up a case, and one of the meals was missing. When I confronted the crew, Bob Steele readily admitted to going through them. I asked why all the boxes had been opened and why we were missing a meal. He just shrugged and looked at his feet, like a kid caught with his fingers in the cookie jar. I thought he had been highly inconsiderate of his fellow crewmen and told him so.

"We always go through a new case of C rats to find the ham and motherfuckers," he replied.

"And do what with them?"

"Throw 'em away," he said.

I reprimanded him again for his lack of concern for his fellow crewmen. Yes, motherfuckers was the worst meal in the case and everyone despised it, but Steele had thrown out the entire meal, together with the can of cheese and crackers, mini-pack of cigarettes, and—the best part of the meal—a can of apricots. Everybody loved their sweet syrup.

Or so I thought.

Truitt came to Steele's defense, "Motherfuckers is the dead man's meal."

"What are you talking about?" I frowned.

"Nobody eats ham and mothers up here on the Z."

"No shit!" I replied. "Nobody eats that meal anywhere in The Nam! But I'll be damned if you're going to throw away a perfectly good can of fruit!"

Then John jumped in. "You don't get it, do you? It's the fruit that's the fuckin' problem!"

Had I inherited a crew of lunatics? "What the fuck're you talking about?" I asked.

The crew suddenly came together on top of the armor plate to confront me, three against one.

"No one on this tank eats apricots," proclaimed my loader. The others nodded in agreement. "I go through the rest of the boxes, just to make sure they ain't got any in them either!"

I couldn't believe what I was hearing. "What the hell is wrong with apricots?" I asked.

"They're bad luck," Steele replied. "Nobody eats them."

"Hell, we don't even touch the can," said Truitt. "That's why we throw away the entire box."

John chimed right in. "Eat a can of apricots, and the guy next to you gets killed—every time!"

The other two crewmen agreed. They were steadfast in their belief and vehement about the power that apricots wielded over the lives of others. This superstition, I later learned, pervaded the entire 3rd Marine Division. Supposedly, the rumor went, it wasn't bad luck for the offender to eat or carry apricots, but it was a death sentence for the guy beside him. The superstition was self-perpetuating, guaranteed to be enforced by the guy next to you.

At the moment, I was convinced my crew was testing me or pulling my leg. "This is bullshit!" I snarled. "You go find that can of fruit you just threw away and return it to the tank! I'll eat them!"

All three crewmen tried to reason with me, over what I thought was about the dumbest thing I ever heard. But they stood their ground, and our argument was about to come to blows. There was no rationalizing with them, so I recalled the old saying, "When in Rome . . ." A cohesive crew was more important than one lousy can of fruit.

I did plead with them to at least drain the juice out of the can before throwing it away. But this very idea was met with a steadfast, "No fuckin' way!"

"Apricots on this tank are totally unacceptable, juice and all!" said John, standing his ground.

"And don't even think about eating them off the tank, either!" Truitt piped in. "Someone eats apricots, the guy next to him gets killed!"

Well, for my crew's overall well-being, I could learn to forego apricots. Their belief was as ingrained as their private religious beliefs—maybe more. So I became a reluctant convert.

THAT HAD ALL TRANSPIRED MONTHS EARLIER, when I first took over the tank. Now we were in the field, north of Con Thien, finishing our apricot-free C rations. Truitt was still bolting on his track blocks while the grunts finished digging their two-man foxholes. To slow down any unwelcome visitors, they had set up trip flares out in front of the perimeter, along with some Claymores. Trip flares were early-warning devices—actually booby traps—that fired off a flare when someone snagged a trip wire stretched across the ground.

When in the field, it was SOP for each tank to have at least two men on watch throughout the night. In case they had to start the tank, the third crewman slept in the driver's seat. Bob Steele and I had the second watch when, off to our right, two voices quickly grew louder and louder. We couldn't see them, nor hear exactly what they were saying, but at midnight, in the middle of the bush, it was totally uncalled for.

Still indistinct, the argument kept increasing in volume. Marines on either side told the boisterous foxhole to shut the fuck up.

"You trying to give away our position?" someone stage-whispered through clenched teeth.

They fell silent after a grunt—their squad leader, I suppose—raced past us, visited the contentious duo for a minute or two, then ran back to his own hole.

I began thinking that this unit's discipline wasn't very good. No wonder they always got hit. Then, after a minute or so, the voices started to argue again. In a loud, clear voice came the first discernible words: "You eat those fuckin' apricots, and I'll kill you!"

"Fuck you and your stupid . . ."

The second voice never got the chance to finish. A sudden flash and the sharp report of a .45 pistol interrupted him. Several feet pounded toward the source of the shot.

Another whispered yell went out into the night. "Corpsman! Corpsman up!"

I could barely make out two Marines leading another away, one on each arm. He was mumbling over and over to himself, "I told him not to eat those fuckin' apricots! I told him, goddamn it!"

With eyes probably the size of ping-pong balls, I looked back at Steele.

"Ah told ya they was serious about apricots up here," he said with a little told-you-so smile.

A medevac was called in on a pitch-black night to save a critically wounded kid who had only wanted some fruit. I never learned what became of his assailant, but I became even more convinced that 1/9 was wired way too tight.

Chapter 16

With the Doggies on the DMZ

Our two-day sweep ended peacefully; we made it back to Con Thien and stayed within the combat base for the next ten days, until another unit arrived to relieve us. We returned uneventfully down the same long road I had so feared two weeks earlier and my two tanks proceeded to return to Oceanview, where we pulled into our old revetment atop of the sand dune.

The South China Sea was our doormat. Sand dunes undulated for miles to the west and north of us and into the DMZ, giving the impression we were Foreign Legionnaires rather than Marines. The little fire base's most prominent feature was the squat wooden tower perched upon the area's highest sand dune. The garrison was alarmingly small for a position that close to North Vietnam. Only a single barrier of razor wire surrounded its perimeter.

Oceanview was two miles north of C-4, the northernmost U.S. position in all of South Vietnam—and the only U.S. position literally on the Z. Oceanview was but a pimple on the ass of the Demilitarized Zone, stuck way north, hanging out there by its lonesome. After our stint with 1/9, somehow the weekly rotation of tanks between C-4 and

Oceanview ceased, and it became almost our permanent home for my remaining months in Vietnam.

Technically, Oceanview wasn't a fire base at all, because it had no artillery there. But we had the largest guns in the world at our beck and call.

WHEN I FIRST ARRIVED I found this little outpost manned by a single Marine rifle platoon of only forty men. I worried what fate had in store for me. Oceanview's other residents included a Navy officer, two Marine ANGLICO (Air-Naval Gunfire Liaison Company) people, and a very small detachment of Force Recon Marines.

Nobody associated with Recon, nor they with us. They even went as far as to rope off their small area with razor wire, thereby isolating themselves even more. These strange men would sneak into North Vietnam for weeks at a time. Often they wore ten-inch long, oblong wire hoops that hung off their belts, strung with what looked like dried prunes. I had no idea until someone clued me in that they were the ears of dead North Vietnamese soldiers.

Supporting this lightly held outpost were my two tanks and a pair of Army Dusters. These Doggie Dusters, as we called them, consisted of dual 40mm antiaircraft guns in an open mount, set on an M41 Walker Bulldog tank chassis.

The M42 Duster's open mount provided little or no protection for the crew—a very undesirable feature in the minds of the tank crews—but as defensive weapons, these little vehicles were worth their weight in gold, one of the factors contributing to our little outpost's very survival. Every evening, just after sunset, the Dusters put on an awesome live-fire display, unleashing their exploding 40mm projectiles into the sand dunes to the west of us. That nightly act of defiance served to de-motivate any would-be attackers outside the wire and was a morale booster for those within.

Intimidating as the Doggie Dusters and our tanks were, the real reason Oceanview wasn't overrun sat offshore from us during the day, and just over the horizon at night. In fact, she was the reason Oceanview and its rickety wooden tower existed at all. During the bombing halt, she sailed down from North Vietnam to sit offshore from us and lobbed shell after shell into the southern half of the Z, the men in the rickety tower directing her gunfire. Oceanview served as the eyes of the world's largest artillery piece on the world's only active-duty battleship. No, it wasn't the Dusters or our tanks that kept Mr. Charles away—it was the battle-ship USS *New Jersey*.

The Jersey was one of those things that can't be described. The only word that comes to mind is "immense." You had to see her, and you had to feel the truly awesome concussion from her guns and projectiles. Her giant guns dwarfed everything in Vietnam—or in the world for that matter. Each of her three huge turrets housed three 16-inch guns, each one able to hurl a 1,900-pound projectile 32,500 meters— or nineteen miles! At night, when she fired a salvo from over the horizon, the reddish glow briefly made it look like the sun was about to rise. We could hear the projectiles as they streaked overhead. Anyone looking carefully could trace their flight, like meteors shooting harmlessly across the night sky.

I was in awe of her size and power. On hot, sultry afternoons, when boredom reached its peak, I would aim our tank's gun at the ship and peer through the gunner's telescope, just to look at her magnificent lines. Thirty years later, I can still see the huge number "62" stenciled on her bow.

One day in late 1968, I received a radio message from my platoon leader, who was back in the safety of the hardened bunkers of C-4. Because I was the section leader and a tank commander, he called to warn me that my two tanks at Oceanview were about to take part in an Army operation that would take place in our tactical area of responsibility (TAOR).

I took that as good news. I hadn't known the Army had any units this far north. But, if so, it was high time they did some of the fighting around here. That afternoon I was summoned to Oceanview's little CP. Inside was the Marine infantry CO, a first lieutenant, with an Army major and several of the major's staff. The Doggie officers all wore crossed sabers on their lapels, indicating that they were from an armored unit.

I was introduced as being from the Marine tanks. The major looked at me in disgust and said, "Corporal, go get your section leader."

"Sir," I said, "I am the section leader."

Having worked with the Doggies before, I knew not to be insulted by the major's remark. Army policy was that if you held the job, you deserved the rank. In the Army, a tank section leader would have been a staff sergeant at least; a mere corporal was only a lowly crewman. Holding a job and receiving the rank that went with it was the only thing I liked about the Army, for the Marine Corps didn't recognize that policy at all.

The major was a little taken back by my response. Shaking his head in disbelief, he went on to review the operation slated for the following morning. Spread out in front of the officers was a map depicting our surrounding area. I listened as the major described how his armored unit would come up the beach at dawn, pass our position, and move into the DMZ. He then indicated on the map where they would begin to move inland across the sand dunes just north of Oceanview.

"Excuse me, sir," I interrupted, "but you can't take tanks in there."

"Corporal," he barked, "when I want your opinion, I'll ask for it! Your job is to sit right where you are and cover our left flank from this outpost," he said, pointing to Oceanview on the map. "You got that?"

Maybe he just didn't realize, I thought. "Sir, you won't get a hundred meters before hitting mines or old shells. That whole area is full of unexploded ordnance."

"You just cover our flank, and leave the war to us!" he said, dressing me down in front of the others, then emphasizing my lowly rank. "If you're through, corporal, may I finish the briefing?"

This smart ass thought he knew more about our TAOR than we did. We had been here for two months, but he knew the area better than us? Yeah, right! Screw you! I thought to myself.

"It's your show, sir," I said, answering his rhetorical question with a melodramatic headshake. Sarcasm always was one of my strongest and least-recognized talents.

After the meeting, I assembled my two crews and gave them the sitrep. I proceeded to unfold my own copy of the same map the major had just used. On it, I diagrammed exactly what I had just been briefed on.

"You gotta be shittin' me!" said the other crew's tank commander. "They'll lose every tank they got!" All the other men shook their heads at the absurd idea of driving tanks over thousands of unexploded bombs and shells, plus countless antitank and antipersonnel mines.

"You know that, and I know that. This could well be the shortest operation we'll ever see," I told both crews, "and we won't even have to leave Oceanview!"

"I hope they don't find an unexploded round from the *New Jersey*," joked one of the crewmen.

"Hey," said another, "if these guys want to clear the Z of mines and spent ordnance, all the better for us!"

I nodded sadly. "They really have no idea what they're in for."

We couldn't wait for the next morning to arrive. The Army would be showing us how to fight the war on the DMZ, and we'd have ringside seats.

I HAD THE LAST WATCH THAT NIGHT. Well into the second hour, the first hint of light began to glow in the eastern sky. Another hour would bring another day, and the outpost would begin to stir.

As the sun began to show itself, I could hear the blowtorch-hiss of burning C4. The men of Oceanview were heating up their morning coffee and cocoa. I was standing in the TC's cupola, eating a can of beans and franks—the most sought-after meal in every case of C's. I had just swallowed my second spoonful when I heard in the distance the faint but distinctive sound of tanks approaching up the beach from the south.

"Here they come!" I yelled to my crew. I got on the radio and alerted my other tank that the Doggies were on their way.

The sound grew louder. Soon it became obvious that substantial numbers of vehicles were approaching. Their noise increased until finally they passed our position, halfway into the surf, the same way we traveled the beach. The ground vibrated as ten tanks and an equal number of APCs (armored personnel carriers) thundered by, each vehicle throwing up a rooster tail of water.

The Army crews waved to us, as if they were out for a sightseeing tour. We could only turn our heads, glance at one another, and look back in amazement as they roared by, going full out. They're going to get a tour, all right, I thought to myself.

We hadn't seen this many armored vehicles in one gathering since leaving the States. It was just like the Army to do everything on a colossal scale—a sledgehammer to kill a mosquito. But there was a hint of envy on all of our minds, for here was armor being used decisively and not in a support role, as we typically were. These vehicles were not encumbered by slow, walking grunts; their grunts were riding on top of the APCs. Unfortunately, this was the wrong place and the wrong war for such foolishness; someone was leading armor as if he was on the plains of Europe.

I called down to my gunner to get me a beer while I pulled out an old ratty lawn chair from the gypsy rack and set it up on the armor plate over the tank's engine. Truitt handed me up a beer, and I gave him my camera. I wanted a photographic record of the hardest operation I'd ever be on—and one that I expected would be the shortest.

Bob Steele, the loader, spread out a blanket and joined me on the back of the tank. I sat in my lawn chair, feet up on the gypsy rack, and beer in hand when Truitt snapped my picture.

As the tail end of the armored column finally passed us, we witnessed a sight that left us totally speechless. The column, which had been heading north into the DMZ, suddenly changed direction without warning. As if on a parade field performing close-order drill, each vehicle made a 90-degree turn to the left, so that the entire column was now moving on line across the Z.

For the second time that morning, the four of us looked at one another, shaking our heads in amazement.

"I don't believe these guys," I said.

"They ain't gonna get far now," said Truitt.

"Charlie will fix their arrogant ass," I told him.

The first explosion occurred some one hundred meters from the ocean's surf or about twenty seconds after their stunning flanking maneuver. A minute later came a second explosion, as one of the tanks tried to come to the aid of the first victim.

The third explosion was smaller, but took out one of the Army crewmen inspecting the damage to his tank. (Secretly, I hoped it was the major.)

The fourth explosion was another antipersonnel mine, stepped on by the Army medic running to aid the wounded man. In three minutes, the Army's armor operation had turned into a cluster fuck.

Our attention was next drawn to the sound of a helicopter approaching over the dunes. It was easy to recognize an Army chopper, thanks to the large red crosses in white squares painted on the bird's sides, belly, and nose. Only the Army troubled to paint its medevacs that way, as if they expected to be granted some immunity from Mr. Charles. Hell, Charlie was an equal-opportunity shooter. Years earlier, we Marines had learned not to bother, a fat red cross on a brilliant white field only helped Charlie to aim.

We had learned three things about the Army: One, they were really good at parade maneuvers; two, they sure could get a medevac in a hurry; and three, as I already knew, they didn't know how to listen.

An hour passed while the Army crews worked on the two damaged tanks, tiptoeing around them in fear of finding more mines. Finally, hours after the mission came to a halt, all twenty vehicles cranked up their engines, came alive again, and moved out—in reverse. They didn't want to risk hitting any more mines by turning around; they hoped to extricate themselves by backing over the tracks they had left coming in. Once back in the surf, they performed another brilliant display of close-order drill, a simultaneous left turn in tandem, and began their full-speed retreat south down the beach.

On this return trip, however, there was no grinning or waving of hands. They ignored the taunting and mocking laughter of Oceanview's two Marine tank crews, as we stood on our armor plate giving them the finger. They wouldn't even turn their heads in our direction. Like dogs with their tails between their legs, they pretended they never saw us as they looked straight ahead. Yeah, that was the day the Army showed us how to fight the war on the DMZ.

Chapter 17

Tiger!

So that our radio messages wouldn't reveal too much to any enemy eavesdropper, the military used code words or phrases. I don't think some of them fooled anybody; they actually described what we were trying to hide better than its actual name would. For example, "fast movers" were jet fighters.

These substitutions were changed only rarely throughout the entire war. Often they became part of our everyday language. "Arc Light," the code name for a B-52 bombing mission, became a universal term throughout Vietnam. Other things were often identified or spelled out by their phonetic alphabet names. Over the radio, it was easy to mix up the many similar-sounding letters like B, C, D, E, and G that all end in an ee sound. Replacing a letter with a word eliminated that problem. The international phonetic alphabet, developed for NATO countries and still in use today, was a set of words that corresponded to each letter of the alphabet.

Often these letter-words became names all by themselves. For example, the four companies in a Marine battalion would be identified by four consecutive letters—A, B, C, and D. But you never called them by their letter-names, as in Bee Company or Dee Company. Instead, you called them by their phonetic alphabet designations: Alpha Company, Bravo Company, Charlie, Delta, Echo, and so on. This practice, universal throughout all the armed services, was an effective way of eliminating errors that could be caused by static, people's accents, and particularly noisy surroundings.

In fact, the phonetic alphabet was responsible for how our Indo-Chinese foe got his nickname. It all began during the late 1950s, when guerrillas calling themselves the Viet Cong first tried to overthrow the South Vietnamese government. American military advisors quickly shortened their name to its initials, VC. Over the radio, though, you wouldn't say "Vee Cee," but instead used the phonetic alphabet equivalent, or "Victor Charlie." Because radio procedure required that words be short and concise, Victor Charlie became simply "Charlie."

As the war progressed from a guerrilla uprising to an all-out invasion from the North, it became necessary to differentiate the local VC from the professional North Vietnamese Army—or NVA—troops. Often, for expediency, we referred to both enemies as "Charlie," but we sometimes called the NVA "Mister Charles" as a sign of respect. Professional courtesy, if you will.

Now that I was up north, I had to get used to a few new terms. Down south around Da Nang, for example, tanks were referred to as "kings" or "beetles" over the radio. Up north, we called them "tigers." Actually I liked the new term better—it was closer to how we really thought of ourselves.

WE RECEIVED ORDERS TO MOVE NORTH of Dong Ha and link up with a grunt unit for a sweep near the Z, somewhere northwest of Con Thien. I was the section leader in charge of three tanks when I got the order to move west on Highway 9 and make contact with a battalion of the 9th Marines.

Hearing that regiment number, I froze. "Which battalion of the Ninth Marines?" I asked. "It's not One-Nine, is it? Anybody but the First!"

In northern I Corps, that was the first question any other normal man would have asked. No one in his right mind wanted to work with the 1/9. But at least the 9th Marine Regiment had three battalions—1st, 2nd, and 3rd, so the odds were two-to-one in my favor. This time, the luck of the draw was with me. "Two-Niner," said the voice over the radio.

We left Dong Ha and drove west past Cam Lo in the direction of the Rock Pile, where we met up with 2/9 and got briefed on the sweep. It was to be a search-and-destroy mission, our main objective being the insertion of two sniper teams during our sweep northeast of the Rock Pile. I'd heard about our Marine sniper teams and their legendary accomplishments of shots farther than 1,000 meters—better than three-fifths of a mile. But until that morning, I never had the chance to meet one.

Each team was made up of two men, the spotter and the shooter. Often they sat for days to wait for a single shot on some unsuspecting North Vietnamese soldier. But sniper teams were one of our best psychological weapons during the war, second only to the B-52 Arc Lights. Imagine the mind-job a good sniper can wreak when the head on the guy next to you explodes—without you hearing a shot! The bullet, traveling faster than sound, arrives before the report from the rifle. Several seconds before the shot is even heard, the body has hit the ground. That would leave a strong impression upon anyone in the vicinity, long after they ducked for cover.

Both of the two-man teams would be riding in on the back of the tanks as we supported the grunts on their search-and-destroy mission. The sweep's covert purpose, however, was to secretly drop—or insert—these two teams as we proceeded onward. At a time of their own choosing, the four men would slip off the back of our tanks and hide in the tall grass. We were to move on without stopping, leaving them behind.

I signaled to the four men approaching the tanks by holding up two fingers and pointing to the tank to my right, and then two fingers again waving them up on the back of Pray for Slack. As the second pair climbed on board, I couldn't help noticing that one of them had stenciled on his helmet, in large black letters, 13¢ KILLERS. Not understanding, I asked him, "What's the thirteen cents for?"

He reached inside his shirt and, from beneath his armpit, pulled out three bullets. "Each one costs Uncle Sam thirteen cents," he said.

"You keep your ammunition under your armpits?" I asked, incredulous.

"Keeps 'em at the same temperature, no matter where you are."

Whoa! I thought to myself. That was really splitting hairs—or did a bullet's temperature make that big of a difference?

The second guy was still on the ground, waiting to climb up on the tank. The aluminum case he carried was five feet long and perhaps four inches thick. I knew a gun case when I saw one, but couldn't fathom why anyone in The Nam would be toting one around. It wasn't like these boys were going out deer hunting.

The first sniper took the case from his partner and sidestepped past the turret with it. His partner climbed up. Working his way over to my side of the turret, he asked if, after the sweep, I wouldn't mind bringing the cases back and leaving them with the grunts.

"No problem," I told him.

I was really surprised to see that this second guy had an M14 slung over his shoulder. He noticed my own M14 hanging from the side of the tank commander's cupola, much like the Winchester on a cowboy's horse, and gave me a thumbs-up to acknowledge that we both knew a good rifle when we saw one.

But I was more fascinated by what kind of surprise was in the aluminum case. "What's in the box?" I asked our new guests.

The team leader set it up on the gypsy rack and lifted the lid proudly, like a surgeon pulling open a drawer to show you his scalpels, then tipped the box to give me a better look. Inside was a Remington Model 700 with a large Redfield telescopic sight. You know how, when a close friend shows you his racy new sports car, you don't ask to drive it until he offers you a spin? This was one of those times. I so wanted to pick it up, but I knew the surgeon wouldn't want his instruments contaminated.

He closed the box and flipped the latches, never offering to let me try it out. "The most cost-effective weapon in the Marine Corps," he said. "One shot, one kill. Thirteen cents."

The regular grunts were ready to move out, and we began the sweep, into an area I had never seen before. The trees and brush began to thin out into tall grass. I constantly scanned the area, checked on my other tanks, and made sure the grunts were well in front of us.

I was looking at the ground when I saw them—tank tracks! They were impressions made in the ground from a vehicle I didn't recognize.

We had yet to see an enemy tank, but all tankers on the DMZ feared meeting one. Whoever shot first would likely be the winner. Reports that they were in the area were taken so seriously that our ready rack had three HEAT rounds in the first three positions, where the loader could reach them the fastest.

I caught the eye of the tank commanders on either side of me, pointed my hand down at the ground, then up to the ridgeline. I keyed my helmet microphone and used the proper code words, "Enemy tiger tracks going up the hill. Be ready, just in case."

We began creeping up a moderately steep ridge. The heads of the grunts in front of us disappeared over the top of ridgeline. I told the loader and gunner to have a HEAT round halfway into the chamber of the main gun and instructed the driver to slow down, creep to the top of the hill, and be ready to stop on my command. I told the other tanks to stop and let me take a gander first: I wanted to scope out the area that was on the other side before driving into a possible ambush. Meanwhile, I wanted my head to be the only thing exposed above the ridgeline. Sitting atop the ridgeline would needlessly silhouette us, making us a juicy target for a would-be NVA tank.

I looked over the rise. The coast seemed clear, but there might be an enemy tiger I didn't see, and I didn't want any single tank of ours to be a lone target. I told the other tanks that we would all crest the ridge-line together—as fast as possible. My last instruction was, "Keep alert and watch out for a possible enemy tiger."

It was the start of a very confusing situation.

All this time, our company CP back in Dong Ha was monitoring our radio conversation. This was standard operating procedure. But because we rarely talked with them, I never gave it much thought.

When we broached the top of the ridgeline, falling away in front of us was an awesomely lush valley. A sea of grass about three feet high was being blown by the wind as if being brushed by an invisible hand. That unbelievably beautiful sight was unlike anything I had ever seen in this miserable country. In this peaceful Eden, there was no place for an enemy tank to hide.

The two sniper teams slid off the back of the tanks, leaving their gun cases behind. We lost sight of them almost immediately, as they melted into the tall grass. I couldn't help but admire and respect those guys. They were the true loners of the Marine Corps, and theirs was the purest form of combat: one man, one rifle, one shot.

"Good luck!" I yelled back, but the noise of the tank's engine drowned out my words. Even if they had heard me, they wouldn't have acknowledged it. This was the most dangerous part of their mission—separating from the main body of troops under the watchful eyes of Mr. Charles. Their life expectancy was directly proportional to the degree of stealth they maintained, and all they wanted to do was disappear.

So as not to be silhouetted on top of the ridgeline, we had stopped fifty meters down from the crest. We were all taking in the view when the grunt CO motioned to me that he wanted to come up on the tank. I waved him toward the front of our tank, then up to my position. Awkwardly he clambered up onto the fender, trying to figure what to grab and where to place his feet, and made his way over to my side of the turret.

Leaning toward him, I pulled one side of my comm helmet away from my ear to hear what he had to say.

But he just stood there, taking it all in. After a minute he said, "Beautiful, ain't it?"

I nodded as I looked down into the lush valley. A sudden blur of motion caught our attention. Something was cutting through the grass at a rapid clip, about two hundred meters out. When the CO and I recognized what it was, we both yelled the same thing—"Tiger!"

The animal was bounding through the grass at amazing speed. Barely visible to us high up the tank, it went unseen by those on the ground. We caught only a glimpse of it as its tail whipped up with each leaping stride.

Immediately I keyed my mike. "I've got a tiger in the grass," I told the other tank commanders. "It's moving from my left to right about two hundred meters out! Can you see it?"

My two other TCs confirmed my sighting. "Roger," they came back over the radio, "Identified! We got the tiger."

I was thinking how cool it would be to have a tiger skin on our tank! "Shoot it!" I yelled to my gunner. "Shoot it before it gets away!"

"Can't get a clear shot," my gunner replied, "I've got grunts in front of me."

"Charlie Two-Two," I asked the other tank, "can you get a shot in?"

"Negative, Two-Four. The tiger just went over the far ridgeline."

Meanwhile, of course, someone back in Dong Ha was monitoring this entire conversation. I never gave a thought to what it must have sounded like, until over the radio came a strange voice, asking for my tank by its number: "Charlie Two-Four? This is Charlie Six."

I was surprised, because our company CP seldom interfered with a tank commander in the field. What the hell can they want with me at a time like this?

"This is Two-Four," I replied. "Go ahead, Six."

"How many tigers can you identify?" the voice asked.

I couldn't imagine what his interest was. "Just one, and it disappeared over a ridgeline about a klick away."

"What's your poz?" he asked. (Poz was short for position.)

I glanced at my map and gave him a coded position report: "From Thunderbird, up eight hundred meters, west five hundred meters. Over."

"Wait one!" he replied, short for wait one minute or hold the phone.

Now, more than ever, I was convinced that the guys in the rear didn't have enough to do. Looking back on it, I don't recall ever seeing a tank officer in the field with us during an operation, except on Allen Brook. They always seemed to have to be at the CP for some reason. Now they wanted to bother me out of the blue. Were they looking to grab my trophy tiger skin?

I looked over at my other TCs, who were gazing back at me with SEGs (shit-eating grins), shrugging, and shaking their heads. But I had the distinct impression they knew what was going on.

After a couple of minutes, the same voice came back on the radio. "Charlie Two-Four, this is Six."

"Go ahead, Six," I replied.

"We've got two fast movers inbound to your position to take out the tiger. Over."

Fast movers meant jet aircraft! The fear of running into an NVA tank was on everybody's mind, and someone back in the rear with the gear had overreacted.

"It's just a . . ." Then it dawned on me: They thought we had been talking about an enemy tank and were about to engage in the first tank-versus-tank confrontation of the war. Two F-4s were now inbound to bag one large feline with stripes.

"Six, negative on the air," I replied. "It's just a tiger."

"There are no friendly tigers in your area," The voice told me sternly. "You'll have air support in five minutes!"

"It's just a tiger!" I yelled. "Like in a zoo! Over!"

"We'll take it out in a few minutes, Two-Four."

"You don't understand, Charlie Six. It's not a machine, it's the animal. You know, the one with stripes, razor sharp teeth, and a tail? Negative on an enemy tiger."

We went back and forth a few more times, until I was able to convince Dong Ha of what we had actually seen. Whoever the voice belonged to, it wasn't the CO, or he would have referred to himself as Charlie Six Actual. He rebuked me mildly for using improper radio procedure. Was there a code word for a live tiger that I wasn't aware of? The other TCs were now in hysterics over the whole situation.

Jeez! I thought. When we wanted air, we couldn't get it—and now that we didn't need it, it was only moments away.

Before it got dark that night, after we had set up a perimeter, I visited with each of my TCs. We all had a good laugh over the whole incident.

Today, older and wiser, I'm grateful the tiger got away.

Chapter 18

Twenty-nine and a Wake-up

"Twenty-nine days and a wake-up" was another way of saying you only had thirty days left in The Nam. Your final day was never counted, because all you had to do was wake up. It was an easy way of reducing the number of days left in this damned place. Twenty-nine days and a wake-up was all that remained of my thirteen-month calendar——just one more month.

Twenty-nine days and a wake-up placed you in a new category, known to all as being a short-timer. All Marines were convinced that reaching this plateau put your life expectancy in grave jeopardy, because in The Nam, only two kinds of Marines ever seemed to get killed—FNGs and short-timers. Anyone in between seemed to be impervious to enemy action. At least it seemed that way, and therefore, it was that way. When you heard of someone's demise, the first question out of your mouth was, "How short was he?"

Twenty-nine days and a wake-up caused early symptoms of paranoia to appear that, for some, became almost debilitating. All of a sudden, decisions that had been a snap were now loaded with implications and what-ifs. Tiny details took on life-threatening implications. Should I pee off the back of the tank as I've done a thousand times before—or use an empty shell casing as a receptacle, inside the safety of the tank? Should I leave the earthen bunker I've slept in for months, or should I take my poncho and blanket inside the tank and sleep on the turret's cramped floor?

You began to try to see if you could wear two flak jackets at the same time. You weren't worried about their bulk keeping you from exiting the tank, because there was no way you were leaving it for the next thirty days.

My last month in The Nam didn't render me ineffective, but I did experience the paranoia. I began to wear my helmet and flak jacket to the latrine. Hey, we all dealt with being short in our own ways. Also, I paid $100—the winning bid—for a flak jacket attachment some guy auctioned off the day he rotated home. This seldom-seen device, sometimes worn over a standard flak jacket by helicopter crews, attached to the front, went between your legs, and connected to the back of your flak jacket—it was basically, a bulletproof diaper.

But it turned out to be a very wise investment, because thirty days later I was able to sell it and double my money off another paranoid Marine. I actually did rather well on my last day in country, because my M14 was also in demand. I would sell it to a grunt for an additional $200—but that was a whole month away. For right now, I had to concentrate on surviving the next twenty-nine days.

I was still way up north at Oceanview. Each day, the wire surrounding the perimeter seemed to get lower. In fact, it seemed to get proportionally smaller and thinner, the shorter I became.

The tank began to look more vulnerable, and I began to wonder if it sat too high on the sand dune. The wall we had built in front of the tank—was it thick enough? Should we make it higher? Or maybe double the men on watch at night?

My mind started to concoct all sorts of ridiculous scenarios that might keep me from going home alive. Suppose the North Vietnamese tried an air attack using their MiGs? Did the NVA have Marines who could perform a beach landing here at Oceanview? I never asked myself why I hadn't worried about this stuff before. Questions like that would have kept things in perspective, could have kept me in touch with reality when I became convinced that everyone was out to kill me—and not only Charlie, either!

I grew convinced that every sweep or search-and-destroy mission was deliberately scheduled just to get as much as possible out of me before my return to civilization. It added to the conviction that someone, somewhere just didn't want me to leave this place. Why else would they send a short-timer out on another sweep? Every time a short-timer ventured outside the wire, any short-timer, he would repeat his mantra, "I'm too short for this shit!" And keep repeating it for his next twenty-nine days.

In what we later termed the "Miracle of the Immaculate Ejection," Pray for Slack's main gun miraculously began to shed tears of red liquid, as if God was trying to prove his existence to me. At first, I hadn't given it much thought, for it wasn't pouring on the floor. It was a couple of dozen drops every day. But each time we fired the main gun, it got worse.

Actually, the gun's recoil mechanism had begun to leak red hydraulic fluid, but it had just as deep an effect on us as if it had been pure hemoglobin. No one, including the mechanic from battalion maintenance who was sent up to try and fix it, had ever seen such a thing before. Left unchecked, the gun could recoil right through the back of the turret—and I definitely didn't want any windows added to my tank décor.

But the true miracle had yet to fully disclose itself. The mechanic who came up from Dong Ha confirmed that the fluid was, in fact, leakage.

"You figured that out all by yourself?" I asked. I loved sarcasm.

He declared that the tank would have to go back to Dong Ha and be looked at by a turret specialist. Because we were a month away from our scheduled PM, it was decided that we should leave the next day and take the mechanic with us.

But the miracle was still unfolding and had yet to reveal its full implication. Going back to Dong Ha meant hot meals, warm showers, and a cot to sleep on. What more could we want? Via the radio, I made arrangements for one of the tanks at C-4 to take our place the next morning. At the same time, we would leave our respective positions and cross paths midway on the beach between the bases. This wouldn't be a happy reunion of two tank crews, because one crew knew it had just been screwed out of an easy stay at C-4.

Next morning, I received word over the radio that the relief tank had departed C-4. I had Pray for Slack cranked up. We left our sand dune position, exited Oceanview, and hung a right, south down the beach.

Five minutes later, we were racing along the shoreline. Soon I could make out the smoke and spray of our "willing" replacements approaching—half in the surf and half out, just as we were. Neither tank wanted to yield for the other and relinquish the safety of the water. Neither wanted to risk slowing down in this no man's land between the fire bases. We charged headlong directly toward each another for a mile, 104 tons on a collision course at sixty miles per hour. It was a game of chicken played by leviathans, each daring the other to turn inland.

I had one pissed-off tank crew coming toward us, and they might just be crazy enough not to yield. After all, what did they have to lose? I didn't want any part of a board of inquiry as to how two tanks managed to run into one another on an isolated stretch of beach in the middle of nowhere.

I told my driver to turn into the deeper surf at the last possible moment, "They'll never expect us to go into the deeper water!"

We were going to Dong Ha and the good life; who cared if we had to eat a little humble pie? At least we could give them a scare.

The two tanks came within a few lengths of each other, then each made a quick turn to avoid one another by inches. The other tank swerved inland; it was surprised by our seaward move. We had both lost the skirmish of nerves, but I had the satisfaction of yelling over to the wide-eyed tank commander, "We'll bring you back a hot meal!"

Both he and his loader promptly gave me a respectful one-finger salute.

After an uneventful trip down the beach, we got lucky once again: The Mike boat was waiting on our side to take us across the Cua Viet River. After crossing the river, we proceeded for another half an hour and pulled into the tank park at Dong Ha, where several tank crews and mechanics were busy working on a half dozen tanks. They were all in various stages of their PMs. After removing our personal gear from the tank, we moved into one of the nearby tents set up for visiting crews. We had a large tent and its half dozen empty cots all to ourselves.

My first duty was to check in at the maintenance shack and find out when we were scheduled for the PM to begin.

"First thing tomorrow morning" was the answer. I was ordered to have everything prepped before dark. That meant that these guys weren't wasting any time. We had to start unbolting our armor plate and getting everything ready so that maintenance could yank out the engine and transmission as soon as it grew light enough.

After my crew started prepping the vehicle, I went to make a few house calls, going from tank to tank to see who was in and to catch up on the latest scuttlebutt from the other TCs. I was surprised to see Crispy Critters, John Wear's tank, in the park; it had sustained mine damage and was off to the side, away from all the other tanks. The track was off the vehicle and the last set of roadwheels was missing on one side.

I found John half under the hull of his vehicle, struggling with the support arm that holds the roadwheels.

"Well, no shit!" I said to the prostrate figure. "If it ain't my pet boy Sherman!"

"Is that you, Mr. Peabody?"

"Well, who else would be calling you his pet boy?"

We hadn't seen each other since that night we polished off my mother's baby bottles. I immediately wanted to know how his crew was. The mine had taken its toll on John's flame tank. What was strange was that all of his tank's damage was at the rear.

Sherman's would be the only tank in The Nam to back over a mine! John seldom did anything the way the rest of us did, so I couldn't help but kid him.

After razzing him for a few minutes and getting caught up on what each of us had been doing, I had to get back and help my crew with their pre-PM work. John and I agreed to meet that night for the long walk over to the mess hall.

Dong Ha's hot, dusty tank park lay inside a huge perimeter atop a ridgeline; its top graded flat to create the park itself. Situated on top of the next ridge, half a mile away, was the mess hall. Many people found it to be too far away to make the long hot walk for noon chow. So during the noon-hour break, many of us racked out in the temporary tents that were provided for visiting tank crews.

John and I met around 6 p.m., for the long walk over to the mess hall. On our stroll over there, John warned me about the noonday and dinner surprises. In the rear—as we line-Marines considered Dong Ha to be—everyone kept to the same working hours they would if back in The World. Everything came to a halt for lunch, something Mr. Charles was very aware of. Several times a week, he aimed his large artillery pieces, hidden across the DMZ in North Vietnam, at the crowded mess hall. Dong Ha may have been the rear for combat troops, but for support Marines it wasn't far enough back. John explained that you could hear the NVA guns when they fired, giving you exactly ten seconds to find a hole. They would try for the mess hall John explained.

We had a good time and quite a few laughs during dinner and our long walk back to the tents.

That next morning, our armor plate was pulled off and the PM began. At that point, the maintenance people took over. We were no longer needed, so I left the crew and went to check on Crispy Critters. It was getting close to noon when I found John rolling a new roadwheel over to his tank. He asked if I wanted to walk over with him for lunch in the mess hall.

I looked at him in disbelief. "Just last night you told me the mess hall's what the NVA aims for!"

"So what are you going to do, starve for the next three days? Besides, they haven't hit the mess hall for a couple of months now."

He was not doing a very good job of persuading me. Actually, without realizing it, he had given me a good reason to stay right there during all my lunches—out of the heat. I spent the next two lunches lying on my cot enjoying a quiet hour in the shade of the tent. I guess it was too hot for Charlie as well, because we experienced none of the shelling that John had warned me about.

In a normal PM, it takes about two days to pull the power train, steam clean the engine and transmission, and change the lubricants. Our main gun's hydraulic leak kept us a day longer, while a senior turret specialist was flown up from Division Force Service Regiment (FSR) in Da Nang for another diagnosis. He confirmed that the gun was leaking.

Another Einstein, I thought.

I was on my cot, with no plans for going to lunch that day either, when John came by to tell me that this was his last day. Next morning, Crispy Critters was to go back into the field. Right away, I knew the implications. Because John was shorter than I was, there was no telling if we would ever run across each other again. I decided to go to lunch with him.

We made the long trek to the mess hall. By the time we got there, a meandering column of men a hundred strong was standing outside the door.

As we approached the end of the line, we heard some very distant and muffled booms. Typical everyday background noises, I thought and I paid them no notice. Hell, there was always some rumbling or distant explosion going off somewhere far away. Just another day in The Nam.

Suddenly the line of Marines scattered in all different directions. I found myself standing alone. Rookies, I thought. FNGs who panic over nothing! I started to move to the door of the mess hall, not believing my luck at now becoming first in line.

I hadn't taken two steps forward when I heard John call. "Mr. Peabody!" He was standing in a slit trench some fifty feet away. "Get your ass in here! Incoming!"

I finally realized this must be that lunchtime shelling he had warned me about. As I took off toward John, I heard what sounded like somebody tearing paper right next to my ear. Except that the sound came from overhead.

Crack! was followed by several more right behind it: Crack . . . crack . . . crack! I jumped into the space John had saved for me in a slit trench already packed with Marines from the chow line.

John pointed north, toward a new series of distant and muffled booms. "Count to ten," he said.

All around us, I heard people counting down, under their breath.

". . . eight, nine . . . " Then I heard the paper-tearing sound of an artillery round coming in, high over our heads.

"Ten!"

Crack! I stuck my head up to see where it landed. If they were trying for the mess hall, obviously they were way off target.

Another shell went streaking overhead, followed by two more. Crack! Crack!

"Sherman, I knew I shouldn't have gone to lunch with you!"

Someone next to me spoke up: "As long as you hear the shells, it's okay. It's the one you don't hear that gets you."

I pondered for a minute and thought what a stupid saying that was. Of course you weren't going to hear it.

The next five incoming shells landed on the ridge south of us. Again I stuck my head up to see where their black bursts were popping.

"Jesus Christ!" I yelled to John. "They're hittin' the tank park!"

"I told you they weren't very good! They're tryin' for the mess hall!" He stuck his head up over the trench just in time to hear another shell streak overhead. We both watched it land—squarely between our two tents.

"Holy shit!" we said together. Looking at John with eyes the size of saucers, I started a mental inventory of everything I had back in my tent.

"Now," he asked, "aren't you glad you came to lunch?"

I nodded my head to his rhetorical question. "I'm too short for this shit!" I added, forgetting I was standing right next to a guy who was even shorter.

Short guys always knew exactly how many days they had left. "Short?" John laughed. "I'm so short I can play handball off the edge of a dime!"

The distant booms and the noise overhead continued, but Charlie's aim never improved. Several of our trenchmates decided they had gone long enough without lunch and began to play a game of chicken. A few guys made a break for the vacated mess hall. They came running back out after the next series of distant "booms" was heard, all carrying the first thing they could grab in the mess hall.

The Marine next to us waited until the next salvo impacted, then went over the top. About thirty seconds later, we heard another flurry of distant booms, and we started to count. To those in the mess hall, we yelled out the seconds remaining until impact.

A paper-tearing sound came overhead. At our count of eight—with only two seconds left—our trenchmate came diving back into the trench, a huge gallon-sized jar of jelly clutched to his chest. Another hungry guy followed him with an industrial-sized jar of peanut butter and yelled, "Who's got the bread?"

"Down here!" came a voice from farther down the trench.

"I got the jelly!" yelled the Marine next to me. It was obvious the bread man was at the wrong end of the trench. Down there at the far end, a commotion started and moved swiftly toward us. Bodies parted. Somebody was making his way through. In his arms was a huge loaf of bread. When he reached where we were, he held up a butter knife from the mess hall.

"I bet none of you were smart enough to stop and get one of these?"

After the Olympic sprinters had finished making their rightfully earned sandwiches, they handed the knife to John, who looked at me and said, "Hey, ya never know how long the show's gonna last!"

We proceeded to fix our own lunch and watch the incoming shells.

"I'm going for milk!" said the peanut butter guy. "Can't eat peanut butter and jelly without milk!"

As soon as the next salvo landed, he jumped up and ran for the door of the mess hall, followed by more distant muffled booms. Our milk-man knew he had less than ten seconds to get in and out. The mess hall's screen door had just slammed shut when it slammed open again. Running back to the trench was the sprinter, each arm wrapped around a cardboard box holding a collapsible bag of milk. Sticking out of it was a short rubber hose; he had pulled it out of one of the milk dispensers.

The shelling lasted about half an hour, but it seemed like all afternoon. The last five minutes were accompanied by the sounds of outgoing 8-inch rounds from our own artillery battery nearby.

From trenches all around us went up cheers: "Get some!" The volume of noise around us increased tenfold; the ground shook with each report from the huge Marine guns. I tried to take it all in: the giant industrial-sized jars of peanut butter and jelly, and the gargantuan loaf of bread. We all shared the oversized container of milk, holding the box over our heads to drink through the rubber hose. All this, accompanied by our huge 8-inch guns, plus incoming shells tearing overhead and exploding on the other ridgeline, made for the most bizarre and surrealistic meal of my life—and we thoroughly enjoyed every swallow. It was the company of the men around me, especially John, that I was so grateful for. And I wasn't on that fuckin' cot!

Finally the shelling ended. Heads popped up around the perimeter like prairie dogs sniffing the air for danger.

By now, John and I had had our fill of milk and sandwiches. We decided to forego lunch and go see what was left of our tents. During the long walk back, we mentally inventoried our gear, neither listening to the other.

"God, I hope my cassette player is alright," I said. It was brand new and the format was very unusual in early 1969.

"Hope my camera is okay," said John.

Our tents were still standing, a little out of whack. Mine, the closest as we approached, was shredded with hundreds of holes. I quickly ducked into the smoky tent. For all I knew, there might be dead and wounded in there. Inside, a hundred shafts of light came beaming through the dust-filled air. It was like a planetarium gone berserk, with stars twinkling all around me.

I saw what was left of my things. Shrapnel had torn my cot to shreds. Several of its wooden legs were severed. . . . "Oh shit!" I said. My most prized possession—the one item I totally forgot to mention to John on our walk over—was a pair of fireman's boots that my mother had sent me. After I sent her snapshots of my tank mired in knee-deep mud, she went to the local firehouse to ask who their supplier was and where she could buy a pair. What a mom!

They were worth their weight in gold. With two top straps on the sides of each boot, they pulled on fast. They could reach as high as my thighs, or I could wear them rolled down to knee-high. They were the envy of every tanker who saw them. When I was about to be rotated back to The World, I expected to sell them for a tidy sum.

Now they were shredded, cut in half! Gone, along with my cassette player, all my clothes, and most of my personal gear. But what if John hadn't talked me into going with him that afternoon? I would have been sacked out on the cot.

His stuff, in a tent next to mine, had survived better, and he came over to see what I was able to salvage. "Hey, do you want to go to chow tonight?" he asked with a knowing smile.

"Buddy, I'll go anywhere you ask!" I answered.

Chapter 19

"Too Short for This Shit"

You would think that the Miracle of the Immaculate Ejection had already occurred in the form my eating sandwiches in the trench instead of lying on my cot and getting cut in half by shrapnel. But no, it had yet to manifest in its true glory.

After the PM on Pray for Slack was complete, one of the mechanics told me to report to the maintenance shack—and there, the rest of the miracle revealed itself. When I reported in, the maintenance officer told me that the gun couldn't be fixed in Dong Ha, that I would have to take the tank to Da Nang!

"Da Nang?" I asked, incredulous. "I'm supposed to drive all the way there? It's over a hundred and fifty miles!"

"No," he said. "The tank will be transported by boat."

Shit, I thought to myself. That meant we would be sitting around until it came back. The last thing you wanted to be found doing was sitting around with nothing to do. No telling what they might have you doing until it got back—if it ever got back.

"You and your driver will take the tank to Da Nang and Division FSR."

I couldn't believe it! We were to proceed to the mouth of the Cua Viet River, where we would be met by a ship and taken back to Da Nang. That meant at least a week away from the Z while our tank was being repaired. I thought I had died and gone to heaven.

The maintenance officer instructed me to unload all of the tank's ammo, because it would not be permitted on the boat. That worried me, because I didn't like driving around with empty guns. On our half-hour drive to Cua Viet, we could run into an ambush, however unlikely that might be. To the rear-echelon officer, I explained that I wasn't about to drive to Cua Viet without taking a couple of canister rounds and a thousand rounds of machine gun ammunition.

The crew and I spent the next couple of hours unloading the rest of the ammo and stacking it in a bunker near the tank park. Over the radio, I updated my platoon leader and alerted him to pick up the two crewmen I would leave behind in Cua Viet. As you might expect, my gunner and loader weren't happy about being left behind, but it wasn't all bad news for them. They would get to stay at C-4 until we got back.

At Cua Viet, I was expecting to meet a large LST that would take us on a leisurely cruise to Da Nang. I was looking forward to getting a warm meal on a large ship. Instead, they pointed us toward the Cua Viet ferry. "That's your ride," said the old Navy chief.

Hell, I didn't think a Mike boat could travel that far.

We were one of several vehicles making the trip, but nothing else aboard the LCM was near our size. The others were a menagerie of hapless jeeps and small trucks, all obvious casualties of the war. Our tank was the only vehicle accompanied by its crew. To keep the boat's weight centered, we were told to stop in the middle of the deck, shut down the engine, sit back, and enjoy the eight-hour pleasure cruise.

Never before had the Navy guys seen a tank up close. Once we got underway, two of them became inquisitive and peered inside the turret. There, surrounded by dozens of empty racks, our two lonely canister rounds stood out like sore thumbs.

I thought the squids were going to pass out. "You got ammo on board!"

"Well, what did you expect?" I asked. "Last I checked, this was still a war zone!"

"Chief!" one yelled toward the bridge. "They got ammo in here!" The squids were waving for the petty officer who ran the boat. He came over and climbed up on the tank. His crewmen pointed out the two projectiles.

"Can't go into Da Nang with that," he said.

Ah, military logic at its finest. I pointed out to him that every day, in that same port facility, dozens of ships were unloading pallets of ammo in wholesale quantities—stuff like aerial bombs with a lot bigger bang than anything we had.

He shrugged. "Hey, I don't make the rules."

I explained why we had brought a couple of rounds for the run from Dong Ha and offered to throw them overboard.

Then I saw an idea cross his mind. "Hey," he said, "don't waste 'em. Wait till we get out a ways, and you can shoot 'em off! We ain't never seen a tank shoot before!"

"Okay," I agreed, "maybe we'll get us a few fish."

About an hour went by. The coastline was already below the horizon when the chief asked, "Wanna let 'er rip?"

I looked around the LCM and its cargo of small, battered vehicles. There was just enough room for me to traverse the gun tube over the side of the boat, with our muzzle barely clearing the edge. I told the driver to jump into the loader's position, put one round in the chamber, and stand by with the second round in his hands. "Let's show these squids just how fast we can pump out two rounds!"

The chief and his crew were standing on their small customized bridge at the rear of the boat. A large tarp, stretched tight over their heads served as an awning to keep the sun off. The bridge also had a home-made windshield of glass panes to shield the helmsman from inclement weather and bow spray.

I checked once more with the chief. He gave me a thumbs-up. "On the way!" I yelled for all to hear—including the driver, who was serving as loader—and pulled on the TC's override control handle.

Wham! As soon as I heard the breech slam shut with the second round, I pulled the trigger again. Wham! Both rounds fired in less than two seconds! God, we're good, I thought. Eager to see the squids' reaction to how we "real men" were fighting the war, I looked over to the bridge—or rather, what was left of the bridge!

Only two of the squids were standing. The third was lying on the deck, and all three were covered with shards of glass. Gone too was the tarp. Every jeep, truck, and other vehicle on the boat was now as windowless as the ship's bridge.

"Oh, shit!" I said. Had my recklessness injured somebody or put someone's eye out? I leaped out of the tank as the three seamen brushed off the slivers of glass that covered them.

"Holy shit!" said one.

"Motherfucker!" said the other.

We last glimpsed the tarp behind the boat, slowly sinking in the South China Sea.

When the squids got over the shock of being hit with the muzzle blast—and once they finally realized they were all right—they were too stunned to do anything but laugh. The windowless vehicles only added to the humor of the situation. They couldn't stop laughing! They couldn't believe the noise and thoroughly loved how fast we had gotten off those two rounds. In fact, one of the knocked-down guys thought we had fired only one until the others convinced him otherwise. We presented them with two souvenirs, the spent brass shell casings.

It was the dumbest thing I'd ever done with a tank, even worse than that searchlight stunt I had pulled, or even knocking the ballistic computer off the bulkhead. Of all people, I should have realized that as the projectile exited the muzzle, the barrel was purposely designed to deflect the blast sideways. The intention was to get the smoke away from the main gun, so as not to block the gunner's view of the target. So even though I was aiming the shells safely out to sea, the gun's blasts had been directed right at the Navy guys.

Well, I thought, it served them right, after all the stunts pulled on us during our voyage on the *Thomaston*. God, all that seemed like five years ago.

With no more ammunition onboard, we made it into Da Nang and were offloaded from the LCM. I waved to the chief, who stood where his bridge once was. Our episode must have given them a whole new impression of what the war was like for some of us. Maybe they would be even more appreciative of the cushy jobs they had.

We proceeded to Division FSR near the Da Nang airport. In the huge repair facility, they told me it would take about three days to pull the main gun, fix the seal, and reassemble it. Great! I thought, off the Z and living in hardback hooches.

Mechanics were assigned to start work removing the gun shield. "Hey, guys," I told them, "take all the time you want! I'd rather have this job done right than have you rush it."

I had the distinct impression that they thought I was serious.

Since first reporting our hydraulic gun-seal leak, however, one thing had gnawed at the back of my mind. Every time someone said, "Shit, I've never seen this before," they never intimated that it was anything more than a defective seal. Nonetheless, that leak was such an odd, unusual quirk that somebody might just wonder if we had deliberately caused it.

There were rumors of crewmen sabotaging their vehicles so as to take them off the line. One story had it that, during a PM, someone put a small rock in the turbocharger of a tank's engine. When the engine started, the rock got sucked in and tore up a cylinder—which took several more days to repair.

My crew and I would never have considered such an act; we would have felt guilty for letting down some grunts who really needed us.

I spent the next day searching out Arthur Weber, the brother of a friend of mine. He was in First Force Recon near Hill 327, just outside Da Nang. Force Recon's reputation made them easy to find. Everyone always knew where the crazy people were; it was like asking people in a small town how to get to the biker bar. You could ask most anyone where Force Recon was located, and they could point you in the right direction. So I started by asking one person after another. It took me only an hour and several lifts from trucks to find Arthur's outfit.

I had never really expected to find Arthur himself, figuring he would be out in the bush somewhere. I came across a sign that proclaimed that I was now in Force Recon country and quickly found the unit's CP, which had an office in one of the hooches. I asked an enlisted guy in the office where I could find Lieutenant Weber.

"He just came off a mission," the clerk said as he pointed to the hooch next door. Its sign proclaimed itself as being the bachelor officers' quarters.

Arthur, just showered, was sitting on a cot when I came in. After we caught up on what each of us was doing in this crazy war, he invited me to join him for drinks in the officers' club.

"You know I can't go in there," I said.

He winked, told me to take off the corporal chevrons on my collar, and went over to one of his roommates, who was lying on a cot reading. After they talked for a minute, Arthur came back with two silver bars. "You are now an officer and a gentleman," he said, pinning the bars in place of my chevrons.

On our way over to the club, it took me a minute to adapt to my new role as an officer. I had two and a half years of conditioning to suddenly overcome. Arthur kidded me about not returning a few salutes from enlisted men.

"I'll get the hang of this," I told him. "All I gotta do is act like an asshole," I said with a smile.

"Not quite," Arthur chuckled. "You're playing the role of a first lieutenant, not a second lieutenant."

When we got near the officer's club, suddenly the door opened, and out came a second lieutenant. I was halfway through my salute when I realized I didn't have to—saluting officers was a reflex every bit as automatic as blinking my eyes.

The second lieutenant didn't know what to make of me, a first lieutenant saluting him. He started to return the salute not once but twice, before catching himself—but still not sure, either.

"Goddamned second lieutenants!" I muttered. Arthur was in stitches.

Inside, we ordered a couple of beers and sat down with a few of Arthur's friends. He introduced me as a back-in-The-World buddy, now with 3rd Marine Division. Like any bunch of enlisted Marines, they wanted to know what unit I was with.

"Third Tanks," I said.

"You're a ways south, aren't you?" one asked.

Arthur was eyeing me, thoroughly enjoying the game. Naturally the conversation drifted around to what I did, and when did I get in-country? But I had trouble with the next question: "Who was in your class at Quantico?"

Of course I had never gone to the boot camp for Marine officers. I stammered for a second, until Arthur stepped in and explained who I really was and my real rank. They all had a good laugh. Then Arthur told them about the saluting incident and how I had confused the second lieutenant coming out the door. They got a big kick out of that. It was comforting to know that even first lieutenants hated second lieutenants.

I enjoyed that civilized evening with Arthur, one very cool guy, and some of his Force Recon buddies. But the longer we talked, the less I understood what drove people to join a bizarre outfit like Force Recon. Their job was to gather information and call in artillery on any NVA units they spotted. They worked in very small, often isolated teams, always miles from any friendly units. If discovered, they were helpless.

I told them about the guys who operated out of Oceanview, with ear collections hung on their belts, who went into North Vietnam for days at a time. The guys around the table didn't say anything, they just looked at each other. It was instantly clear I had mentioned something that wasn't supposed to be talked about, so I changed the subject.

Before leaving the next morning, I shook Art's hand and returned the collar emblems. "If I thought it was that easy," I said, "I'd have put them on a long time ago. Thanks for the best evening I've had in The Nam!"

I went back to being a corporal once again—more than ever convinced that when I got back to The World, I was going to college. The officer's lifestyle was more to my taste, and I liked the perks that rank brought with it.

I hitched a ride back to Division FSR. What progress had the maintenance people made? By the time I arrived that afternoon, the main gun had already been pulled out of the turret—a procedure seldom done, if ever, and certainly something few tank crews ever witnessed. Inside were exposed areas that hadn't seen daylight since the assembly line. With a large hole gaping in front of the turret where the gun once protruded, the tank had a strange, far less intimidating appearance.

Now that they had the main gun out, they could take apart the recoil system and discover why the seal was leaking. I was relieved when they told me the cause—a scratch caused when the gun was assembled back at the factory. There was no way it could have been caused in the field.

But the mechanics were far too efficient for my taste. After the third day, right on schedule, they declared us ready to return. We boarded another LCM at the Da Nang docks. The Mike boat backed out, and we headed to open waters for the cruise back to Cua Viet.

The driver and I took off our shirts and sunned ourselves on the back of the tank. As we took in the cooling breeze, I told him about my twelve-hour stint as an officer.

Several hours later, the chief informed me that we were approaching the harbor.

"Would you mind dropping us off on the north side of the river?" I asked.

He looked at me like I was crazy. "Ain't you gone north far enough?"

We rolled off the LCM, waved our thanks, and raced north up the beach with the same precious few rounds of machine gun ammo we started out with. Reporting to my platoon leader at C-4, I learned that we would be returning to Oceanview the next morning. We had no problem with that. After all, we had just spent five days off the Z.

The crew and I spent the next few hours reloading all sixty-two rounds of ammunition and all our small-arms ammo from a nearby bunker. Next morning, we sped on up the beach, back to our old position atop the sand dune. It was good to be home, even if it was the DMZ.

Two days later, my platoon leader came up to brief me on an operation about to get underway. We'd be going with a Marine battalion on a sweep into the northern area of Leatherneck Square. Immediately I got a sinking feeling. Leatherneck Square was the area between Con Thien and Gio Lihn at its northern corners, and Dong Ha and Cua Viet at the southern corners. The Square was infamous for its large-unit battles, more reminiscent of World War II than Vietnam.

Worse still was being told we were going out with a grunt unit from the 9th Marines. Of course my first question was, "Please tell me it's not One-Nine?"

The look on his face telegraphed the answer I deeded. "One-Nine it is. Hope you had a nice vacation in Da Nang."

"Sir," I muttered, "I'm too short for this shit!"

Late the next morning, we joined up with the Walking Dead and went on line with them to sweep through the northern portion of the Square. As we advanced through a lot of low scrub mixed with tree lines we encountered the usual sniper fire that always followed a grunt unit around. We moved north at a slow walk with the grunts a hundred feet in front of us, everyone tense . . . waiting for the first sign of Charlie. Reportedly, an NVA battalion was in the area, and we were trying to flush it out.

Around ten in the morning, the grunts—previously close by—had distanced themselves from us. It was a common mistake for them, and you couldn't blame them. A bad feeling washed over me; I didn't like the looks of this at all.

Ten feet away, up jumped an NVA with an RPG launcher. He was at the one o'clock position, almost in front of our tank!

I reached for my M14, which lay across the top of the TC cupola. The driver reacted at the same time, adding full throttle and jerking our tank to the right. The NVA soldier was bringing up his RPG when we lurched toward him. The tank's abrupt swerve and acceleration was something I never expected, but it definitely grabbed the NVA's attention; it's hard not to be distracted with fifty-two tons bearing down on you. I'm sure the noise of our engine's revving and our tracks coming straight at him, block by block, had its effect on his aim.

His RPG fired wildly over us. He had started to turn when the track grabbed him and flung him to the ground like a rag doll. Without the slightest hesitation in the tank's movement, the tracks pushed him down. I couldn't see over our fenders, but I assumed we ran over the lower half of him.

"Got the motherfucker!" yelled the driver at the top of his lungs. He jerked the tank back to the left.

The adrenaline was really pumping in all of us now! "Nice job, driver! You probably saved us with that move," I said over the intercom. Positive he had squished the shooter like a bug, I shot a quick glance back over my right shoulder. I thought it odd that I didn't see a body, but I didn't waste time looking for our freshly minted waffle. There could be more idiots like him out there, armed with RPGs.

I yelled to get the grunt sergeant's attention and signaled him to bring his men in closer to us. But as the day wore on, the grunts kept edging farther and farther away from the tank. I had to snag the sergeant's eye again and again; I didn't want another eye-to-eye face-off with an RPG. Later that afternoon, they distanced themselves from us yet again, and once more I had to signal him to bring his men back in.

The sergeant walked over and looked up at me. "I can't keep my guys around you!" he said with a smile, "The smell is killing them."

"What are you talking about?" I asked, incredulous.

"Can't you smell it?"

I had been so anticipating another RPG shooter that my brain had switched off my sense of smell. Suddenly the odor overwhelmed me, almost making me nauseous.

"You got about eighty pounds of hamburger in your sprocket."

Then I realized what had become of the RPG gunner. Somehow, the edge of our track had pulled him into the tank's sprocket—which, we discovered later, was far more effective than any meat grinder.

The loader was standing next to me. "You think that gook has become attached to our tank?"

"Yeah," I said, "He fell head over heels for us!" If there was one thing we all loved, it was sick humor. "Do you think we made a good impression?" Asked my driver over the intercom.

The afternoon heat had gotten to the raw meat, and our tank was really rank. Noisy as we were, you wouldn't hear us coming before you smelled us.

"Hey!" I called to the sergeant. "We wouldn't smell like this if your guys had been doing their job!" He grinned, held his nose, and directed his reluctant men to stick closer to us.

We continued the sweep, using our machine gun to recon-by-fire on suspected areas of scrub bushes. We fired at a tree line and suddenly tripped an ambush. They returned fire, and the grunts went down to protect themselves. Then a large artillery round landed two hundred meters off to our right. A minute later, several more shells followed, now coming toward us. An NVA artillery spotter—probably in the tree line—was making adjustments, walking the rounds toward us. We had no choice but to close with the enemy; it was our only hope of avoiding his artillery.

I didn't have to give the order to button up. Our loader and driver had already closed their hatches. We fired while the grunts assaulted the tree line in rushes. We stopped about fifty meters in front of the trees and provided supporting fire. The incoming artillery got lighter. That meant we had gotten their forward observer, or he had simply taken off.

At almost the same time, two RPG shooters jumped up out of their grass-covered holes about twenty feet away. I grabbed my M14 and took out one of the NVA. The other one came under fire by the grunts assigned to our tank. This was getting too hairy; I was way too short for this shit.

That night, we learned we would spend two more days in the field. In the darkness, Mr. Charles probed us, looking for a weak spot and trying to get us to react to his poking around. But 1/9 was too good a Marine outfit to fall for such mind games. Their automatic weapons remained quiet, as did the tanks. It would take a full ground assault before these guys would open up.

The only reaction Charlie got from within the perimeter was one single rifle shot, by a sniper specially equipped with a Starlite scope. The following morning, it was discovered that Mister Charles had turned around most of the Claymore mines that 1/9 had placed out in front of them. The NVA were hoping we would fire them off and have all the ball bearings come back our way.

The remainder of the sweep was uneventful. We were none the worse for wear, except for being tired from lack of sleep. We were reassigned back to Oceanview. The run north along the ocean, half in, half out, helped clean up the mess we had in our sprocket. Taking up our familiar position atop the sand dune, we quickly downed a meal of C rats as the sun set behind the mountains to the west.

We all felt drowsy as we started our watch routine; I had the second watch, from midnight to 2 a.m. Around 12:30 the ARVN fire base at Gio Lihn, about five miles west of us, came to life. Green and red tracers flew in both directions. The hill was under attack, and sporadic flashes of artillery silhouetted it against the dark horizon. I immediately woke up the crew to be ready in case this wasn't an isolated incident.

I was standing in the TC's position, with Steele next to me in his loader's position. Suddenly we heard a buzzing noise that grew louder and louder, until finally we all ducked without knowing why. The buzz ended with a Thud!, impacting the ground right next to the tank.

"What the fuck was that?" I asked the crew over the intercom, trying to get back in my own skin. "Did anybody see where it came from?"

A few minutes later, another buzz was followed by a similar Thud. This one landed a little farther away, but behind the tank, inside the compound.

I immediately contacted the CP on the radio and told them we were taking some kind of incoming fire, except their rounds appeared to be duds. Just then, another buzz grew in intensity and ended with the same Thud!—this time, only five feet from my side of the tank.

Some kind of projectile had hit the sand dune with a very sharp impact, again without exploding. Even so, this one really scared the shit out of me. "Jesus Christ!" I yelled, still on the radio. "That son of a bitch just missed me!"

Whatever they were, they sounded large, and they were getting too goddamned close and scaring the hell out of all of us. We were being shot and bracketed, the target of some weapon that gave no indication where it was located. At least its ammunition was defective—so far!

I had the driver start the tank and was prepared to move, but then I realized something didn't add up. I had seen no muzzle flashes. We could hear the rounds coming, so they were traveling too slowly to be fired at us. That, plus the unlikelihood that all of them were duds, kept me from moving the tank from this key position.

These things kept impacting all around and inside the perimeter. Their rhythm was almost predictable. A terrifying buzzing grew in volume until it impacted the ground, solidly. It was that approaching sound that really freaked us out.

Yet another buzz was getting louder and louder. We all ducked inside the turret and immediately heard—as well as felt!—a loud clang.

"Motherfucker!" screamed the driver. "Did you hear that? We just took a hit!"

"Of fuckin' course I fuckin' heard it!" I yelled back. "I might be short, but I ain't fuckin' deaf!"

Whatever these things were, one had just made a direct hit on my tank. If this was some NVA kind of psychological warfare, it was working marvelously. Man, I thought, I'm too short for this shit!

Again, I got on the radio and explained the hit we had just taken. I had both the driver and the loader button up, but somebody had to keep a lookout. First I peeked over the very lip of the cupola, keeping the TC's hatch down on my head with one hand. Then I decided to get out of the turret and at least investigate where the thing had hit.

From the direction of the sound, I was sure it was the tank's right fender. The rest of the crew agreed with me, so I climbed outside. I crawled on hands and knees, feeling my way around the top of the tank, groping for the impact site to get some idea of what in hell it was—scared shitless that I would be this thing's first victim.

We weren't the only ones with the shit scared out of us. Down from where we sat, the grunts along the perimeter had only a hole to hide in; they were totally vulnerable to whatever these things might be.

I found a dent pushed in about a half-inch in diameter on the fender, near the driver's position. What could have made such a pronounced dimple? I felt around in the dark to see if I could learn what it was. Jumping down off the fender, I got on my hands and knees, and groped around in the dark, but didn't find anything odd, much less solid—just sand.

I felt like a damned idiot. If it was a dud projectile, did I really want to find it?   Buzz-z-z-z . . .

I dropped to the ground and covered my head, feeling absolutely helpless and totally vulnerable, like a deer caught in the headlights of an eigh-teen-wheeler.

Finally——thunk! Another one impacted, just behind the tank. This was doing nothing for my short-timer's paranoia. I had had enough of this crap. I scampered up on the tank and into the safety of the turret.

A minute went by, then buzz-z-z-z . . . thud! This one landed out in the wire, directly in front of us. The grunts were getting vocal about the mysterious buzz bombs.

Meanwhile, the firefight going on at Gio Lihn had died down. The sky above the base was still illuminated with the flares that hung over it.

Another minute brought another buz-z-z-z and thud! One more of those whatever-they-were landed even closer to the front of our tank. Now that I thought about it, the sounds had been evenly spaced—almost clocklike in their regularity. I looked back at Gio Lihn, where the firefight had simmered down to a few sporadic flashes. Then it suddenly dawned on me what these things were.

I told the crew. They didn't believe the idea, so I had them all look toward Gio Lihn. "Wait for the next illumination flare to go up."

Just as the last flare was about to burn out underneath its parachute, we saw a new one burst in the sky above it.

"Get ready," I told the crew. "One of the buzz-bombs is about to pay us a visit." As if on cue, the buzzing sound began its approach, terminated by a now-familiar thud! behind our tank.

My crew didn't say a word. They wanted to confirm my hypothesis with a second example, so they waited for that far-off flare to extinguish itself. Sure enough, just before it started to fade and go out, another flare broke above it. After a few seconds went by, buzz-z-z-z . . . thud!

I dropped into the turret, switched on the red light, and got out my maps. Mentally, I drew a line between Oceanview and Gio Lihn, then extended it on past Gio Lihn. When I unfolded and joined the next map, my straight line continued on to Con Thien.

Over the radio, I gave the Oceanview CP my hypothesis: The ARVNs were getting their illumination from either The Washout or Con Thien. I figured that an illumination round fired from Con Thien was crossing over Gio Lihn when it released its flare, illuminating the battlefield. But the projectile itself continued on course and fell to earth at Oceanview.

It took a few minutes before the CP could confirm it: A gun battery at Con Thien was indeed providing the illumination. The CO was able to get the illumination lifted, and the mysterious buzz bombs finally ceased.

The next morning revealed the mystery thud makers—as I'd suspected, howitzer illumination projectiles. This place was getting crazier and crazier. Now I had to worry about being conked on the head by a five-pound projectile from one of our own guns!

Just as I had suspected all along, everybody was out to get me—even the friendlies. I could just see my mother opening the letter: Dear Mrs. Peavey, We regret to inform you that your son, who almost made it out of Vietnam, was killed during enemy action while serving in northern I Corps on the Demilitarized Zone. He was hit in the head by a buzz bomb.

THE FOLLOWING MORNING, via the radio, the message I'd awaited for thirteen months finally found its way to me: "Papa 2283 was to report to the Battalion CP in Quang Tri the next day."

Papa stood for the first letter of my last name; 2283 was the first four digits of my serial number—a way of identifying an individual over the air without revealing his name, lest the enemy possibly use that information on the home front. It was my orders to return to Dong Ha on the next day's resupply run, without my tank, for the start of my long trip home.

The next morning we left our position and drove down to C-4. There, my crew would pick up a new TC and turn around and go right back to Oceanview.

It would be the last time I would ever see them. On their part, the goodbyes were genuine, but all I wanted to do was get the hell out of there.

The next part of my trip was by truck down to Cua Viet. Never had a ride down that familiar beach taken as long as it did that morning. Mysteriously, the shore had tripled in length and was strewn with dozens of unseen mines, each one with my name engraved on it. I was hunkered down in the back of the truck, never more grateful to be inside my two-part flak jacket, M14 at the ready, and pistol holstered under my left armpit. My eyes, just above the truck's sidewalls, scanned the sand dunes, looking for an NVA I just knew was out there—and who didn't want to let me go home.

I made it to Cua Viet and, eventually, to Dong Ha.

Next morning, after a sleepless night back at the company CP, I reported to the airstrip to wait for the first C-130 destined for Quang Tri. I knew that I was still facing the most dangerous part of the trip, for if my journey was going to get interrupted anywhere, it would be at the Dong Ha airstrip. Often, when a plane landed, NVA artillery opened up and tried to catch it on the ground, where it was most vulnerable. So at Dong Ha, planes never "stopped" in the traditional sense of the word. They just kept taxiing while their crews pushed out pallets of supplies. To catch a plane at Dong Ha, you chased after it and literally caught the plane as the last pallet rolled off.

We were told, to my surprise, that our plane had to take on some cargo and would actually stop for a few seconds. Ten of us were waiting for that same flight, half heading home and the rest going on R&R. We were all waiting in a slit trench running parallel to the runway. I was surrounded by nine very anxious men as the Marine C-130 began its steep approach to the runway.

A gunnery sergeant who ran the strip came over and said, "If you guys want to get out of here, ya gonna have to help with loadin' some cargo. We can't sit around here waitin' for Charlie to shell us."

"Shit, Gunny, we don't mind. This is our bird out of here!"

With half of us going home and the others leaving for R&R, what did we care? We were only too happy to lend a hand, because none of us wanted to be caught on the ground by Charlie's artillery. I had almost forgotten the first day I had landed at Dong Ha, six months earlier—but I was in for a quick refresher.

The C-130 touched down, immediately roared its engines in reverse to bring it to a stop at the end of the runway, and turned toward us. We were brought around the edge of the slit trench and told to kneel down behind a sandbag wall. The plane raced back up the runway, which was more like a straight dirt road. Billowing clouds of brown dust followed the plane as it taxied toward us at an alarming speed.

We were led around the revetment in a half-crouched run to muscle whatever cargo had to accompany us on the flight. Turning the corner, we ran right into two rows of . . . body bags!

We all came to an abrupt halt. "Oh, fuck!" I said.

"No fuckin' way, man!" said another guy. "I'm outta here!"

In unison, several men yelled to the gunny, "You motherfucker!"

"Let's go!" he yelled back. "Two men to a bag! Ya ain't leavin' till they're all on!"

To load all twelve bags, we had to make several trips in and out of the aircraft. With the first five, we paired ourselves and tried to carry them at a run onto the plane. It was difficult, because one man had to run backward while carrying that weight up the ramp. As we hurried back and forth, we were all grumbling and bitching—"I don't believe this shit!" and "I'm too short for this!"—and cursing out the cargo master. We hated anyone with a cushy job who hadn't seen combat, especially any asshole who took advantage of us, like this one. Making us, the ones who did the fighting, load the dead was the final outrage.

The plane sat there too long. We had just gone back for the third haul when the first shell landed at the far end of the runway.

"Oh, shit!" I said, as my partner and I struggled with another bag.

"Charlie, you motherfucker," he said. "You're gonna make sure we don't leave this place, aren't you?"

From the front of the plane, the pilots screamed at us to get on. Already the crew chief was raising the ramp. Quickly we lugged the last bag up the ramp and set it in the middle of the floor along with the others. Out of breath, we sat on one of the two benches running along the airplane's bulkhead.

Swiftly the plane taxied to the end of the runway, all of us praying that we would make it through the shelling. The plane turned. Its engines went to full power.

Crack! Crack! Two more rounds landed, one hundred meters off to the side of the runway. The plane rolled forward, engines going full bore. Inside, we hung on to keep from sliding backward.

Come on, I thought. Come on, you can make it! Others verbalized the same thing. We were going to will this goddamned plane off the ground.

Faster and faster we rolled down the dirt runway. Finally, we left the ground in a steep climb. To keep the cargo from sliding to the rear of the plane, everybody had to lean forward and grab a bag. Finally airborne, the ten of us sat back, glad that we didn't have to cling to the bags any longer. We all sighed in relief, but it was restrained. There wasn't the normal joy that ten guys leaving The Nam would display, not with the bags at our feet.

Nobody looked down, ignoring the silent cargo we had just loaded into this flying hearse. Each guy just stared at the man sitting across from him.

We each kept to ourselves, willing the plane to keep on flying. Our minds kept running through all the things that could easily still go wrong—and make us join up with those twelve who lay at our feet. We were the lucky ones, and we knew it. None of us talked. We wouldn't insult those less fortunate who traveled with us, also going home.

The flight to Quang Tri took only ten minutes. No sooner were we up and we were landing again. Independently of one another, without uttering a word, all ten of us had arrived with the same game plan. They had gotten us to do their dirty work once, but there was no way they were going to get us again. At the first moment a survivable escape offered itself, each of us planned to exit that plane.

On the ground, as our taxi speed began to slow, the crew chief began to lower the ramp. Before the C-130 stopped, even before the ramp was all the way down, we scampered through the opening and leaped to the ground.

A few guys tripped, but they rolled and jumped up again. We all broke into a run, leaving behind a dumbfounded crew chief who screamed for us to stop and help with the cargo.

Pretending not to hear his shouting over the propeller noise, we ignored him and kept running, not making eye contact with anyone on the ground. We weren't getting suckered into doing their dirty work again. Let those wing-wipers get a taste of the war.

I grabbed the first truck I could get to 3rd Tank Battalion CP. Once there, I hated having to turn in my .45, but I had been careful to hide my M14 outside the battalion office. For the first and only time, I met the battalion CO. He presented me with a certificate and thanked me for my ser-vice with his battalion.

I stayed there one night, then trucked back to the airfield for an uneventful flight to Da Nang. On the tarmac they directed me to an area that did nothing except handle the rotation of troops.

I was assigned to a hooch, where I grabbed a vacant cot and was instructed to hang loose while waiting for our "back to The World" flight information. Only then did it really hit me: I was immersed in a bunch of guys who were going home, delirious with knowing that they had survived the ordeal.

They were the most upbeat group I had ever been around. None of us imagined this would be the last time ever we could all share our experiences with men who understood, who knew the rush of still being alive. It was the last time we would have to wake up in this god-awful country. No more standing watch or burning shitters. We were outta here!

That evening, we tried to sleep but were like kids on Christmas Eve. We knew dawn would come faster if we slept, but we were all too pumped up. The jokes, particularly those about how short we were, lasted all through the night. We talked about our girls back home and what kind of cars we were going to buy. I had wedding plans in the making; I was due to get married on March 29—only nine days away. I still had to spend four or five days on Okinawa before we caught our plane for California, so my bride-to-be was getting a little nervous that I wouldn't make it in time.

At 10:30 p.m. we all jumped at the familiar ga-womp of an incoming rocket. All through the hootch went the cry of "Incoming!" We piled out of the building and into a slit trench nearby.

Out loud, each of us was saying the same thing: "I'm too short for this shit!" One guy, in a trance, had squatted down against the sandbag wall. Another was weeping that he'd never make it home. The entire trench turned on him and told him to shut up, which he did—but he continued to whimper.

It was impossible to tell where Charlie's rockets landed, but they were somewhere in the distance, maybe at the other end of the airbase. A likely target was the hundreds of helicopters and fixed-wing aircraft that packed the airfield. With so much hardware parked all over, it would be hard to miss. And every combat veteran in our trench knew that rockets sometimes preceded a ground attack. Not one of us had a weapon. Probably for the first time in thirteen months, everyone was totally defenseless—except me. I still had my M14 with four full magazines, each holding twenty rounds.

All of us watched the night sky, looking for the dreaded red star cluster that signaled an enemy ground attack. I positioned myself at one end of the slit trench, waiting for anyone or anything that came our way.

So far, the rockets were impacting a long way off. Men were speculating that it would affect tomorrow's flight.

Someone said loudly, "Charlie, you can't even let me get out of here without more shit, can you?" That drew a big laugh, because we were all thinking the same thing. All were praying, Please, just let me get out of here!

If I report the phrase, "I'm too short for this shit," just one more time here, that night I must have heard it five thousand times. It was a mantra that we uttered over and over again.

The rockets subsided after about ten minutes and an all-clear sounded, and we went back inside our hooches. After that, no way was anyone getting any sleep!

Late the next morning, an Air Force bus took us out to the tarmac, where we stood in a loose formation next to a Continental Airlines DC-8, waiting for it to unload its cargo—a fresh batch of FNGs. It was a changing of the guard. They had all just enjoyed twelve hours of airborne air-conditioning, so when each new guy reached the doorway to exit the plane, he usually took a step back, as if he'd been hit in the face with the blast of a Pittsburgh coke furnace.

One by one, they staggered down the stairs and past a gauntlet of mangy veterans, calling out to them, "Hey, you think this is hot?

You ain't seen shit yet!" They were taunted with questions like, "Hey, FNG! Don't you wish you was us? We're so short we could use a blade of grass for a hammock!" And reminders like, "Look at the bright side; you've only got three hundred and ninety-four and a wake-up!" And horrible threats like, "They got a plastic bag with your name on it!"

It was then that I realized just how fortunate I had been twelve months earlier to arrive by sea. I had never had to face a chanting group of happy short-timers, nor the sudden plunge into this hellhole's heat. I never had to face a crowd of men my own age wearing tattered uniforms, whose eyes looked ten years older than they had looked only a year before.

We climbed the stairs to the DC-8, thanking God we were not one of those men, who each had a whole year in front of him. There was a lot of joking, singing, and grab-assing as the first in our group entered the plane. Something has to go wrong, I thought. This plane just has to have some mechanical problem—something bad has to happen!

No sooner did the first guy disappear into the plane's door, than he bounded back out. "Round eyes!" he yelled down to the rest of us. "We got us some round-eyed ladies on this here plane!"

From below him, the assembled horny souls let out a collective scream of catcalls. We couldn't believe it—female stewardesses . . . American female stewardesses . . . in dresses!

We taxied out. Our freedom bird started down the runway. Inside, there was an absolute hush. No one uttered a word—yet silently, to ourselves, each of us said the same thing: Don't fuck with me now, Charlie. Just let me get out of here!

We held onto our armrests for dear life. The guy next to me had his fingers crossed on both hands. Some had their eyes shut, others just glanced from one face to another, seeking reassurance that we were going to make it.

Gaining speed, the airplane made a slow turn and began to climb—out of the Stone Age. The higher we got, the safer we each began to feel. But nobody uttered a peep.

Finally the captain came over the intercom: "Guys, we have just left the airspace of the Republic of Vietnam!"

Cheers, whistles, yells, and foot stomping engulfed the cabin. Hats were thrown in the air. We had made it! Never have I had such an exhilarating feeling. The uproar lasted for five straight minutes, unabated.

When it finally died down, one of the stews announced that there could be no playing of radios or cassette players. They could affect the plane's navigation equipment, she explained.

A few seconds later, her announcement was followed by a voice I could only assume was the captain's: "Hey, guys, don't worry about it! We don't know how to navigate anyway!"

With that, the entire cabin broke into hysterics.

"Ma'am, could you get me a pillow, please?"

After that first guy, everyone wanted a pillow or a blanket, just to watch the stews lean forward and reach up into the overhead bins, their skirts raising up a little. With every request, the whistling started anew.

I felt sorry for the girls, but they were very gracious about the whole thing. After all, their passengers had just been through hell. They even looked as if they enjoyed it just a bit.

AND SO ENDED MY THIRTEEN-MONTH TOUR. Waiting for me was my future bride and the chance to go to college. I was twenty-two, going on forty.

We were all returning heroes—or so we thought. We never imagined what awaited us when we landed in the States. I had no anger at the moment. That would come later, not to be overcome until I wrote this book.

I was alive. I sat next to the window and gazed out among the clouds, a million thoughts running through my mind. I pulled out a pack of Camels, flicked the wheel on my Zippo, and lifted the flame to my cigarette.

Engraved on my lighter were the words from that sign outside Con Thien:

For those who must fight for it, life has a certain flavor the protected will never know.

Yes it does, I thought.

Yes, it does.